Copyright Policies

CLIP Note #39

Compiled by

Patricia Keogh
Long Island University
Brooklyn, New York

Rachel Crowley
Briar Cliff University
Sioux City, Iowa

College Library Information Packet Committee
College Libraries Section
Association of College and Research Libraries
A Division of the American Library Association
Chicago 2008

The paper used in this publication meets the minimum requirements of the American National Standard for Information Sciences-Permanence of Paper for Printed Library Materials, ANSI Z39.48-1992.

Library of Congress Cataloging-in-Publication Data

Keogh, Patricia.
  Copyright policies / compiled by Patricia Keogh, Rachel Crowley.
    p. cm. -- (CLIP note ; #39)
  Includes bibliographical references and index.
  ISBN 978-0-8389-8459-8 (pbk. : alk. paper) 1. Library copyright policies--United States. 2. Fair use (Copyright)--United States. 3. Academic libraries--United States--Case studies. 4. Library surveys--United States. I. Crowley, Rachel. II. Title.
  Z649.L53K46 2008
  346.7304'82--dc22

                                                2008009308

Copyright © 2008 by the American Library Association. Portions of this publication may be photocopied for the noncommercial purpose of scientific or educational advancement granted by Sections 107 and 108 of the Copyright Revision Act of 1976.

Printed in the United States of America.

12 11 10 09 08   5 4 3 2 1

Cover design by Jim Lange Design

TABLE OF CONTENTS

INTRODUCTION   1

SURVEY ANALYSIS   3

CONCLUSION   17

SURVEY RESULTS   21

SELECTED BIBLIOGRAPHY   35

COPYRIGHT POLICY DOCUMENTS   39

    Albion College   40
    Assumption College   85
    College of Mount St. Joseph   91
    Earlham College   95
    Emmanuel College   107
    Goucher College   111
    Middlebury College   129
    Moravian College   137
    Oberlin College   153
    Randolph-Macon College   157
    Smith College   167
    SUNY@Plattsburgh   183
    Trinity University   189
    Washington and Lee University   195
    Wheaton College   221
    Winthrop University   255

CLIPNote Committee

Amy J. Arnold, Chair
Sherrod Library
East Tennessee State University
Johnson City, Tennessee

Ms. Gillian S. Gremmel, Lead Editor
EH Little Library
Davidson College
Davidson, North Carolina

Jennie Elaine Callas
McGraw-Page Library
Randolph-Macon College
Ashland, Virginia

Rachel C. Crowley
Bishop Mueller Library
Briar Cliff University
Sioux City, Iowa

Eleonora Dubicki
Monmouth University Library
Monmouth University
West Long Branch, New Jersey

Cherie Alexandra Madarash-Hill
Torreyson Library
University of Central Arkansas
Conway, Arkansas

Leslie L. Morgan
Hesburgh Libraries
University of Notre Dame
Notre Dame, Indiana

Doris Ann Sweet
Simmons College Library
Simmons College
Boston, Massachusetts

Nancy J. Weiner
David and Lorraine Cheng Library
William Paterson University
Wayne, New Jersey

The authors would like to gratefully acknowledge the contributions of Edward Kownslar and Margaret Sylvia to the work presented here.

INTRODUCTION

INTRODUCTION

OBJECTIVE

Creating and updating copyright policies for libraries and college campuses can be daunting: practical advice on and examples of copyright policies are paltry compared to the overwhelming amount of information available on actual copyright law. Although copyright law is subject to frequent revision, a copyright policy drafted with sufficient care should contain a relatively stable structure; future updates or additions required in response to changes in the law should be relatively minor. The information provided in this College Library Information Packet (CLIP) Note is meant to assist in the creation and improvement of academic library copyright policies. Included are the results of a survey administered to college and university librarians who had previously agreed to participate in the CLIP program. The survey focuses on the content of college and university campus and library copyright policies, as well as the associated activities of educating about and monitoring copyright. Sample copyright policies offered by survey participants are included, in keeping with the purpose of the CLIP Note series, "to share information among smaller academic libraries." (Morein) While this CLIP Note has been written to assist college and university personnel to develop copyright policies, neither the work as a whole, nor the example policies that have been included, constitute legal advice.

BACKGROUND

It is often said, correctly, that copyright law seeks to balance the rights of copyright holders, in order to spur continued innovation, with the rights of users of copyrighted works, to allow for potentially broader scope of such innovation. Librarians' ability to provide many current services depends on knowledge and defense of users' rights.

A typical scenario of how copyright becomes a concern to librarians begins with an advance in technology. This advance allows users greater capability to access, copy, or share copyrighted works in a particular medium. Libraries or their parent institutions receive pressure from patrons to assist in providing or acquiring such expanded access. Some copyright holders of the more broadly available works, perceiving such change to the status quo as infringements on their rights, typically sponsor legislation to restrict such activities or file suit. Whether motivated by actual or potential legislation or legal action, librarians may be compelled to respond in turn. Their response is likely to include instituting or updating library or institution copyright policy.

Past efforts to provide examples of copyright policies include two ARL SPEC kits devoted to the topic, the most recent in 1987; although a SPEC kit on electronic reserves was published in 1999. Johnston and Roark's *A Copyright Sampler*, published in 1996, contains a short survey and sample policies from community and junior college libraries.

The increasing pace of technological innovations has resulted in an ever greater need for copyright policies to serve as reference tools for librarians who must address these problems successfully on behalf of both their users and their institutions.

Because copyright issues have become so pervasive, responsibility for addressing the activities affected by them is generally allocated rather widely throughout an academic library. Questions about making photocopies are generally addressed by the reference librarians, although personnel involved in interlibrary loan and periodicals must often confront them as well. Questions about reserve items are generally the province of circulation personnel. Interlibrary loan staff must be familiar with the CONTU (National Commission on New Technological Uses of Copyrighted Works) guidelines regarding journal title, age of article, requesting/supplying institution, and time frame of requests. Questions regarding videos and CD-ROMs, including the right to make archival copies and the permissibility of playing clips or entire works in class, may need to be addressed by reference librarians, circulation librarians, media librarians, and even systems/electronic services librarians. The wider use of computers and the Internet has raised the stakes because interested parties can find out about infringements more easily – and, of course, infringements can be expected to increase along with expanded access. Issues relating to database articles, such as limiting access to qualified patrons, rules for copying and/or downloading, the impact on print sales of journals, and blackout periods must be confronted by serials/periodicals librarians, electronic resources librarians, and need to be explainable by reference librarians. Questions about e-reserves generally devolve to circulation librarians. Issues relating to distance education, which may include all of the above problems as well as questions relating to faculty work product, may have to be dealt with by systems/electronic services librarians, circulation personnel, and possibly reference librarians as well. Popular activities associated with multimedia and music, such as "sampling," copying, downloading, sharing, incorporation by students in assignments, and inclusion by professors in course e-reserves are also likely to be widely problematic and need to be addressed by access services, electronic services, and so on. These librarians should be able to expect leadership and guidance in resolving these issues from the head of the library (i.e. Dean of the Library, Library Director, College or University Librarian) or from a copyright policy, whether developed for the library or for the campus. In the case of a campus policy in particular, it would be appropriate for the college or university legal department and campus administration to be involved as well.

SURVEY PROCEDURE

The authors designed a survey on copyright policies using SurveyMonkey, a service that permits users to respond to online questionnaires and facilitates the compilation of results. The survey was reviewed and approved by the CLIP Notes Committee. E-mails were sent to participating schools asking them to respond to the survey and to provide sample policies. Reminder emails and follow-up letters were sent out a month later to those who had not completed the survey. Once the deadline arrived and a sufficient number of completed surveys were received, the survey was closed and the authors began to analyze the results.

In cases where the same individual responded twice or two individuals from the same institution answered the survey, the set of answers considered less complete was discarded; these discarded results are not included in any of the reported statistics, which reflect at most one response from each college or university. Statistics reported for each question are based on the number of responses to that particular question, with the exception of the "check all that apply" questions (Questions 6-11, 15, 17-19).

SURVEY ANALYSIS

SURVEY ANALYSIS

The survey link was emailed to 207 committed participants, of whom 175 (84.5% of requests sent) responded and 144 or 69.6% completed the survey. This disparity may be attributable, at least in part, to the specialized knowledge the survey requires: some respondents wrote to say that they were referring the matter to someone else at their institution with greater knowledge of copyright.

General Information (Questions 1-5)
The first question solicits general contact information about the individual taking the survey and the institution represented. Results of the question on type of institution yielded fifty-six (32.6%) responses of "public" and 116 (67.4%) responses of "private."

As Questions 2-5 are open-ended, the responses have been grouped in ranges for evaluation purposes. Responses to the question about number of full-time equivalent enrolled students range from 600 to 14,000. The median number reported is 2,450.5 and the average is 3,129.0. This disparity is attributable to one outlier, a medium-sized college that recently merged with another college. Although, the resulting newly combined student population of this institution places it outside the parameters of the CLIP Note series, its responses have nonetheless been included in this study's results. According to the responses, the number of full-time equivalent (FTE) librarians ranges from 1 to 33.5, with a median of 7.0 and a mean (average) of 7.9; the number of FTE library support staff ranges from 0 to 69.7, with a median of 8.25 and an average of 10.7.

Campus policy and library policy questions (Questions 6-12)
These questions list copyright-related topics beside boxes to be marked to indicate inclusion in the campus policy, the library policy, or both. A no-response to any part of these questions functions as a "no" rather than a "skipped question." Each of these questions is multi-part and addresses a general theme; therefore, each will be discussed in detail.

Question 6 inquires about library or campus copyright policy references to: copyright basics (such as fair use); the TEACH (Technology, Education, and Copyright Harmonization) Act, under which accredited not-for-profit educational institutions enjoy the leeway of fair use standards if they have a copyright policy in place; CALEA (Communications Assistance for Law Enforcement Act of 1994), which "further defines the existing statutory obligation of telecommunications carriers to assist law enforcement in executing electronic surveillance pursuant to court order or other lawful authorization" (Commission on Accreditation for Law Enforcement Agencies Implementation Unit); the Digital Millennium Copyright Act of 1998, or DMCA, which criminalizes "circumvention of technological measures used to protect copyrighted works, and to prevent tampering with the integrity of copyright management information," (Digital Millennium Copyright Act of 1998) but contains important exceptions for non-profit libraries, archives and educational institutions; United States Copyright Law (Title 17, U.S. Code Sect. 101, et seq.); and Creative Commons licensing, a non-profit organization that "provides free tools" that permit creators of copyrighted works to "mark their creative work with the freedoms they want it to carry[,]… to change [their] … terms from 'All Rights Reserved' to 'Some Rights Reserved.'" (Creative Commons) [Author's note: A category for interlibrary loan was inadvertently included twice in the online survey – in this question, where it has since been removed – and in Question 8 where it was intended.]

"Copyright basics" are referenced in seventy-six campus-wide copyright policies (51.7% of those who answered the question) and in ninety-six library copyright policies (65.3% of those who answered the question). Among campus copyright policies, twenty-five reference the TEACH Act (17.0%); fourteen library copyright policies (9.5%) made reference to the TEACH Act. CALEA appears in fourteen of the campus copyright policies (9.5%), but in only a single library copyright policy (less than 1% of responses). DMCA is specified in thirty-four campus copyright policies (23.1%) and in eighteen library copyright policies (12.2%). United States Copyright Law (Title 17) appears in sixty-four campus copyright policies (43.5%) and in ninety-eight library copyright policies (66.7% of question respondents). Creative Commons licensing is included in nine campus copyright policies (6.1%) and in ten library copyright policies (6.8% of question respondents).

Question 7 investigates whether copyright policies address the following topics: downloaded music, printed music, sound recordings, audiovisual recordings, photos/images/art works, multimedia projects, digital works, dramatic works, musical performances, and public lectures on campus. Given the propensity of college students to download and share music and other media and the litigious activities of relevant copyright holder organizations (Bridges, 2007) it is hardly surprising that downloading music is the most frequently addressed topic by either campus or library copyright policies (ninety-six responses or 91.4% overall); next were audiovisual recordings (seventy-nine responses or 75.2%), sound recordings (seventy-five responses or 71.4%), and photos, images and artworks (seventy-two responses or 68.6%); least mentioned were dramatic works (forty-nine responses or 46.7%) and public lectures on campus (forty-three responses or 41.0%).

Based on the 105 responses to this question, topics more frequently addressed by library copyright policies than campus copyright policies were: printed music (thirty-three library copyright policies or 31.4% of question respondents versus twenty-three campus copyright policies or 21.9%); sound recordings (forty-four library copyright policies or 41.9% versus thirty-one campus copyright policies or 29.5% of respondents); audiovisual recordings (forty-five library copyright policies or 42.9% versus thirty-four campus copyright policies or 32.4% of question respondents); and use of photos, images or art works (thirty-seven library copyright policies or 35.2% of respondents versus thirty-five campus copyright policies or 33.3% of question respondents).

Topics occurring more frequently in campus copyright policies than library copyright policies were: music downloads (eighty-one campus copyright policies or 77.1% of question respondents versus fifteen library copyright policies or 14.3%); multimedia projects (thirty-one campus copyright policies or 29.5% versus twenty-eight library copyright policies or 26.7% of respondents); digital works (thirty-five campus copyright policies or 33.3% of respondents versus twenty-nine library copyright policies or 27.6%); dramatic works (thirty-three campus copyright policies or 31.4% versus sixteen library copyright policies or 15.2% of respondents); musical performances (thirty-nine campus copyright policies or 37.1% of respondents versus twelve library copyright policies or 11.4%); and public lectures on campus (thirty-eight campus copyright policies or 36.2% of question respondents versus five library copyright policies or 4.8%).

The issues more frequently addressed by library copyright policies – printed music; sound recordings; audiovisual recordings; and photos, images, and art works – refer to items more likely to be physically located in and available for use at the library. Therefore, these findings are consistent with what one might expect. The topics more frequently addressed by the campus copyright policy – music downloads, multimedia, and digital resources – involve activities which could take place anywhere on campus, due to the ubiquity of internet access, or are associated with other parts of the campus outside of the library – musical performances, dramatic works, public lectures. It is important to note that a topic could be covered by both campus policy and library copyright policy.

Question 8, which received 147 responses, focuses on traditionally library-centric activities – reserves, electronic reserves, microform, interlibrary loan, database downloading, and library archives and collections. As expected, in every one of these categories, the number of library copyright policies that addressed these topics exceeded the number of campus copyright policies that did so. Surprisingly, in no case was there a topic that was addressed by all library copyright policies: reserves, the most broadly represented topic among library copyright policies, was specified by 136 of 147 respondents (92.5%) and fifteen (10.2%) of campus copyright policies; interlibrary loan was a close second in frequency (135 or 91.8% of responses for library policies and nine responses or 6.1% among campus policies). Electronic reserves were addressed in 101 respondent library copyright policies (68.7%) and sixteen campus copyright policies (10.9%: the highest frequency category for mention in campus policies for this question). Library archives and collections were mentioned in eighty-eight library copyright policies (59.9% of responses) and nine or 6.1% of campus policies. Microforms were next-to-last for inclusion in library copyright policies (fifty-seven responses or 38.8%) and last among campus policies (three responses or 2.0%). Database downloading was mentioned least frequently among this question's categories (fifty-six responses or 38.1%), but comparatively frequently among campus policies (ten responses or 6.8%).

Question 9 elicits information about activities – campus software, classroom use, course packs, course management systems, document reproduction, computer scanning, and photocopying – that the authors considered more likely to be widely dispersed across campus and, therefore, more likely to be addressed by a campus-wide policy, rather than a library copyright policy. Results of the survey indicate that two of the categories would have been more appropriately placed in Question 8, as discussed below. This question was answered by 135 respondents. Campus software was addressed by 114 campus copyright policies (84.4% of respondents) and nine (6.7%) library copyright policies; classroom use was included in eighty-one (60%) campus policies and fifteen (11.1%) library policies; course packs were found in sixty-nine (51.1%) campus policies and nineteen (14.1%) library policies; course management systems were addressed by seventy-four (54.8%) campus policies and eleven (8.1%) library policies; and computer scanning was addressed by thirty-six (26.7%) campus policies and twenty-six (19.3% of respondents) library policies. Document reproduction and photocopying are the two topics that evidently fit better under the library umbrella: document reproduction was addressed by forty-two (31.1% of question responses) campus copyright policies, but forty-three (31.9%)

library policies; photocopying was covered by fifty-eight (43.0%) campus policies, but 100 (74% of question responses) library copyright policies.

Question 10 concerns faculty-related activities and asks about policy coverage for works for hire, ownership of faculty work, and unpublished works. These topics are less likely to be included in either a campus-wide or library copyright policy than those associated with students, based on the fact that the number of survey responses dropped to eighty-three. (It seems likely that faculty-related issues are being addressed by other means, such as a faculty handbook, hiring agreement, or intranet site.) However, based on the survey results, the frequency of occurrence in campus copyright policies of each of the faculty-related categories is markedly higher than in library copyright policies: forty-four campus copyright policies (53% of responses) address works for hire versus three library policies (3.6%); ownership of faculty work is addressed in seventy-six campus policies (91.6% of results) but only four library policies (4.8%); and unpublished works are covered in twenty-two (26.5% of question responses) campus policies versus six (7.2%) library policies. These findings are consistent with the fact that most campus activities of teaching faculty occur outside the library.

Responses to **Question 11** indicate that the activities of student use and student publications are, again, more likely to be covered by a campus copyright policy than a library copyright policy. Student use appears in fifty-five campus policies (76.4% of question responses) and twenty-four (33.3%) library policies; student publications are addressed in forty-six (63.9%) campus policies, but only six (8.3%) library copyright policies. These topics are, in turn, even less frequently encountered in library and campus copyright policies than those discussed in the previous question, as evidenced by the survey results; out of 144 surveys completed, there were only seventy-two responses to this question – an indicator that only 50.0% of campus or library copyright policies address them. By comparison, in Question 10, faculty-related activities are addressed in 57.6% of the policies.

Question 12, an open question, allows respondents to list any additional relevant areas or topics for which their campus or library has a copyright policy. It elicited comments, as well as the following results: two responses specified a campus-wide acceptable use policy for the campus network and internet access; one response mentioned "archives and manuscripts copying"; and another listed an intellectual property policy. Interesting comments received include one describing an institution with no unique campus or library policies, instead using those of the state university system; another institution "refers to Library of Congress for specifics of various aspects of copyright"; one institution reports it has completed a draft of an intellectual property policy. While one respondent wrote that "in nearly every case the campus policy IS the library policy"; another wrote that the "library is responsible for all policies on copyright – both campus level and library specific"; and yet another wrote that "our policy is not a lot of 'thou shalt not' rules, but, rather asks individuals to apply the fair use guidelines rationally." This diversity of responses suggests that multiple approaches are being employed for both campus and library copyright policies.

Two respondents mentioned "acceptable use agreements," web-based computer use policies, covering topics that range from such copyright-pertinent activities as downloading music and software to behavioral guidelines seeking to curb spam, profanity, forgery, and so forth. It should be borne in mind that, while "acceptable use agreement" may appear as an alternate term for a campus copyright policy, it should not be presumed to constitute such without closer examination.

Copyright Monitoring (Questions 13-19)

In response to **Question 13**, which asks if there is a "campus copyright liaison or someone who is in charge of overseeing copyright regulations," fifty-nine respondents (42.8%) affirm and seventy-nine (57.2%) deny the existence of such a position on their campus.

In reaction to these surprising results, the authors searched the online directory of designated agents maintained on the United States Copyright office website. Among the seventy-nine respondents reporting that their institution had not designated an agent, thirty-three (41.8%) were incorrect and, in fact, have an agent designated by their institution. However, the fact that nearly 60% (46 or 58.2%) of survey respondents' institutions have evidently not designated an agent is rather alarming. Among these respondents, four (5.0%) represent state universities that belong to statewide systems in which another system member has designated an agent; it is not clear if this fulfills the requirement for the reporting institutions. This development is alarming because the limitations on online service provider liability for copyright infringement provided by Section 512 (C) of the United States Code apply only if "the service provider has designated an agent to receive notifications of claimed infringement by providing contact information to the Copyright Office and by posting such information on the service provider's publicly accessible website." (United States Copyright Office, "Online Service Providers")

A follow-up question seeking the job title of this person and whether or not they are associated with the library received sixty-seven responses, which contradicts the fifty-nine affirmative responses to the original question. Four of these responses, including a "don't know," had to be discarded; of the retained responses, one began with "not really" but proceeded to describe a complex relationship of shared responsibility among several departments "by default." These results reveal a lack of clarity among respondents with regard to a question that was intended to be straightforward.

In reporting the job title of the individual acting as campus copyright liaison, eighteen respondents (28.6%) cite the titular head of the library (Dean of the Library, Library Director, College Librarian/University Librarian, etc.). Writes one librarian: "I am not an 'official' liaison, but I attend conferences on a regular basis and enforce copyright in my department despite the lack of an enforced campus policy." Another states that the "Library Director tends to function in this capacity, but very informally." Five (7.9%) more respondents report that this responsibility resides in the titular head of the library in combination with one or two individuals; these include: "the Office of Risk and Safety Management [authors' note: comparable in this instance to University General Counsel] oversees contracts, licenses, etc. when [they] need signatures from the vendor and the institution"; the "Associate Director of Libraries [and the] Networks Director [who] deals with issues related to purported copyright violations on network or web sites"; the "Deputy Director of the Libraries"; the "Director of Instructional Media"; and the Vice President for Academic Affairs. The latter respondent commented: "The Vice President for Academic Affairs has taken responsibility for this area, but most of the work [was] done by the Library Director, in consultation with the college legal counsel." Two respondents (3.2%) reported cases where the library head bears responsibility in combination with a committee: "The college auditor leads a Copyright Team that includes the Dean of the Library"; the "Library Director and a committee including the IT Director and Instructional Media Director." In one (1.6%) unique instance, a single individual who heads both the library and the information technology departments holds the position of copyright liaison as well. At another institution (1.6%), the Fair Use Committee is assigned this charge – with no mention of library involvement.

Five respondents (7.9%) report that the Chief Technology Officer, the Director of Information Technology, or other IT personnel alone bears responsibility for copyright monitoring and enforcement on campus. Six respondents (9.5%) report that copyright is the responsibility of the Office of General Counsel of their respective institutions. Nine responses (14.3%) indicate that the individual responsible for institutional copyright is an administrator – Vice President, Dean, etc. – not associated with either the library or information technology.

Four responses (6.3%) report that (non-administrative) library personnel – Head of Public Services, Library Circulation Supervisor, or unspecified library staff – bear responsibility for copyright oversight in combination with other non-library departments or administrators on the campus. Finally, twelve responses (19.0%) indicate that library personnel are charged with overseeing copyright at the respondents' institutions; these titles include: Coordinator of Scholarly Communication; Collection Manager; "University Copyright Officer – a librarian currently holds this position"; Catalog/Metadata Librarian; Head of Public Services; Head of Circulation & Interlibrary Loan; Library & Information Services Policy Advisor; Circulation/Reference Librarian; Access Services Librarian; Bibliographic Instruction Librarian; Senior Catalog/Reference Librarian; and Library Director of Public Services. In summary, library personnel, whether administrators or non-administrators, are charged with exclusive copyright oversight in thirty-one or 49.2% of the sixty-three usable responses; library personnel are reported to share this responsibility with others on campus in eleven or 17.5% of reported instances. In addition, overall, non-administrative library personnel are involved in twenty (31.7%) of the sixty-three reported responses.

Question 14 asks for the title of the person responsible for enforcing and monitoring agreements with vendors. Nineteen of the ninety-three usable responses (20.4%) specify that the responsible party is head of the library (Dean of the Library, Library Director, College/University Librarian, etc.). In eleven reports (11.8%), the head of the library shares this responsibility with non-library personnel: four with the Chief Technology Officer, Chief Information Officer, or Director of Information Technology; another four with both the CTO (or local equivalent) as well as another individual – in one case, the Director of Computing Services; in another, the Director of the Center for Teaching and Learning, in the third, the Instructional Media Director, and in the fourth, the Chief Financial Officer of the college. At three institutions, the head of the library shares responsibility for copyright oversight and enforcement of vendor agreements with another campus administrator (Vice President, Dean, etc.) or campus department from neither the library nor information technology: in one case, the office of the general counsel; in another, the Director of Purchasing; and, in the third, the Vice President for Business & Treasurer [a single individual]. In three cases (3.2% of responses), the library head shares vendor agreement enforcement responsibility with non-administrative library personnel: in the first case, the Library Collections Coordinator; in the second case, with the Head of Reference; and in the third, with the Heads of Technical Services and Public Services.

At two institutions (2.2%), respondents report the Associate Library Director is responsible for enforcing these agreements; at another campus (1.1%), the responsibility is shared by the Assistant Director of Libraries, the Associate Director of Libraries, the Purchasing Agent, and the Chief Financial Officer; on three other campuses (3.2% of responses), the Chief Technology Officer equivalent – also styled "Chief Information Officer," and, in one case, a single individual is both "Associate Vice President of Information Technology *and* Chief Information Officer" [italics added for emphasis] – is reported to bear sole responsibility for monitoring and enforcing vendor agreements; two other respondents (2.2%) state that this responsibility resides in the campus legal counsel.

One respondent (1.1% of responses) reports that the authority for monitoring and enforcing vendor agreements is dispersed among "individual departments under general counsel"; another respondent (1.1%) reports that "various college departments handle these agreements, in consultation with the area vice presidents and the college legal counsel."

Three respondents (3.2%) indicate that the library's acquisition manager or purchasing division is solely responsible for enforcing the terms of vendor agreements; another three respondents (3.2%) report this as the responsibility of the Collection Development Librarian. In two more instances (2.2% of responses), the Collection Development Librarian shares this duty – in one case, with the Heads of Circulation, Technical Services & Systems, and Reference Services, and the Reference/Electronic Services Librarian; in the other, with the Vice President for Technology and Planning. The Electronic Resources Librarian (or local equivalent) reportedly bears sole responsibility for monitoring and enforcing vendor agreements on seven campuses (7.5% of responses), shares this duty with a non-library administrator in two cases (2.2%) – with the Vice-President for Business, Finance & Technology and the CTO local equivalent; and on one campus (1.1%), shares responsibility with the Collection Development Librarian and a non-library administrator, the Purchasing Director local equivalent. According to one report (1.1% of responses), the function was shared between the Manager of Interlibrary Loan & Digital Resources [one individual] and the Director of Client Services [CTO local equivalent]. Three or 3.2% of responses indicate that the Head of Periodicals/Serials Librarian/Head of Serials Acquisitions is responsible for enforcing vendor agreements. In five reported cases (5.4%), the lead public services librarian (Head of Reference/Public Services Librarian/Head of Reference & Instructional Services) enforces and monitors vendor agreements – although in one of these cases, the same individual functions as both the Head of Reference and the Circulation Manager; on three other campuses (3.2%), reference librarians share this responsibility with other non-administrative librarians – the Collection Development Coordinator, the Systems Librarian, and the Heads of Technical Services and Access Services. Three respondents (3.2%) report that the Systems Librarian is in charge of vendor agreements for their institutions, and another (1.1%) indicates that both the Systems Librarian and the Access Services Manager share this responsibility. In five instances (5.4% of respondents), the Head of Technical Services local equivalent is responsible for monitoring and enforcing vendor agreements.

Four responses (4.3%) indicate shared responsibility for vendor agreement enforcement between the library, in general, without specifying any individual titles, and another department: on one campus, the library and information technology are so charged; at another, it is the library, information technology, and the Resource Center; at a third, the library and the purchasing department bear responsibility; and at the fourth, the library, the purchasing department, and campus general counsel all share in the monitoring and enforcement of vendor agreements. At three other institutions (3.2% of responses), the purchasing department is charged with monitoring and enforcing agreements with vendors. Finally, five of the usable responses (5.4%) indicate that this responsibility resides in another administrative unit of the campus separate from the library, information technology, and the purchasing department – although the majority mentions the business office of the campus which, presumably, has some relation to the purchasing department.

In summary, library administrators are involved in the vendor agreement process in thirty-nine reported instances (41.9% of usable responses); non-administrative library personnel are involved in forty-two reported instances (45.2%); in the aggregate, library personnel are involved in the monitoring and enforcement of vendor agreements in eighty-one of ninety-three usable reports (87.1%).

In response to **Question 15**, in which survey takers are asked to choose all the document delivery or other service providers that are used to maintain compliance with copyright law, ninety-nine respondents (75.6% of the 131 question respondents) indicate "Copyright Clearinghouse" [i.e. the Copyright Clearance Center]; fifty (38.2%) use ILLiad; thirty-five (26.7%) use CLIO; thirteen (9.9%) use CISTI Document Delivery; none (0%) indicate CTRC; one (0.8% of respondents) uses Carolina Library Services; forty-seven (35.9%) use EBSCO-EJS; sixty-seven (51.1%) use FirstSearch; five (3.8%) use Infotrieve; twenty-eight (21.4%) use Ingenta; one (0.8%) uses Research Associates; none (0%) use TDI Library Services, Inc.; and eleven (8.4%) chose "other." However, once again, more elaborated under "other, specify" (seventeen) than would logically be expected. Among the "other" answers that are elaborated on, four specify BRI /British Library; three specify eRes/Docutek eRes; two respondents specify Ariel; two specify their library's OPAC/ILS; two report that they use library records and/or an in-house database; one specifies the Copyright Clearance Center, which is what the authors intended when writing "Copyright Clearinghouse"; one specifies the IP authentication software, EZProxy; one specifies AOTA-American Occupational Therapy Association; and one specifies Odyssey, an electronic ILL delivery service. [Authors' note: Some of the user-supplied responses, such as Ariel and Odyssey are not, strictly speaking, related to copyright.]

When asked, in **Question 16**, if their document delivery service keeps track of usage statistics, ninety-six or 76.8% of the 125 respondents report that it does; twenty-nine or 23.2% report that theirs does not. A follow-up question for those who answered in the negative asks if the library then keeps its own statistics. This question met with twenty-seven responses, of which twenty-six were yes, including five respondents who failed to answer the first part of the question. One respondent, who had answered "yes" to the first part of the question, answered in the second part, the "library also keeps statistics." Another "yes" respondent to the follow-up question wrote: "Yes. Not sure what you mean here. The only thing I can think of is the Orbis Cascade Alliance [author's note: a regional consortium in the Pacific Northwest] through which we share books. That doesn't need copyright tracking but Orbis does track use of materials. We also use a [courier] system to transport ILL requests, but they don't know what is in the packages we send." The single negative response reported that no document delivery service is used.

Question 17 asks respondents to rate, on a scale of 1-5 (1=least, 5=most), how closely their library monitors and/or enforces copyright in particular activity categories. The majority of respondents rate their library a 5 in interlibrary loan (eighty-one out of 142 respondents or 57%), electronic reserves (fifty-five out of 119 responses or 46.2%), database licensing (sixty-two of 138 responses or 44.9%) and reserves (sixty-three of 143 responses or 44.1%). Photocopying and database downloading are the least closely monitored activities, with a majority of institutions rating themselves a 2 (forty-one of 141 responses or 29.1%) for photocopying and rating a 3 for database downloading by forty-two of 129 respondents (32.6%). Furthermore, the four categories most frequently rated "5" all have their second highest frequency at rating "4"; in two of these categories the sum of ratings 1-3 ranges between 25% and 30% of responses; in the other two categories (reserves and electronic reserves), the sum of ratings 1-3 in the other two categories (interlibrary loan and database licensing) is below 20%. These findings indicate confidence in the ability to monitor and enforce copyright in the areas of interlibrary loan, database licensing, reserves, and e-reserves. It is interesting to note that, with the exception of traditional reserves, all of these activities are conducted with software or significant interaction with agencies or companies beyond the campus – agents with the ability to monitor and report on infractions connected with these activities. It is not particularly surprising that photocopying is the least strictly enforced, given the considerable effort that would be required to monitor this activity and the ease of meeting institutional copyright requirements. As related by Gasaway and Wiant, "Section 108(f)(1) frees a library from liability for unsupervised photocopy machine use by patrons if the library posts a notice of copyright near all unsupervised copiers." (1994, 51) The findings for database downloading have a few possible explanations: respondents' agreements with database vendors may allow for this activity to be monitored by the vendor; the agreements may allow unlimited downloading by authorized users (which would have rendered appropriate a follow-up question about authentication); or, the findings may simply reveal that a lack of negative consequences associated with this activity has caused it to receive less attention.

In response to **Question 18** regarding how often respondents have received notice of copyright violations from publishers or music publishers, the responses are both reassuring and thought-provoking: 122 of 141 responses (86.5%) indicate 0-1 times per year; seven respondents (5.0%) indicate 2-5 times per year; five responses (3.6%) indicate 6-10 times per year; and seven respondents or 5.0% indicate at least eleven times per year. On the one hand, it is comforting to conclude that the preponderance of answers indicates that this is currently not an area of great concern; on the other, for the institutions where this is occurring relatively frequently, it must be a cause for concern. Incidentally, the authors applaud the courage and honesty of the respondents, as they had wondered, in developing the survey, if anyone would respond to this question or the next. Willingness to admit that the problem exists and has consequences is an important incentive to confront the thorny topic of copyright.

Question 19 asks how often respondents consult legal counsel regarding copyright. One hundred twenty-nine of 144 respondents (89.6%) report 0-1 times per year; twelve of 144 or 8.3% report 2-5 times per year; three of 144 or 2.1% report 6-10 times per year; and no respondents (0%) report more than 10 times per year. These results are somewhat consistent with the responses to Question 13, if we assume that there is not a one-to-one relationship between a complaint and seeking counsel. For example, a publisher reporting multiple violations at one time could lead to academic legal counsel being consulted once or, at any rate, fewer times than the total number of violations being reported.

Copyright Education (Questions 20-23)

Question 20 inquires if the library educates faculty on copyright policy. Of the 144 responses received, 106 (73.6%) are positive and thirty-eight (26.4%) are negative. A follow-up question asks those who answered "yes" how often such training is provided. In descending order of frequency, thirty-three of seventy-six responses (43.4%) answer annually; eleven responses (14.5%) indicate more frequent training – 2-5 times per year; eight (10.5%) provide it "on demand," "as requested," or "as needed"; six (7.9%) responses indicate training is offered "occasionally"; four (5.3%) responses indicate that training is offered "every few years," "every other year," or, in general, less frequently than annually; four more responses (5.3%) characterize training as "ongoing" – a decidedly vague response; three (3.9%) respondents indicate that this faculty training in copyright is only offered once – presumably as part of new hire orientation; and one respondent (1.3% of positive follow-up responses) reports that training is offered monthly; the remaining six (7.9%) "yes" follow-up responses are difficult to characterize: one states that faculty training is "not systematic or compulsory"; another reports that faculty training occurs "in conversations with them"; the others report that faculty training occurs in relation to "reserve only," that training for faculty is offered "three times (through email about reserves)," and that faculty bear the responsibility for securing copyright permissions for articles and "they place their reserve material on WebCT so the library is not in danger of violating copyright." Two of the responses coded as "ongoing" also contain interesting comments: one respondent states that information for faculty on copyright is "currently in [the] Faculty Handbook, [with] programs [offered] through [the] Teacher Excellence Center and Distance Learning and currently under revision"; the second, more ambiguous answer indicates that faculty training is "ongoing, by informing them about policies" but also replies to the follow-up question for those who answered "no" (i.e. that their college or university does not educate faculty about copyright. This respondent states that there are "no plans to create a specific program for faculty in the next twelve months." Finally, one "yes" respondent, whose follow-up was coded as "other," states that "plans are in the works." The "no" follow-up question received eleven responses: nine (81.8%) respondents report that there are no plans to offer copyright training within the next twelve months, but two (18.1%) report that there are such plans.

Question 21 asks if staff receive education on copyright policies. Ninety-eight of the 143 respondents to this question, or 68.5%, indicate that they do; forty-five or 31.5% indicate that they do not.

Among those who responded "yes," six responses to the follow-up question on frequency had to be discarded as unresponsive. In answer to a follow-up question on how often such training is offered, four respondents, or 6.9% of the fifty-eight valid responses received to this portion of the question, indicate that this training occurs once – presumably as part of the new hire/orientation process; twenty-four or 41.4% indicate that training occurs yearly; five or 8.6% indicate a higher frequency than yearly – at least once a year, once a semester, or one or two times a year; two respondents (3.4%) report that training occurs monthly; three or 5.2% indicate that training is "ongoing," however one of these responses is less than clear: "Ongoing, as needed. No specific education program for staff planned"; three responses (5.2%) state that training occurs "occasionally"; twelve or 20.7% report that training is provided "as requested," "as needed," "as necessary," or "on demand" – one of these responses includes the comment: "Only staff involved in reserves and ILL are aware of copyright policies"; three respondents (5.2%) report that training is provided "regularly" or "periodically"; two responses (3.4%) state that training occurs "irregularly" or "once every few years."

In answer to the follow-up question (if training is not currently provided, does the campus plan to create such an education program for staff within the next twelve months), seven responses indicate that the campus is not planning to do so; one indicates that it might; and one answer had to be discarded as not appropriate to the question.

There were 143 responses to **Question 22**, which asks if respondents educate students on copyright policy: ninety-three (65%) report "yes"; fifty (35%) report "no." Of those who answered "yes," fifty-four responded to the follow-up question of how often such training occurs: thirteen responses (24.1%) indicate that such training occurs in information literacy, library instruction, or freshman orientation classes – which presumably could be presented once or be repeated; ten responses (18.5%) specify "as requested," "as needed" or "on demand"; eight (14.8%) respondents state that training occurs annually and another eight (14.8%) report that it occurs a few times a year to several times a year; three (5.6%) answered that training occurs occasionally; four (7.4%) report that training is only provided once; and one (1.9%) states that copyright training is presented to students monthly. There seems to be some blurring between this question of how often training occurs and the next, which asks how it occurs, as evinced by the first set of answers about library instruction, as well as three (5.6%) more which report that training is limited to signage. This confusion between questions was most evident in four (7.4%) unclassifiable responses: two allude to the student handbook; one states that training is confined to conversation; and one states that training is limited to student workers. Subsequent to a "no" response to the original question – that the library does not educate students on copyright policy – a follow-up question, asking if such training is planned in the next twelve months, yielded six (60%) "no" responses, two (20%) "yes" responses, one "maybe" response, and one comment that training currently occurs: "serendipitously but revision underway includes improving student education."

In brief, faculty and staff generally receive copyright education annually, although "on demand" was also frequently reported. Students appear to receive their copyright education during library instruction, although, again, "on demand" is reported frequently. However, it seems likely that such requests are made by faculty, rather than by students.

Question 23
Although most of the respondents do not explicitly state who initiates copyright education at their institutions, by analyzing the responses in terms of how copyright education is provided we can infer that it is initiated by a number of actors: by faculty and the library together, when an information literacy or bibliographic instruction session is presented as part of another course; by library users and staff together, via "'teachable moment' education when students (or faculty or staff) ask [library personnel] to provide items or services which would be violations of copyright"; by campus administration and the library, when education is presented as part of orientation for freshmen and new faculty, or part of a required core course for students; and by

the library, who may convey it via formal workshops and presentations, as part of library staff training, or through signage. Administration, information technology, and the library may all be involved in copyright information presented via the Web, in brochures, or in departmental, faculty, or staff meetings. Although many responses include only some of these elements, one fairly typical respondent who includes almost all methods mentioned by others writes: "The library has had workshops for faculty; we answer queries about copyright; we make our written policies available. We [instruct] staff, especially ILL, on copyright compliance. Students receive copyright instruction in the course of library instruction classes."

CONCLUSION

CONCLUSION

Drawing from results of the survey, topics most frequently mentioned in library copyright policies include reserves; electronic reserves; interlibrary loan; photocopying and other forms of document reproduction; permissible use of archives, collections, and microforms; and restrictions on downloading from databases. Both library and campus copyright policies emphasize copyright basics and United States copyright law. Campus copyright policies tend to emphasize campus-wide activities such as classroom use, campus-purchased software, course packs, music and media downloads, reproduction of musical performances, public lectures, dramatic works, and faculty- and student-centered activities.

Library personnel – whether solely or in part – occupy the position of campus copyright liaison or individual in charge of overseeing copyright regulations on 71.2% of campuses where survey respondents report that such a position exists. Furthermore, survey results tell us that library personnel bear responsibility for monitoring and enforcing agreements with vendors on 83.9% of campuses: library administrators account for 46.1% of these; non-administrative library personnel comprise the remaining 53.9%.

When providing education on copyright, even in the case of faculty, it is important to associate this information with the learners' self-interest (cf. Smith [2006]). According to the results of the survey, students, faculty, and staff receive copyright education from a variety of sources – with the library preeminent among these. As a result, familiarity with copyright is both desirable and necessary for library personnel who serve as educators in this area.

This CLIP Note has been designed to assist in the production of library or campus copyright policy and includes example policies for convenient reference. In addition to library policies, we have included one exemplary university policy, for the benefit of interested readers. The policies provided herein, and this publication as a whole, are intended to convey general information concerning copyright law and do not constitute legal advice.

SURVEY RESULTS

SURVEY RESULTS

Survey: Copyright Policy

GENERAL INFORMATION (Questions 1 – 5)

Where appropriate, statistics should be taken from the most recent Integrated Postsecondary Education Data System (IPEDS)

1. **Please supply the following general information.**

    Name: (175 responses)

    Title: (175 responses)

Library Director/Library Chair/Dean *and related titles*	(131)	(74.9%)
Access Services Librarian *and related titles*	(9)	(5.1%)
Public Services Librarian *includes Instruction*	(8)	(4.6%)
Technical Services Librarian (*Serials, Acquisitions, Cataloging, etc.*)	(6)	(3.4%)
Associate Dean/Associate Library Director *and related titles*	(5)	(2.9%)
Reference Librarian *and related titles*	(5)	(2.9%)
Librarian *miscellaneous*	(3)	(1.7%)
Systems Librarian *and related titles*	(2)	(1.1%)
Collection Development Librarian *and related titles*	(2)	(1.1%)
Documents Librarian *and related titles*	(1)	(0.6%)
Special Collections Librarian *and related titles*	(1)	(0.6%)
Administrative Assistant *and related titles*	(1)	(0.6%)
Vice President of Academic Affairs *and related titles*	(1)	(0.6%)

    Telephone Number: (172 responses)

    Institution Name: (175 responses)

    City/Town: (175 responses)

    State/Province: (175 responses)

    E-mail Address: (173 responses)

2. **Please select the type of institution to which your library belongs**

                                                                             (172 responses)

Public	(56)	(32.6%)
Private	(116)	(67.4%)

3. **Number of full-time equivalent (FTE) students enrolled**   (166 responses)

<1,000	11	(6.6%)
1,000 – 1,999	55	(33.1%)
2,000 – 2,999	40	(24.1%)

3,000 – 4,999	29	(17.5%)
5,000 – 6,999	18	(10.8%)
7,000 – 14,000	13	(7.8%)

4. Number of FTE librarians (171 responses)

1 – 2.9	13	(7.6%)
3 – 4.9	26	(15.2%)
5 – 6.9	43	(25.1%)
7 – 8.9	31	(18.1%)
9 – 10.9	20	(11.7%)
11 – 12.9	14	(8.2%)
13 – 14.9	11	(6.4%)
15 – 33.5	13	(7.6%)

5. Number of FTE library support staff (171 responses)

0 – 2.9	12	(7.0%)
3 – 4.9	27	(15.8%)
5 – 6.9	26	(15.2%)
7 – 8.9	27	(15.8%)
9 – 10.9	17	(9.9%)
11 – 12.9	13	(7.6%)
13 – 14.9	13	(7.6%)
15 – 16.9	11	(6.4%)
17 – 69.7	25	(14.6%)

CAMPUS/LIBRARY POLICY(IES)   (Questions 6 – 12)

6. LAWS

	Campus Policy(ies)	Library Policy(ies)
Copyright Basics	76 (51.7%)	96 (65.3%)
TEACH Act	25 (17.0%)	14 (9.5%)
CALEA	14 (9.5%)	1 (0.7%)
DMCA	34 (23.1%)	18 (12.2%)
Creative Commons Licensing	9 (6.1%)	10 (6.8%)
United States Copyright Law (Title 17, U.S. Code Sect. 101, et seq.)	64 (43.5%)	98 (66.7%)
Total Responses		147

7. FORMATS

	Campus Policy(ies)	Library Policy(ies)
Downloading of Music	81 (77.1%)	15 (14.3%)
Printed Music	23 (21.9%)	33 (31.4%)
Sound Recordings	31 (29.5%)	44 (41.9%)
Audiovisual Recordings	34 (32.4%)	45 (42.9%)
Photos/Image/Art Works	35 (33.3%)	37 (35.2%)
Multimedia Projects	31 (29.5%)	28 (26.7%)
Digital Works	35 (33.3%)	29 (27.6%)
Dramatic Works	33 (31.4%)	16 (15.2%)

Musical Performances	39 (37.1%)	12 (11.4%)
Public Lectures on Campus	38 (36.2%)	5 (4.8%)
Total Responses		105

8. LIBRARY	**Campus Policy(ies)**	**Library Policy(ies)**
Reserves	15 (10.2%)	136 (92.5%)
Electronic Reserves	16 (10.9%)	101 (68.7%)
Microform	3 (2.0%)	57 (38.8%)
Interlibrary Loan	9 (6.1%)	135 (91.8%)
Database Downloading	10 (6.8%)	56 (38.1%)
Library Archives/Collections	9 (6.1%)	88 (59.9%)
Total Responses		147

9. CAMPUS	**Campus Policy(ies)**	**Library Policy(ies)**
Campus Software	114 (84.4%)	9 (6.7%)
Classroom Use	81 (60.0%)	15 (11.1%)
Course Packs	69 (51.1%)	19 (14.1%)
Course Managements Systems	74 (54.8%)	11 (8.1%)
Document Reproduction	42 (31.1%)	43 (31.9%)
Computer Scanning	36 (26.7%)	26 (19.3%)
Photocopying	58 (43.0%)	100 (74.0%)
Total Responses		135

10. FACULTY	**Campus Policy(ies)**	**Library Policy(ies)**
Works Made for Hire (for definition and example see: http://www.copyright.gov/circs/circ09.pdf)	44 (53.0%)	3 (3.6%)
Ownership of Faculty Work	76 (91.6%)	4 (4.8%)
Unpublished Works	22 (26.5%)	6 (7.2%)
Total Responses		83

11. STUDENTS	**Campus Policy(ies)**	**Library Policy(ies)**
Student Use	55 (76.4%)	24 (33.3%)
Student Publications	46 (63.9%)	6 (8.3%)
Total Responses		72

12. List any additional relevant areas or topics for which your campus or library has a policy.
(9 responses)

1. Acceptable Use Agreement - Faculty, Staff, Students (computing facilities and services); Acceptable Use Agreement - Network ([college] campus network); EDUCOM Code PLEASE NOTE: New intellectual property policy has just been entirely revamped and submitted to attorneys, will be

presented to [the college's] Board of Trustees in October; new policy addresses issues such as works for hire, ownership of faculty work, and student publications.

2. NO UNIQUE COMPUTER OR LIBRARY POLICIES; all of our policies come from the [state university system]...

3. Institution refers to materials available from sources such as Library of Congress for specifics of various aspects of copyright. We have a university acceptable use policy for the campus network and Internet access

4. Archives and manuscripts copying, policy linked below intellectual property policy under development

5. We are in the process of developing a campus wide copyright policy and have a draft of an intellectual property policy, but nothing is official yet.

6. In nearly every case the campus policy IS the library policy.

7. Note library is responsible for all policies on copyright - both campus level and library specific... Specific policies are posted in library as well as on web pages.

8. Many of those checked [in questions 6-11] are under an overall campus copyright policy.

9. The survey is too fine grained for our situation. We have a general copyright policy that covers all (or almost all) of the individual items listed above. Our policy is not a lot of "thou shalt not" rules but rather asks individuals to apply the fair use guidelines rationally.

COPYRIGHT MONITORING   (Questions 13 – 19)

13. Does your campus have a campus copyright liaison or someone who is in charge of overseeing copyright regulations?

	Responses
Yes	59 (42.8%)
No	79 (57.2%)

If yes: a. What is the job title of this person?
          b. Is the position associated with the library?   (63 usable responses)

Dean of the Library, Library Director, College/University Librarian	18 (28.6%)
Library Personnel	12 (19.0%)
Administrator not associated with the library	9 (14.3%)
Legal Counsel	6 (9.5%)
Library in combination with one or two individuals	5 (7.9%)
Chief Technology Officer and related titles	5 (7.9%)
Library Personnel with other non-library personnel	4 (6.3%)
Library Director with a committee	2 (3.2%)
Library and IT Director same person	1 (1.6%)
Fair Use Committee	1 (1.6%)

Summary:

Library Personnel alone	31 (49.2%)
Library Personnel shared with others on campus	11 (17.5%)

14. What is the title of the person(s) responsible for enforcing and monitoring agreements with vendors?   (93 usable responses)

Dean of the Library, Library Director, College/University Librarian, etc	19 (20.4%)
Head of Library with non-library personnel (see below)	11 (11.8%)
Chief Technology Officer or equivalent (4)	

Chief Technology Officer and another individual   (4)
Campus administrator (Vice President, Dean, etc.) or campus department
    from neither the library nor information technology   (3)

Head of Library with non-administrative library personnel (see list below)   3 (3.2%)
    Library Collections Coordinator (1)
    Head of Reference (1)
    Head of Technical Services and Public Services (1)

Associate Library Director   2 (2.2%)

Assistant Director of Libraries, Associate Director of Libraries, Purchasing   1 (1.1%)
    Agent, and the Chief Financial Officer

Chief Technology Officer equivalent and either Chief Financial Officer,
    Chief Information Officer, or both   3 (3.2%)

Legal Counsel *(and related titles)*   2 (2.2%)
Legal Counsel and departments under legal counsel   1 (1.1%)
Legal Counsel in consultation with area vice presidents   1 (1.1%)
Library's acquisition manager or purchasing division   3 (3.2%)
Collection Development Librarian   3 (3.2%)
Collection Development Librarian shares this duty   2 (2.2%)
Electronic Resources Librarian *(and related titles)*   7 (7.5%)
Electronic Resources Librarian shares this duty   2 (2.2%)
Manager of Interlibrary Loan & Digital Resources and the Director
    of Client Services   1 (1.1%)
Head of Periodicals/Serials Librarian/Head of Serials Acquisitions   3 (3.2%)
Head of Public Services Librarians *(and related titles)*   5 (5.4%)
Reference Librarians shares with other non-administrative librarian   3 (3.2%)
Systems Librarians   3 (3.2%)
Systems Librarians and Access Services Manager   1 (1.1%)
Head of Technical Services   5 (5.4%)
Library, in general, without specified titles, and another department on campus   4 (4.3%)
Purchasing Department   3 (3.2%)
Administrative Unit on Campus separate from the library, information
    technology and the purchasing department.   5 (5.4%)

Summary:
Library Personnel   78 (83.9%)
    Library administrators   36 (38.7%)
    Non-administrative library personnel   42 (45.2%)

**15. Select all document delivery services or other services that you use in order to maintain
    compliance with copyright law.**

                                                                    (131 responses)
                                                                    Responses

        Copyright Clearinghouse [i.e. Copyright Clearance Center]   99 (75.6%)
        ILLIAD   50 (38.2%)

CLIO	35	(26.7%)
CISTI document delivery	13	(9.9%)
CTRC	0	(0.0%)
Carolina Library Services	1	(0.8%)
EBSCO – EJS	47	(35.9%)
First Search	67	(51.2%)
Infotrieve	5	(3.8%)
Ingenta	28	(21.4%)
Research Associates	1	(0.8%)
TDI Library Services, Inc.	0	(0.0%)
Other:	11	(8.4%)

(Please specify):   (17 responses)

BRI /British Library	4
ERes/Docutek ERes	3
Ariel	2
Library's OPAC/ILS	2
Library records/in-house database	2
Copyright Clearance Center	1
EZProxy (IP authentification software)	1
AOTA-American Occupational Therapy Association	1
Odyssey	1

16. Does your document delivery service keep track of usage statistics?

(125 responses)
Responses

Yes	96 (76.8%)
No	29 (23.2%)

If not, does the library keep its own usage statistics?   (27 responses)

Yes	26 (96.3%)

17. On a scale of 1(least) – 5 (most) how closely does your library monitor/enforce copyright in the following areas?   (143 responses)

	1	2	3	4	5	Rating Average	Response Count
Reserves	6.3% (9)	7.0% (10)	12.6% (18)	30.1% (43)	44.1% (63)	3.99	143
Electronic Reserves	10.9% (13)	7.6% (9)	9.2% (11)	26.1% (31)	46.2% (55)	3.89	119
Interlibrary Loan	2.8% (4)	1.4% (2)	9.2% (13)	29.6% (42)	57.0% (81)	4.37	142
Photocopying	22.7% (33)	29.1% (41)	27.0% (38)	10.6% (15)	10.6% (15)	2.57	141

Database Downloading	28.7% (37)	20.2% (26)	32.6% (42)	10.1% (13)	8.5% (11)	2.50	129
Database Licensing	2.2% (3)	4.3% (6)	12.3% (17)	36.2% (50)	44.9% (62)	4.17	138

18. How often have you received notices from publishers/music publishers of copyright violations? (141 responses)

	Responses
1-1 times per year	122 (86.5%)
2-5 times per year	7 (5.0%)
6-10 times per year	5 (3.6%)
>10 times per year	7 (5.0%)

19. How often have you gone to legal counsel regarding copyright? (144 responses)

	Responses
0-1 times per year	129 (89.6%)
2-5 times per year	12 (8.3%)
6-10 times per year	3 (2.1%)
>10 times per year	0 (0.0%)

COPYRIGHT EDUCATION (Questions 20 – 23)

20. Do you educate faculty on copyright policies? (144 responses)

	Responses
Yes	106 (73.6%)
No	38 (26.4%)

If yes, how often? (87 responses)

Yes, Comments: *combined into similar categories.* (76 responses)

Annually	33 (43.4%)
2-5	11 (14.5%)
On Demand	8 (10.5%)
Occasionally	6 (7.9%)
Miscellaneous	6 (7.9%)
Ongoing	4 (5.3%)
Less frequently than annually	4 (5.3%)
Once	3 (3.9%)
Monthly	1 (1.3%)

If not, is your campus planning on creating an education program for faculty in the next 12 months? (11 responses)

	Responses
Yes	2 (18.1%)
No	9 (81.8%)

21. Do you educate staff on copyright policies?   (143 responses)

	Responses
Yes	98 (68.5%)
No	45 (31.5%)

If yes, how often?   (73 responses, 66 usable responses)

Yes, Comments: *combined into similar categories.*   (58 usable responses)

Annually	24 (41.4%)
On demand	12 (20.7%)
More than annually	5 (8.6%)
Once	4 (6.9%)
Ongoing	3 (5.2%)
Occasionally	3 (5.2%)
Regularly	3 (5.2%)
Irregularly	2 (3.4%)
Monthly	2 (3.4%)

If not, is your campus planning on creating an education program for faculty in the next 12 months?   (8 usable responses)

No	7 (87.5%)
Maybe	1 (12.5%)

22. Do you educate student on copyright policies?   (143 responses)

	Responses
Yes	93 (65.0%)
No	50 (35.0%)

If yes, how often?   (64 responses)

Yes, Comments: *combined into similar categories.*   (54 responses)

Unknown *(during library instruction)*	13 (24.1%)
On demand	10 (18.5%)
Annually	8 (14.8%)
Few to several times a year	8 (14.8%)
Once	4 (7.4%)
Miscellaneous	4 (7.4%)
Occasionally	3 (5.6%)
Training is limited to signage	3 (5.6%)
Monthly	1 (1.9%)

If not, is your campus planning on creating an education program for faculty in the next 12 months?   (10 responses)

No	6 (60.0%)
Yes	2 (20.0%)
Maybe	1 (10.0%)
Serendipitously	1 (10.0%)

23. Please describe how this education occurs and indicate who initiates it? (109 responses)

1. Education is done on an ad hoc basis, rather than systematically. Librarians and library staff, primarily the library director and the reserve staff, provide copyright information to faculty, staff and students as they request it, give presentations to classes and at meetings, etc. Requests may be faculty/staff/student initiated, library initiated, or department head initiated.
2. The librarians principally reach the students through web information and library instruction classes.
3. Workshops for faculty on open access touch on copyright issues; various staff attends copyright-related workshops on an irregular basis.
4. Student workers in twice yearly organizational meetings; library department meetings; campus as violations are observed
5. Orientation
6. Annual in new student orientation; and continuously through signage at photocopy machines
7. We make announcements at Faculty Council, post information on our website and at every copier and computer area, discuss it in classes, and one-on-one when people are referred. Our librarians have attended workshops to stay current on the laws.
8. Information sessions given by librarians
9. Case by case basis
10. Students get materials at registration and in dorms. Faculty are invited to copyright lectures.
11. We have signage and documentation and review policies at opening meetings to faculty and during library instruction sessions for students.
12. The education is coming from various sources. Usually initiated by the administration or a member of the faculty.
13. All faculty who place items on reserve or e-reserve are informed of copyright policies. More extensive copyright education is planned for the next 12 months.
14. During orientation, through the academic year, by librarians and the Center for Teaching and Learning staff.
15. The University Librarian (i.e., me) will be organizing a copyright policy/education working group made up of faculty and staff to develop the eponymous documents and programs.
16. Integral part of info lit course required for all students Integral part of info lit course required for all students
17. The English Department emphasizes it in their freshman courses and there is a session during JumpStart, our institution's freshman orientation program. Focuses mostly on plagiarism, though.
18. Instruction sessions for students. Case-by-case consultations with faculty. Periodic educational events, primarily for staff.
19. Faculty are educated on copyright through the Information Technology Group and through information on the college web site. Staff can find information on copyright on the college web site as well. Incoming students are directed to a podcast on copyright and piracy.
20. Faculty are responsible for educating students. Academic integrity is a required part of each course and section.
21. We have hosted seminars on fair use and educational use of copyright. Library initiated.
22. New Faculty Orientation, Training for Staff, Student Handbook - all [initiated] by library staff
23. Copyright basics are covered in two 75-minute library workshops required for all freshmen.
24. We have information workshops in academic programs/classes when copyright is a subject covered.
25. Mostly via the web and occasional announcements/articles in campus publications.
26. As the Scholarly Communications Coordinator, I will be visiting a faculty meeting in the next year to talk about copyright issues. We will also be formulating a campus-wide copyright policy in the next year or so.
27. The Bibliographic Instruction Librarian outlines some of the requirements.
28. [For faculty:] New faculty orientation and faculty emails when services change. [For library staff:] Continuing education as available, e.g. ALA web cast, etc. [For students:] Instruction sessions.
29. During orientation, workshops, and info lit sessions Librarian initiates. Student Info lit classes Staff info lit sessions faculty info lit sessions
30. Librarian initiates. Student Info lit classes. Staff info lit sessions. Faculty info lit sessions
31. Faculty is usually done through faculty meetings. Actually, it's usually the Provost/Academic VP who does it, but he consults with me and the IT people. I educate staff through staff meetings, mostly reminding them what they can and cannot do. Students are not educated per se, but we do have the appropriate signage up around copiers and through ILL.
32. It has been done [by] our Systems Librarian who has recently left our employ.

33. The Library provides up-to-date links on the website to recognized and reliable entities that provide detailed information relating to copyright and intellectual property issues.

34. Policies are posted in handbooks and online. Otherwise we have no specific education programs.

35. During annual meetings and bibliographic instruction

36. At point of need or use, such as when faculty request items to be placed on reserve or users request a service that exceeds fair use.

37. [Director] of Law Library give talks to Faculty on occasional basis. New staffs in Access Services are trained in copyright compliance. We have copyright information posted on Library's website and Title 17 information posted at each photocopy machine and near scanning equipment.

38. Documentation and discussions

39. Workshops, documents, web pages

40. Campus legal office in [consultation] with Library and IT

41. During orientations we discuss copyright; Library instruction sessions cover copyright; Campus efforts include copyright/appropriate use questions before students can register a computer on the campus network. Discussion is lively and initiated from various offices (e.g. Dean of Students, Library, Academic Computing Services)

42. Access Services department sends information to faculty regarding compliance with reserves. We monitor ILLiad requests and contact patrons when we reach our Fair Use limits and need to pay copyright fees.

43. Education is done in the course of the information literacy program.

44. Informal. Often simply a conversation about what is and is not permitted in terms of reserves and via interlibrary loan. No formal efforts.

45. No real education program; copyright notices posted

46. Posted signs; yearly sessions for faculty and staff

47. We include issues of copyright and plagiarism in all our library instruction classes. The Provost's office also sponsors an annual Call to Honor, which has first-year students publicly sign the University Honor Code. Respecting others' intellectual property is part of that code.

48. The Copyright Chat program: an informal monthly meeting with staff & faculty to ask questions and learn about copyright. In addition to the meeting itself, various people who can't attend contact me with questions.

49. The information literacy instructional program includes ACRL Standard 5

50. Faculty handbook policy materials, staff on a case-by-case basis, students as part of library research instruction.

51. Library staff makes annual presentation to faculty. Librarians educate staff.

52. This education is typically initiated by librarians and is carried out through pamphlets, integrated class instruction, newspaper articles, individual consultations, etc.

53. At the beginning of each semester we contact faculty about the applicable copyright laws. Our staff are trained by staff trained in copyright.

54. We are currently revising our campus copyright policies and guidelines. When we "roll out" those guidelines this fall there will be programs to instruct faculty. New faculty are also given an overview and put in touch with librarians. All of this has emanated from the Dean of Faculty office

55. Library faculty in the process of information literacy activities.

56. Nothing is official - I would like to offer such instruction. Currently it is a case-by-case instruction.

57. As noted above, through email messages or handbook language; also, copyright articles appear in LIS newsletters, campus newspaper articles, etc.

58. We do this individually with students, [faculty], and staff as needed when they request something that deals with copyright. We did have a faculty meeting two years ago and did have a copyright specialist do a two hour session with our faculty. We also have a copyright information page on the web that was with the library home page and it seems to move around on the university home page.

59. Library handouts, emails, and presentations

60. New Faculty Orientation and during fall faculty workshop at each school

61. All members of the information literacy team provide copyright education in information literacy sessions. In addition, we provide "teachable moment" education when students (or faculty or staff) ask us to provide items or services which would be violations of copyright.

62. Workshops, email postings, etc., from the library

63. Through library instruction and our webpage has the information needed on copyright.

64. Faculty: in faculty meetings and on request; staff: as part of in house training; students: as part of Information Literacy classes

65. In printed information and in answer to direct questions by librarians
66. Credit-bearing information literacy instruction, taught by librarians, required for graduation
67. Copyright signs at copiers and printers and copyright notices on interlibrary loan forms and materials.
68. Student education takes place in the info lit sessions and one-on-one if folks ask
69. Policies are printed in student and faculty handbooks
70. Faculty informed during New Faculty library orientation session and as needed if they place material on reserve that requires permission.
71. Done in faculty and staff orientation sessions, in bibliographic instruction activities, and in letters and other notices to the campus community at large. Initiated by copyright officer and by librarians/technologist engaged in instructional work.
72. Part of the library's research tutorial.
73. The Library Director has initiated this education through the Faculty assembly or faculty on the library advisory committee. The policy was also put up on the college web page in the past year to make it more accessible for all faculty.
74. [Instruction] [is] a routine, though brief, part of [bibliographic] instruction.
75. Frequent contacts and reminders and posting of policies with regular reminders at point of service.
76. I advise faculty about copyright issues if they ask. I train my staff so they can deal with copyright as part of Reserves, E-Reserves, and Interlibrary loan. I have never been asked about copyright by a student.
77. Sessions are held for faculty and staff each year. Students are given notices of database terms of use and copyright notices/links with reserves, ILL, etc.
78. Student education is handled, if at all, by individual faculty members and tends toward countering accidental and intentional plagiarism.
79. Articles and information in the Library's newsletter.
80. Faculty: I lead a session for all new faculty on copyright Staff: Staff is updates 4-6 times a year on any changes Students: in student handbook
81. Up to the individual librarian during instructional classes.
82. The library has had workshops for faculty; we answer queries about copyright; we make our written policies available. We [instruct] staff, especially ILL, on copyright compliance. Students receive copyright instruction in the course of library instruction classes.
83. New Faculty orientation and follow-up orientation
84. Bibliographic Instruction Librarian provides instruction during BI sessions. It is initiated by both teaching faculty and library faculty.
85. Library Director
86. Presentations to all members of the college community, through the campus website and intranet, through official policy as published in student and faculty handbooks, and orientations to new staff. These efforts have been jointly developed by administrators, librarians, IT staff, and other staff (bookstore managers, copy center managers, etc.)
87. The education for students happens during orientation week. It lasts 1.5 hours, is done in small groups and is a [PowerPoint] presentation presented by a variety of faculty. It is handled by the VP of Academic Affairs.
88. The [state university system] has a very good web site on this issue; we conduct short introductory workshops or one-on-one instruction basically walking people through the most relevant parts of the web site.
89. The library maintains a university web site on copyright. The topic is covered during new faculty orientation sessions, and this year a brochure on Retaining Your Copyright was printed, distributed to all faculty, and made available to the campus at various locations.
90. In discussions with faculty, staff, and students.
91. When the copyright policy was written, it was discussed with college administration and with academic department chairs. It is commented on at new faculty orientation. It is referred to in the student, staff, and faculty handbooks. The full text of the policy is on the college intranet.
92. During library and internet research instruction
93. The University Librarian talks to all students in an introductory Computer Science course, we have information on our website and we distribute information to faculty. That doesn't mean that the campus respects it, however.
94. We've had speakers and "brown bag" lunches and plan workshops
95. Our policies are included in the faculty handbook which all faculty receive at employment with annual updates.
96. Orientation - librarians and tech trainers. Web sites. Tech training - tech trainers. Information Literacy classes – librarian. Policies sent electronically to faculty from Dean

97. All faculty receive a copy of "Questions and answers on copyright for the campus community" published by National Association [of] College Stores. We do library session on fair use and copyright for various classes. The library director answers questions about copyright from anyone on campus.

98. We have had visiting specialists come to address the campus; librarians deal with individual situations as they arise; librarians address copyright together with plagiarism in instruction. Some faculty also include elements of copyright in their courses.

99. Library & IT give an intro to all new [faculty]. Library staff have discussion at staff meeting

100. Presentation by Director of Library Services in required freshman course.

101. Librarians cover copyright in our freshman seminar.

102. Library instruction sessions by a librarian & in various classes by the professor.

103. Education on copyright happens in new faculty/staff orientation; new student orientation; as a part of all bibliographic instruction in specific classes; and one-on-one as needed.

104. Basic course for freshman and at faculty meetings

105. [Web] site, part of new faculty and new student orientation, brochures. Information Services [initiates].

106. Email

107. Librarians discuss this when we teach information literacy sessions in courses.

108. Library instruction sessions – Librarians. Photocopying - information statements. Reserves – librarians. E-Reserves - librarians / software restrictions

109. Faculty/staff in-service day (annual)

SELECTED BIBLIOGRAPHY

SELECTED BIBLIOGRAPHY

Anderson, Judy and Lynne DeMont. "Treading Carefully Through the Murky Legalities of Electronic Reserves." *Computers in Libraries* 21, no. 6 (June 2001): 40-42, 44-45.

Ardito, Stephanie C. and Paula Eiblum. "Royalty Fees Part III: Copyright and Clearinghouses—Survey Results." *Online* 29, no. 4 (July-August 1998): 86-90.

———. "Royalty Fees Part IV: Authors' Rights." *Online* 22, no. 6 (November-December 1998): 70-74.

Belastock, Tjalda Nauta. "Writing a Copyright Policy for the Campus." *College & Research Libraries News* 57, no. 5 (May 1996): 297-299.

Bridges, Andy. "E-reserves Threatened at Cornell." *College & Research Libraries News* 68, no. 5 (May 2007): 317.

Bruwelheide, Janis H. "Do You Have a Copyright Policy?" *School Library Journal* 35, no.7 (March 1989): 129.

Commission on Accreditation for Law Enforcement Agencies Implementation Unit. "Commission on Accreditation for Law Enforcement Agencies, AskCALEA." CALEA Implementation Unit, Federal Bureau of Investigation. http://askcalea.net.

CONTU (National Commission on New Technological Uses of Copyright Works). "CONTU Guidelines on Photocopying under Interlibrary Loan Arrangements." Coalition for Networked Information. http://www.cni.org/docs/infopols/CONTU.html

Creative Commons. "Creative Commons Home Page." Creative Commons. http://creativecommons.org

Crews, Kenneth D. *Copyright Essentials for Librarians and Educators.* Chicago: American Libraries Association, 2000.

Dames, K. Matthew. "Copyright Clashes on Campus." *Information Today* 24, no. 5 (May 2007): 19-20.

———. "Copyright Clearances: Navigating the TEACH Act." *Online* 29, no. 2 (March-April 2005): 25-29.

Eiblum, Paula and Stephanie C. Ardito. "Royalty Fees Part I: The Copyright Clearance Center and Publishers." *Online* 22, no. 2 (March-April 1998): 83-86.

———. "Royalty Fees Part II: Copyright and Clearinghouses." *Online* 22, no. 3 (May-June 1998): 51-56.

Gasaway, Laura N. and Sarah K. Wiant. *Libraries and Copyright: A Guide to Copyright Law in the 1990s.* Washington, D.C.: Special Libraries Association, 1994.

Graves, Karen J. "Electronic Reserves: Copyright and Permissions." *Bulletin of the Medical Library Association* 88, no. 1 (January 2000): 18-25.

Harris, Lesley E. "Finding Your Way Out of the Copyright Maze." *Computers in Libraries* 18, no. 6 (June 1998): 20-22, 24-25.

Hodgins, David. "Copyright Resources on the Web: Sites to Keep You Current." *College & Research Libraries News* 68, no.3 (March 2007): 164-168.

Hoffmann, Gretchen M. "What Every Librarian Should Know about Copyright Part IV: Writing a Copyright Policy." *Texas Library Journal* 79, no. 1 (Spring 2003): 12-15.

Hudock, Sandra. L. and Gayle L. Abrahamson. "Embracing Fair Use: One University's Epic Journey into Copyright Policy." *Journal of Interlibrary Loan, Document Delivery & Electronic Reserves* 15, no. 1 (2004): 65-73.

Johnston, Wanda K. and Derrie B. Roark. *A Copyright Sampler*. Chicago: American Libraries Association, 1996.

Lipinski, Tomas A. *The Complete Copyright Liability Handbook for Librarians and Educators*. New York: Neal-Schuman Publishers, 2006.

Morein, P. Grady et al. "What is a CLIP Note?" *College & Research Libraries News* 46, no. 5 (May 1985): 226-229.

Nollan, Richard. "Campus Intellectual Property Policy Development." *Reference Services Review* 32, no. 1 (2004): 31-34.

O'Hara, Eileen. "Eliminating e-Reserves: One Library's Experience." *Technical Services Quarterly* 24, no. 2 (2006): 35-43.

Russell, Carrie. *Complete Copyright: An Everyday Guide for Librarians*. Chicago: American Libraries Association, 2004.

Seaman, S. "Impact of Basic Books v. Kinko's Graphics on Reserve Services at the University of Colorado, Boulder." *Journal of Interlibrary Loan, Document Delivery & Information Supply* 5, no. 3 (1995): 111-118.

Smith, Kay H., Rajia C. Tobia, T. Scott Plutchak, Lynda M. Howell, Sondra J. Pfeiffer and Michael S. Fitts. "Copyright Knowledge of Faculty at Two Academic Health Science Campuses: Results of a Survey." *Serials Review* 32, no. 2 (June 2006): 59-67.

Smith, Millison. "Fair Use and Distance Learning in the Digital Age." *The Journal of Electronic Publishing* 5, no. 4 (June 2000). http://www.press.umich.edu/jep/05-04/smith.html (accessed August 25, 2007).

United States Copyright Office. "Copyright Law of the United States. Title 17." United States Copyright Office. http://www.copyright.gov/title17/

United States Copyright Office. "The Digital Millennium Copyright Act of 1998." United States Copyright Office. http://www.copyright.gov/legislation/dmca.pdf

United States Copyright Office. "Online Service Providers. Service Provider Designation of Agent to Receive Notification of Claims of Infringement." United States Copyright Office. Copyright Office. http://www.copyright.gov/onlinesp/

COPYRIGHT POLICY DOCUMENTS

Albion College

Albion College
Copyright Policy

*TABLE
OF
aaaCONTENTS*

F.A.O.

PURPOSE OF THIS
HANDBOOK

TOC1

COPYRIGHT
POLICY OF ALBION
COLLEGE

TOC2

RIGHTS OF
CREATORS:
COPYRIGHT

TOC3

RIGHTS OF USERS:
FAIR USE

TOC4

MATERIALS IN THE
PUBLIC DOMAIN

TOC5

STUDENT USE OF
COPYRIGHTED
MATERIALS FOR
CLASS PROJECTS

TOC6

PRINTED
MATERIAL:

MAKING PHOTOCOPIES
OF COPYRIGHTED
MATERIAL

TOC7

Copying for Classroom
Use

TOC8

Copying for Library
Archives and
Collections

TOC9

PURPOSE OF THIS HANDBOOK

This handbook of information, guidelines and procedures has been compiled as a reference guide for Albion College faculty, staff and administrators to help answer everyday questions about the use and reproduction of copyrighted materials and to provide information about College policy regarding the reproduction of copyrighted materials in various formats. It has been developed to guide faculty and staff by setting out their rights to copy and distribute material under fair use guidelines, specifying the exemptions granted to educators, and clarifying the responsibilities of faculty and staff for understanding the restrictions on copying and the need to obtain permissions.

In light of the many questions which are arising with the proliferation of information in electronic form, we urge all members of the community to familiarize themselves with this handbook. It is far too brief to encompass the law, and it should not be used as a substitute for sound legal advice, but it provides a brief summary of the points most likely to concern faculty and staff at Albion College.

Much of the text of this handbook is taken with permission from Bucknell University, Mercer University and the *Copyright Sampler,* and from copyright legislation and legislative guidelines. Some of the text has been adapted from policies and guidelines such as The Association of Research Libraries' *Briefing Paper on Copyright* and the American Library Association's *Model Policy Concerning College and University Photocopying.* These documents address copyright issues of interest to institutions of higher education with a clear and balanced approach.

Copyright exists for three basic reasons:

1. to reward authors for their original works;
2. to encourage availability of the works to the public; and
3. to facilitate access and use of copyrighted works by the public in certain circumstances.

The copyright statute balances the creator's interests against the public interest in the dissemination of information and ideas. As educators, we must maintain the fair and proper balance between owners' rights and public rights that copyright law is intended to embody.

The first copyright law was enacted in 1790, and four major revisions have followed. The 1976 revision of the 1909 law has itself has been substantially amended in 1998 by the Sonny Bono Copyright Term Extension Act and the Digital Copyright Millennium Act, which attempts to address technological advances. Copyright law is constantly changing, so be aware that details in this handbook could quickly become outdated.

Further information, including the full text of the laws, is available in Stockwell-Mudd Library together with numerous other materials which provide more specificity. Routine inquiries may be channeled through the Library Director, Information Technology, Campus Programs & Organizations or the Dean of Students, the Vice-President & Dean of Faculty, the Music and Theater Departments, and the bookstore. Complex questions will be referred to College Counsel.

COPYRIGHT POLICY OF ALBION COLLEGE

In the context of higher education, there are many circumstances in which such uses of copyrighted material as duplication, distribution of copies, public display or performance, and preparation of derivative works, are perfectly appropriate. However, as we exercise our rights to fair use as individual members of the public, or as educators using materials in the classroom, we need to be sure that we are not violating the rights of authors and/or distributors or the privacy

Copying for Library
Reserve Use

TOC10

Copying for
Interlibrary Loan

TOC11

Copying for Course
Packs and Customized
Anthologies

TOC12

UNPUBLISHED
WORKS

TOC13

COPYING MUSIC
FOR EDUCATIONAL
PURPOSES

TOC14

PERFORMANCES

TOC15

MUSIC

TOC16

AUDIOVISUAL
MATERIALS

TOC17

MICROFORMS

TOC18

SOUND RECODINGS
(OTHER THAN
MUSICAL)

TOC19

ART WORKS

TOC20

INTERNET USE AND
THE WEB

TOC21

MULTIMEDIA

TOC22

rights of individuals.

Members of the Albion College community are prohibited from using copyrighted works in any way that is not authorized by (a) specific exemptions in the copyright law, (b) fair-use guidelines, including those specifically granted to educators in classroom settings, or (c) licenses or written permission from the copyright owner.

Faculty and staff are reminded that it is unlawful for staff members (e.g., secretarial staff and student assistants) to copy material for which necessary written permission to copy has not been obtained. Both the individual requesting such services and the individual performing them may be liable for copyright infringement.

Members of the Albion College community who willfully disregard the institution's Copyright Policy do so at their own risk and assume all liability, including the possibility of disciplinary actions for copyright infringement.

Back to Table of Contents

RIGHTS OF CREATORS: COPYRIGHT

Copyright is a form of legal protection for authors of original works, including literary, dramatic, musical, artistic, and other intellectual property. **Publication is not essential for copyright protection, nor is the well-known symbol of the encircled ©**. Section 106 of the Copyright Act (90 Stat 2541) generally gives the owner of copyright the exclusive right to do, and to authorize others to do, the following:

- Reproduce copies of the work.
- Prepare derivative works based on the copyrighted work.
- Distribute copies of the work by sale, rental, lease, or lending.
- Publicly perform the work (if it is a literary, musical, dramatic, or choreographic work or a pantomime, motion picture or audiovisual work).
- Publicly display the work (if it is a literary, musical, dramatic, choreographic, sculptural, graphic, or pictorial work--including the individual images of a film--or a pantomime).

The rights to reproduce the work in copies and to distribute the work refer to the act of copying the work into material objects and to distribute copies publicly. The most common manifestation of the reproduction and distribution rights occurs when an author transfers to a publisher the right to reproduce a novel in book copies and to distribute the copies through sale to bookstores and libraries. The adaption right is the right to prepare derivative works, i.e., works that are derived from an existing copyrighted work. Common examples of derivative works are new editions, translations and condensations. The adaptation right also involves the right to create new arrangements of copyrighted musical compositions, the right to prepare the motion picture script from a novel and the right to transform the format of an audiovisual work such as converting a phonorecord to audiotape, a 16mm film to videotape or 3/4-inch videotape to 1/2-inch format.

The right to perform the work publicly means to recite, render, play or dance the work. The definition covers performance whether done directly or by means of a machine or device. For motion pictures or other audiovisual works, performance means to show its images sequentially or to make its sounds audible. Display is defined as the showing of a copy of a work either directly or by means of a television image, slide, etc., or if the work is a motion picture or other audiovisual work, to show the images nonsequentially. The performance and display right is limited to *public* performance or display which is defined as a performance or display in a place either open to the public or at any place where a substantial number of persons outside the normal circle of family and friends might be gathered. Transmission or other communication to the public of a performance or display also is included in the definition. These rights together encompass all economically significant uses of copyrighted works 1

The copyright owner retains these rights even when the physical manifestation of the work itself

COMPUTER
SOFTWARE

TOC23

COMPUTER
SCANNING

TOC24

DATABASE
DOWNLOADING

TOC25

REQUESTING
PERMISSION TO
USE COPYRIGHTED
MATERIAL IN
EXCESS OF FAIR
USE

TOC26

CONCLUSION

TOC27

APPENDIX A
SAMPLE
PERMISSION
LETTER

TOC28

APPENDIX B
AGREEMENT ON
GUIDELINES
FOR CLASSROOM
COPYING IN NOT-
FOR -PROFIT
EDUCATIONAL
INSTITUTIONS

TOC29

APPENDIX C
AMERICAN
LIBRARY
ASSOCIATION
LIBRARY RESERVE
GUIDELINES:
SECTIONS A & B

TOC30

APPENDIX D
CONTU
GUIDELINES ON
PHOTOCOPYING
AND
INTERLIBRARY
ARRANGEMENTS

TOC31

APPENDIX E

belongs to someone else. **However, these rights are not absolute**. The public in general and scholars in particular have the right to copy under Fair Use guidelines which apply to all media, and under guidelines which apply to a specific medium.

Back to Table of Contents

RIGHTS OF USERS: FAIR USE

The doctrine of fair use, embedded in section 107 of the Copyright Act of 1976, addresses the needs of scholars and students by limiting the rights of copyright ownership. The statute specifies these purposes as acceptable for fair use: criticism, comment, news reporting, teaching, scholarship, or research. However, what constitutes fair use is expressed in the form of guidelines rather than explicit rules. To determine fair use, you will need to consider the following four factors [reprinted with permission from *What Educators Should Know About Copyright*, Virginia Helm (Bloomington, IN: Phi Delta Kappa Educational Foundation, 1986)]:

1. The **purpose and character of the use**, including whether the copied material will be for nonprofit, educational, or commercial use. This factor at first seems reassuring; but unfortunately for educators, several courts have held that absence of financial gain is insufficient for a finding of fair use.
2. The **nature** of the copyrighted work, with special consideration given to the distinction between a creative work and an informational work. For example, photocopies made of a newspaper or newsmagazine column are more likely to be considered a fair use than copies made of a musical score or a short story. Duplication of material originally developed for classroom consumption is less likely to be a fair use than is the duplication of materials prepared for public consumption. For example, a teacher who photocopies a workbook page or a textbook chapter is depriving the copyright owner of profits more directly than in copying one page from the daily paper.
3. The **amount, substantiality, or portion** used in relation to the copyrighted work as a whole. This factor requires consideration of 1) the proportion of the larger work that is copied and used, and 2) the significance of the copied portion.
4. The effect of the use on the **potential market** of the copyrighted work. This factor is regarded as the most critical one in determining fair use; and it serves as the basic principle from which the other three factors are derived and to which they are related. If the reproduction of a copyrighted work reduces the potential market sales and, therefore, the potential profits of the copyright owner, that use is unlikely to be found a fair use.

Back to Table of Contents

MATERIALS IN THE PUBLIC DOMAIN

Some categories of publications are in the public domain; that is, their use is not protected by copyright law. The following types of material may be freely copied:

• U. S. publications more than 75 years old.

• Works published in the U. S. that a) were first published before January 1, 1978 and b) do not include a copyright notice.

• United States government documents issued by the Superintendent of Documents.

Once a work has acquired public domain status it is no longer eligible for copyright protection. Occasionally, scholarly publications such as journal articles include a note offering the right to copy for educational purposes.

FAIR USE
GUIDELINES FOR
EDUCATIONAL
MULTIMEDIA

TOC32

APPENDIX F
GUIDELINES FOR
OFF-AIR
RECORDINGS OF
BROADCAST
PROGRAMMING
FOR EDUCATIONAL
PURPOSES

TOC33

APPENDIX G
WEB ADDRESSES

WHEN WORKS PASS INTO THE PUBLIC DOMAIN

Date of Work	Protection in Effect from	Term
Created 1-1-78 or after	When work is fixed in tangible medium of expression	Life + 70 years (or if work of corporate authorship, 95 years from publication, or 120 years from creation, whichever is first)
Published 1922 or earlier	Now in public domain	None
Published between 1923-1963	When published with notice	28 years + could be renewed for 67 years; if not so renewed, now in public domain
Published 1964-77	When published with notice	28 years for first term; now automatic extension of 67 years for second term
Created before 1-1-78 but not published	1-1-78, the effective date of the 1976 Act which eliminated common law copyright	Life + 70 years or 12-31-2002, whichever is greater
Created before 1-1-78 but published between then and 12-31-2002	1-1-78, the effective date of the 1976 Act which eliminated common law copyright	Life + 70 years or 12-31-2047, whichever is greater

[Adapted, on the basis of 1998 amendments to 1976 copyright law, from *Libraries and Copyright: A Guide to Copyright Law in the 1990s*, Laura N. Gasaway and Sarah K. Wiant (Washington, D.C.: Special Libraries Association, © 1994).]

Back to Table of Contents

STUDENT USE OF COPYRIGHTED MATERIALS FOR CLASS PROJECTS

While the law does not specifically address student uses of copyrighted works, the Senate Report accompanying the Copyright Revision Act of 1976 identifies "special uses" by students:

> "There are certain classroom uses which, because of their special nature, would not be considered an infringement in the ordinary case. For example, copying of extracts by pupils as exercises in a shorthand or typing class or for foreign language study . . . Likewise, a single reproduction of excerpts from a copyrighted work by a student calligrapher . . . in a learning situation would be a fair use of the copyrighted work." (Senate Report No. 94-473)

Based upon that statement, a consensus has developed in higher education that students may copy copyrighted works as a learning exercise (see Appendix E: Fair Use Guidelines for Educational Multimedia). This suggests that students can integrate all types of materials into sound/slide, film, or television productions and other multimedia products. Programs made under this exemption may be submitted to the teacher for a grade and may be shown to the other students in the class, including distance learning transmission over the college's secure electronic network in real time as well as for after-class review or directed self-study. However, the paper or product must remain the property of the student. Copies may not be retained by the teacher or the institution; it may not be shown, transmitted, or broadcast outside the classroom; and no copies may be sold or given away. Students may perform and display their own educational multimedia projects created under Section 2 of the Fair Use Guidelines (see Appendix E) for educational uses in the course for which they were created and may use them in their own portfolios as examples of their academic work for later personal uses such as job and graduate school interviews. Students who wish to make copies beyond these narrow constraints, or who wish to make additional uses of their student projects, must get permission for all elements used.

Back to Table of Contents

PRINTED MATERIALS

MAKING PHOTOCOPIES OF COPYRIGHTED MATERIAL

Copyright law applies to all forms of photocopying, whether it is undertaken at a commercial copying center, at departmental copying facilities, or at a self-service machine such as those in the Library. Guidelines in this handbook aim to give faculty members an appreciation of the factors which weigh for and against fair use. The College does not condone a policy of photocopying instead of purchasing copyrighted works where such photocopying would constitute an infringement under the copyright law, but it does encourage faculty members to exercise good judgment in serving the best interests of students in an efficient manner. It is the policy of this College that the user (faculty, staff, or librarian) secure permission to photocopy copyrighted works whenever it is legally necessary.

Photocopying and Duplication which Require Permission:

1. Repetitive Copying: The classroom or reserve use of photocopied materials in multiple courses or successive years will normally require advance permission from the copyright owner;
2. Consumable Works: The duplication of works that are consumed in the classroom, such as standardized tests, exercises, and workbooks, normally requires permission from the copyright owner;
3. Creation of Anthologies as Basic Text Material for a Course: Creation of a collective work or anthology by photocopying a number of copyrighted articles and excerpts to be purchased and used together as the basic text for a course will, in most instances, require the permission of the copyright holders. Such photocopying is more likely to be considered as a substitute for purchase of a book and thus less likely to be deemed fair use. See the section "Course Packs and Customized Anthologies" below.

Back to Table of Contents

Copying for Classroom Use

Copying for classroom use is governed by the "Agreement on Guidelines for Classroom Copying in Not-for-Profit Educational Institutions" (see Appendix B). Although the guidelines refer to teachers, they are also applicable to librarians and other instructional specialists working with teachers. The guidelines provide a *minimum*, based on three standards: brevity, spontaneity, and cumulative effect. Copying for classroom use that exceeds the guidelines may also be justified in special circumstances under the rubric of fair use.

The negotiated safe-harbor guidelines for classroom uses spelled out in Appendix B are in many ways inappropriate for the college level. "Brevity" simply cannot mean the same thing in terms of grade-school readings as it does for more advanced research. Because university professors were not specifically represented in the negotiation of the classroom guidelines, in 1982 the American Library Association published a *Model Policy Concerning College and University Photocopying for Classroom, Research and Library Reserve Use*. In general, the *Model Policy* with respect to classroom uses suggests following the standard guidelines, recommending that

1. the distribution of the same photocopied material does not occur every semester;
2. only one copy is distributed for each student;

3. the material includes a copyright notice on the first page of the portion of material photocopied;
4. the students are not assessed any fee beyond the actual cost of photocopying.

The photocopying practices of an instructor should not have a significant detrimental impact on the market for the copyrighted work. To guard against this effect, the professor should usually restrict use of an item of photocopied material to one course and should not repeatedly photocopy excerpts from one periodical or author without the permission of the copyright owner. It is reasonable to believe that fair use should apply to library reserves to the extent that it functions as an extension of classroom readings; see the section "Copying for Library Reserve Use" below.

Back to Table of Contents

Copying for Library Archives and Collections

In addition to exercising fair use rights as listed in Section 107 of the Copyright Act, non-profit libraries and archives are authorized to reproduce copyrighted works without permission under the circumstances indicated in Section 108 of the law and according to provisions of the Copyright Term Extension Act of 1998.

Under the following circumstances, the copyright law allows a library to make or request a copy of an entire copyrighted work:

- the library has determined that an unused copy cannot be obtained at a fair price from the usual trade sources, the publisher, copyright owner or authorized reproducing service, [17 U.S.C. Section 108(c)].
- a copy for the library's collection must be made or requested for the purpose of replacing a damaged, deteriorating, lost, or stolen copy [17 U.S.C. Section 108(c)].

Single copies of works or portions of works may be reproduced and distributed by a library employee:

- if there is no direct or indirect commercial advantage;
- if the library or archive is open to the public or available to researchers working in a specific field;
- if the copy contains a notice of copyright.

Library rights under Section 108 are for isolated and unrelated reproduction or distribution, e.g., a single copy of the same work may be distributed on separate occasions. Libraries may not engage in or knowingly be a party to the systematic reproduction or distribution of single or multiple copies of copyrighted material. Libraries may, however, participate in interlibrary loan arrangements under certain conditions. These conditions are outlined in the section of this handbook entitled "Copying for Interlibrary Loan."

Back to Table of Contents

Copying for Library Reserve Use

Photocopying for library reserve use is not mentioned specifically in the Copyright Act. In an attempt to offer guidance to faculty and libraries, the American Library Association issued a recommendation to libraries regarding photocopying for reserve shelf activities. This model policy has been adapted for use by the College's Library and is reproduced below. See also Appendix C.

At the request of a faculty member, the library may place on reserve photocopied excerpts from copyrighted works in its collection in accordance with guidelines similar to the guidelines for classroom copying for face-to-face teaching found in Appendix B. The College believes that these guidelines apply to the library reserve shelf to the extent that it functions as an extension of classroom readings or reflects an individual student's right to photocopy for his/her personal scholastic use under the doctrine of fair use. In general, the library may use photocopied materials for reserve shelf use for the convenience of students both in preparing class assignments and in pursuing informal educational activities which higher education requires, such as advanced independent study and research.

If the faculty request asks for only **one copy** to be placed on reserve, the library may place a photocopy of an entire article, an entire chapter from a book, or an entire poem. Requests for **multiple copies** on reserve should meet the following guidelines:

> 1) the amount of material should be reasonable in relation to the total amount of material assigned for one term, taking into account the nature of the course, its subject matter and level;
>
> 2) the number of copies should be reasonable in light of the number of students enrolled, the difficulty and timing of assignments, and the number of other courses which may assign the same material;
>
> 3) the material should contain a notice of copyright;
>
> 4) the effect of photocopying the material should not be detrimental to the market for the work. (In general, the library should own at least one copy of the work.)

For example, a faculty member may place on reserve, as a supplement to the course textbook, a reasonable number of copies of articles from academic periodicals or chapters from books. A reasonable number of copies will in most instances be less than six, but factors such as the length or difficulty of the assignment, the number of enrolled students, and the length of time allowed for completion of the assignment may permit more in unusual circumstances.

In addition, a faculty member may also request that multiple copies of photocopied copyrighted material be placed on the reserve shelf if there is insufficient time to obtain permission from the copyright owner. For example, a professor may place on reserve several photocopies of an entire article from a recent issue of *Time* or *The New York Times* in lieu of distributing a copy to each member of the class.

Please keep in mind: if there is any doubt as to whether a particular instance of photocopying can be considered fair use in the reserve shelf context, the copyright owner's permission should be sought. (See Appendix A for advice on how to obtain permission.)

Materials placed on reserve will be returned to the faculty member at the end of each semester.

Back to Table of Contents

Copying for Interlibrary Loan

The sections of the 1976 copyright law especially pertinent to reproductions that may be requested or supplied through interlibrary arrangements are sections 107 and 108. Section 108(d) specifies that a library may copy "no more than one article or other contribution to a copyrighted collection or periodical issue, or . . . a small part of any other copyrighted work." The copy must become the property of the requester, and its use is limited to "private study, scholarship, or research."

The Library must have an Interlibrary Loan request form completed by the requester for each photocopy to be requested from another library. The Interlibrary Loan office is legally obligated to display prominently the following notice, and to include the same text on all request forms:

Under the 1976 CONTU guidelines (see Appendix D), systematic photocopying of copyrighted materials is not permitted, but certain copying may be considered fair if there is no intent to avoid purchasing or subscribing to a publication. Some of the important elements of the CONTU guidelines may be summarized as follows:

- The guidelines apply to periodicals published within five years of the interlibrary loan request. (Copying from periodicals older than five years is not unlimited; it remains subject to the provisions of Sections 107-108 of the copyright law.)

- Filled requests from any single periodical title (not single issue), or from any other material described in 108(d), including poetry and fiction anthologies, may not exceed six copies within a calendar year.

- The library may request a loan if an item that it owns is currently unavailable or if a periodical is currently on order.

- Unless the library requesting a photocopy acknowledges COPYRIGHT COMPLIANCE on the request by indicating either CCG (conforms to the copyright guidelines) or CCL (conforms to the copyright law), the supplying library may refuse to fill the request.

When research needs require copying beyond the limits of fair use, permission to copy must be obtained from the copyright owner and/or payment of royalties may be necessary. Examples of copies requiring permission are:

- the reproduction of several articles from a recent issue of a journal;

- the duplication of a substantial portion of a copyrighted work that is available for purchase at a reasonable price.

Back to Table of Contents

Copying for Course Packs and Customized Anthologies

Copyright litigation involving academic users has focused on this type of "anthologies" (collections of articles, or chapters bound together), which are perceived as substituting for textbooks and thus as reducing the potential market for copyrighted publications.

The Courts' decisions in the 1989 lawsuit against Kinko's and the 1992 lawsuit against Michigan Document Services and James M. Smith clearly reinforce the necessity of obtaining copyright owners' permission before producing such customized anthologies. This holds true whether the course pack is produced by an individual or by a copying service.

More information can be obtained through the College's campus bookstore, but some basic guidelines are as follows:

- Every article or chapter in a course pack, if derived from copyrighted material, requires permission, either from the copyright owner (usually the publisher) or through a royalty fee paid to the Copyright Clearance Center. Each item in the packet also must include a notice of copyright--e.g., "Copyright 1990 by Academic Books, Inc." **Permission needs to be requested for each semester in which the course pack is assigned.**

- Adequate time (6 to 8 weeks at a <u>minimum</u>) should be allowed for obtaining copyright permissions. The College's campus bookstore, through its contracted printing center, is able to obtain the necessary permissions on behalf of the faculty or staff member. Whether a bookstore, copy center, or an individual handles requesting permissions from copyright holders, these must be obtained before proceeding with the compilation.

- Course packs must be sold to students at or below cost. Under no circumstances can a faculty member, bookstore, or institution make a profit by selling them. The cost of a course pack includes the cost of processing copyright permissions, any royalty fees required by the copyright holder, and actual photocopying charges.

Back to Table of Contents

UNPUBLISHED WORKS

Manuscripts, letters, and other unpublished materials are likely to be protected by copyright regardless of age, even if they lack a notice of copyright. Unpublished works created before January 1, 1978 are protected through December 31, 2002, or life plus 70 years, whichever is greater. But, if the unpublished work is published before December 31, 2002, then it will be protected for life plus 70 years or until December 31, 2047, whichever is greater.

Unpublished works that belong to the Library Archives may be reproduced in facsimile format for preservation purposes or for deposit for research use in another library or archives. Copies may usually be made for individual researchers under the law's Fair Use provisions. Ownership of the physical object does not signify ownership of intellectual property rights. **Beyond individual fair use, permission must be granted.**

Back to Table of Contents

COPYING MUSIC FOR EDUCATIONAL PURPOSES

Separate copyrights usually exist for sheet music and recordings of musical performances. Additional copyrights may exist for the lyrics. Music dealers usually sell sheet music in sets (e.g., band sets, chorus sets, etc.); hence, single copies may not be available, but can be ordered directly from the publisher. Copying sheet music without permission deprives the composers of royalties.

Fair use guidelines authorize limited copying and altering of sheet music. They also authorize recording student performances. What can be copied varies in accordance with circumstance as follows:

For a Performance:

Emergency copying is permitted so long as replacement copies are subsequently purchased.

Academic Purposes Other than Performance (single copies for personal or library reserve use):

An entire performable unit (section, movement, aria, etc.) if the unit is out of print or available only in a larger work.

Multiple Copies for Classroom (Non-performance) Use:

Excerpts may comprise no more than 10% of a whole work and may not constitute a performable unit.

Music Recordings:

A single copy may be made for the purpose of constructing aural exercises or examinations. Otherwise, the restrictions on copying non-music recordings apply. [See the section in this handbook on Sound Recordings (Other than Musical).]

Back to Table of Contents

LIVE PERFORMANCE AND MEDIA

PERFORMANCES

Public performance of a copyrighted work may also constitute copyright infringement. A performance that takes place at the College will generally be considered a public performance. Albion College has performance agreements for music and dramatic performances with ASCAP and BMI. Copies of these agreements are on file with the Office of the Vice President for Finance and Management. Any music or dramatic work not covered by these agreements requires permission from the copyright owner, and individuals or groups desiring to use such works must seek permission of the copyright owner. Public performances of copyrighted works, however, are permitted under certain circumstances. The statute distinguishes between dramatic works and nondramatic works, grouping musical performances (but not musicals) with the latter. The college has determined that the following activities are permitted without first obtaining copyright permission:

Dramatic Works:

- when a performance takes place in the course of a face-to-face teaching activity (i.e. instructional performances and displays that are not transmitted); and

- when it is conducted in a classroom or similar place (such as a library) devoted to instruction; and

- in the case of an audiovisual work, when the copy (e.g., film or videotape) has been lawfully made. (See also the section in this handbook on Audiovisual Works.)

Performances of dramatic works at the College must meet the above three criteria. If in doubt, you should seek permission from the copyright holder. If the three criteria of this exception are not met, performance of a dramatic work will constitute copyright infringement.

Permission to perform a dramatic work does not automatically give license to videotape the performance and add that videotape to the College's library or drama department collection. If the dramatic work is protected by copyright, permission is required to videotape a performance as well as to retain and distribute that videotape.

Nondramatic Works:

In addition to the exemptions discussed above, performances of nondramatic works at nonprofit educational institutions may be:

- transmitted to other classrooms and to handicapped persons unable to be present in the classrooms, if the performance and the transmission are part of the instructional program; or

- open to the public if the performance is not broadcast, the performers are not compensated, there is no admission charge, any proceeds go to educational purposes, and the copyright owner does not object in writing at least seven days before the performance.

Back to Table of Contents

MUSIC

The use of music raises several issues under copyright law. First of all, when music is performed live, the performance will be governed by the rules discussed in the preceding section. When pre-recorded music is played before a group, there is not only a performance of the musical work but also of the particular recording. Under copyright law, however, the owner of a copyright in a musical recording, as distinct from the underlying composition, does not have the exclusive right to perform the record publicly. Therefore, when pre-recorded music is performed, only the performance of the underlying composition need be analyzed under the statutory provisions governing performances to ensure compliance with copyright law.

On the other hand, the owner of a copyright in a musical recording does have the exclusive right to reproduce the recording. Therefore, when pre-recorded music is copied, for example by making a tape of a song on a compact disc, the exclusive rights of both the owner of the copyright in the recording and the owner of the copyright in the composition may be infringed.

Fair Use Rules Governing Music:

1. Emergency copying is permitted to replace purchased copies that for any reason are not available for an imminent performance, provided that purchased replacement copies shall be substituted in due course.

2. For academic purposes other than performance, single or multiple copies of excerpts of works may be made, provided that the excerpts do not comprise a part of the whole which would constitute a performable unit such as a section, movement, or aria, but in no case more than ten percent of the whole work. The number of copies shall not exceed one copy per pupil.

3. Printed copies that have been purchased may be edited or simplified, provided that the fundamental character of the work is not distorted and that the lyrics, if any, are not altered, or lyrics added if none exist.

4. A single copy of recordings of performances by students may be made for evaluation or rehearsal purposes and may be retained by the college or individual professor.

5. A single copy of a sound recording (such as a tape, disc, or cassette) of copyrighted music may be made from sound recordings owned by the college or an individual professor for the purpose of constructing aural exercises or examinations and may be retained by the college or professor.

Special Fair Use Prohibitions:

- Copying to create or replace or substitute for anthologies, compilations or collective works.

- Copying of or from works intended to be "consumable" in the course of study or of teaching, such as workbooks, exercises, standardized tests and answer sheets and like materials.

- Copying for the use of performance, except as in "Emergency Copying" above.

- Copying for the purpose of substituting for the purchase of music, except as in "Emergency Copying" and "Academic Purposes" above.

- Copying without inclusion of the copyright notice that appears on the printed copy.

Back to Table of Contents

AUDIOVISUAL MATERIALS

Classroom Use of Films and Videotapes:

Possession of a film or video does not confer the right to show the work. The copyright owner specifies, at the time of purchase or rental, the circumstances in which a film or video may be "performed." For example, videocassettes from a video rental outlet usually bear a label that specifies "Home Use Only." However, whatever their labeling or licensing, use of these media is permitted in an educational institution so long as certain conditions are met. Section 110(1) of the Copyright Act of 1976 specifies that the following is permitted:

> Performance or display of a work by instructors or pupils in the course of face-to-face teaching activities of a nonprofit educational institution, in a classroom or similar place devoted to instruction, unless, in the case of a motion picture or other audiovisual work, the performance or the display of individual images is given by means of a copy that was not lawfully made . . . and that the person responsible for the performance knew or had reason to believe was not lawfully made.

Additional text of the Copyright Act and portions of the House Report (94-1476) combine to provide the following, more detailed list of conditions [from Virginia M. Helm, *What Educators Should Know about Copyright* (Bloomington, IN: Phi Delta Kappa Educational Foundation, 1986)]:

1. They must be shown as part of the instructional program.

2. They must be shown by students, instructors, or guest lecturers.

3. They must be shown either in a classroom or other school location devoted to instruction such as a studio, workshop, library, gymnasium, or auditorium if it is used for instruction.

4. They must be shown either in a face-to-face setting or where students and teacher(s) are in the same building or general area.

5. They must be shown only to students and educators.

6. They must be shown using a legitimate (that is, not illegally reproduced) copy with the copyright notice included.

Further, the relationship between the film or video and the course must be explicit. Films or videos, even in a face-to-face classroom setting, may not be used for entertainment or recreation, whatever the work's intellectual content.

Use Outside the Classroom:

The Library has a license from the Motion Picture Licensing Corporation (MPLC) which permits videocassettes in its collection which are covered under that license to be viewed by students, faculty or staff at workstations or in small-group rooms inside the Library. These videos may also be viewed at home (e.g., in a dorm room), so long as no more than a few friends are involved. Larger audiences, such as groups that might assemble in a residence hall living room, require explicit permission from the copyright owner for public performance rights. No fees for viewing a video are permitted even when public performance rights are obtained.

Copying Films or Videotapes:

Permission from the copyright holder must be obtained prior to copying any copyrighted film or videotape. College departments will not duplicate any film or videotape without written authorization indicating that the copyright holder possesses all applicable rights to the work, including literary rights upon which the work is based; music rights (composition and performance); rights to all visual and graphic elements (slides, graphs, still photographs) contained in the work; and performing artists' releases. When you obtain written authorization, make sure that the number of copies of the work that can be made and the length of time they can be retained is indicated. You should also request that the copyright holder indemnify the College against any infringement actions pertaining to the work.

One copy of a purchased foreign-standard videotape may be made to transfer the program to NTSC (U.S.) format. One copy of a purchased U.S. format videotape may be made for use by Albion faculty use while teaching in a foreign country.

Copying Television Programming Off the Air for Classroom Use:

In 1981, an Ad Hoc Committee on Copyright Law negotiated guidelines for off-air recording of broadcast programming for educational purposes. These guidelines represent the committee's "consensus as to the application of 'fair use' to the recording, retention, and use of television broadcast programs for educational purposes. They specify periods of retention and use of such off-air recordings in classrooms and similar places devoted to instruction and for homebound instruction. The purpose of establishing these guidelines is to provide standards for both owners and users of copyrighted television programs."[2]

These guidelines are not embedded in the Copyright Act and it is unclear how courts may choose to apply them. In the absence of explicit legislative or judicial acts, **strict adherence** to the guidelines may serve as some protection should the issue of infringement arise. See Appendix F, "Guidelines for Off-Air Recording of Broadcast Programming for Educational Purposes."

Filmstrips and Slide Sets:

Copying filmstrips and slide sets in their entirety, or altering a program, requires written permission. Transferring a program to another format (e.g., filmstrip to video, filmstrip to slides) also requires permission. Copying a few frames or slides may be a fair use, if the four fair use criteria are met.

Back to Table of Contents

MICROFORMS

Microforms (microfilms, microfiche, etc.) are protected under the copyright act. The rules governing microforms are determined by the nature of the work contained therein (e.g., a literary work, graphic work, etc.). Microform copies of old books, periodicals, and manuscripts may be copied freely if the original works are in the public domain. If the original publication is copyrighted, copies may be made using the rules that apply to books and periodicals.

Back to Table of Contents

SOUND RECORDINGS (OTHER THAN MUSICAL)

Cassettes or disks may not be copied unless all of the following conditions are met:

- the library currently has or had the item in the library's collection;

- the library's copy is lost, damaged, deteriorating, stolen, or its current format is obsolete;

- a replacement recording from a commercial source cannot be obtained at a fair price.

For example, the fact that a replacement cannot be obtained at a fair price does not entitle students and faculty to make copies of copyrighted audiotapes in the Library's collection. Recording brief excerpts is considered fair use, however. For guidelines applicable to musical recordings, see the section "Copying Music for Educational Purposes."

Back to Table of Contents

ART WORKS

Art works are subject to copyright. The duplication of such works in their entirety by photography, sketching, rendering, casting, or printing is a violation of the copyright law. The only exception is for copying illustrations in a book or periodical under the terms of the "Agreement on Guidelines for Classroom Copying" (see Appendix B) or the library photocopying section of the law.

Back to Table of Contents

ELECTRONIC INFORMATION AND COMPUTER SOFTWARE

INTERNET USE AND THE WEB

Internet use and intellectual property rights are the subject of current intense debate, and there are no guidelines other than those we may infer from the use of other media. Use of the Internet, specifically the ease with which data can be transmitted to others and/or altered without permission, gives rise to concerns regarding intellectual property in the global information infrastructure. If you send a message on the Internet you hold the copyright, but realistically you must expect that others will forward it to other users. Material copyrighted to others should not be used other than under fair use, nor should Internet users forward information that they suspect is copyrighted. When creating home pages on the Web, care should be taken not to incorporate copyrighted material, because mounting on the Web is often interpreted as providing multiple copies, not the single copy allowed under fair use. Privacy rights of individuals, e.g., subjects of photographs, must be observed.

Back to Table of Contents

COMPLIANCE WITH THE DIGITAL COPYRIGHT MILLENNIUM ACT

As an Online Service Provider (OSP), Albion College is required by the Digital Copyright Millennium Act of 1998 to establish limitation of liability for copyright infringement by:

- designating an agent to receive statutory notices from copyright owners about infringements and to send statutory notices to affected subscribers;

- advising the Copyright Office of the agent's name and address and posting that information on the OSP's website;

- developing and posting a policy for termination of repeat offenders and providing network users with information about copyright laws;

- complying with "take down" and "put back" notice requirements;

- ensuring that the system accommodates industry-standard technical measures used by owners to protect their works from unlawful access and copyright infringement.

As an OSP, Albion College has limited liability for copyright infringement by third parties, which may include faculty under some circumstances. **Limitation of liability applies to the college as an institution, not to individuals.** The Act determines that the knowledge or actions of a faculty member will not be attributed to the institution when all of the following conditions are met:

- the faculty member's infringing activities do not involve providing online access to course materials that were required or recommended during the past three years;

- the institution has not received more than two notifications over the past three years that the faculty member was infringing;

- the institution provides all of its users with information describing and promoting compliance with copyright law.

The statutory rules do not require the College actively to monitor material on the Internet. The limitation requires an OSP to take action when it has "actual knowledge" of an infringement (by facts brought to its attention or by notice from the copyright owner), but it does not impose the burden on the OSP to monitor or discover infringing behavior. The law also gives immunity from third party user claims, provided there is good faith compliance with the statutory rules.

Back to Table of Contents

MULTIMEDIA

We define multimedia as a computerized format which combines various types of media, including but not limited to graphics, film, sound, television, and text. Some see it as a newly emerging format, but the combining of media in multimedia's predecessor, audiovisual presentation, is not new (see the section "Student Use of Copyrighted Materials for Class Projects"). How copyright and intellectual property rights are defined in this format, however, is currently a matter of intense discussion. There is little, if any, case law providing definitive parameters. In addition, we must be aware of other pertinent concepts, such as privacy rights and complex contracts, which protect individuals.

For use in a class as part of a syllabus, you will be relying on precedents in copyright established for other formats (see the section "Audiovisual Materials" as well as Appendix E). They require that the multimedia be presented only in the classroom setting to class members and the instructor. If you are planning to use the multimedia package in other settings, you need to be aware of the need to get permission for all clips of any kind that you are using. You may be taking profit away from those who own the intellectual property and distribution rights. Furthermore, as with all graphics, especially photographs, you must respect privacy rights of individuals portrayed, and permissions must be gained.

Back to Table of Contents

COMPUTER SOFTWARE

Albion College negotiates site licenses with software vendors whenever possible for software products that are selected for extensive use. These arrangements provide the college community with efficient access to computer programs that support the curriculum while assuring the copyright owner a fair royalty. Check with Information Technology to determine the availability of particular software and the license restrictions that apply.

Other products may be licensed on an individual or limited basis. However, copying is strictly limited except for backup purposes. The Copyright Act allows the purchaser of software to:

- make one and only one copy of software for solely archival purposes in case the original is destroyed or damaged through mechanical failure of a computer. However, if the original is sold or given away, the archival copy must be destroyed.

- make necessary adaptations to use the program.

- add features to the program for specific applications. These improvements may not be sold or given away without the copyright owner's permission.

Printed documentation is covered by copyright as indicated inside each volume of documentation.

In many cases, software may be lent but only for temporary use, not for copying. If the borrower transfers the software to a hard disk, the program must be deleted when the borrowed item is returned. Check the software license for restrictions. Circulating software in the Library's collection must include, and computer labs and other public facilities must post, the following warning to caution against illegal copying of software:

SOFTWARE COPYRIGHT WARNING

Software is protected by the copyright law. In general, software may not be copied without the copyright owner's permission. Read the software license for further restrictions that may apply.

The College strictly prohibits the illegal copying of software. You will be held liable for damages from the illegal duplication of software. Violators will be referred to the College's judicial process.

Copyright law presently is acknowledged to be inadequate in relation to the complexities of software use. EDUCAUSE, a nonprofit organization that supports the use of technology in education, launched the EDUCOM Software Initiative, which developed a statement of principle intended for use by individual colleges and universities and which is endorsed by Albion College.

The EDUCOM Code

Software and Intellectual Rights

Respect for intellectual labor and creativity is vital to academic discourse and enterprise. This principle applies to works of all authors and publishers in all media. It encompasses respect for the right to acknowledgment, right to privacy, and right to determine the form, manner, and terms of publication and distribution.

Because electronic information is volatile and easily reproduced, respect for the work and personal expression of others is especially critical in computer environments. Violations of authorial integrity, including plagiarism, invasion of privacy, unauthorized access, and trade secret and copyright violations, may be grounds for sanctions against members of the academic community.

Software Classifications:

The EDUCOM Code defines four broad classifications of software and applies different principles to each classification as follows:

1. COMMERCIAL SOFTWARE - software for which a license has been purchased allowing use. Minimally, the license will stipulate that the software is covered by copyright; one backup copy of the software may be made, although it cannot be used unless the original package fails or is destroyed; and modifications to the software are not allowed. Other restrictions may apply; read the license for specific limitations.

2. SHAREWARE - the copyright holder specifically allows you to make and distribute copies of the software, but demands payment if, after testing the software, you adopt it for use. In general, all license restrictions for commercial software apply. Selling software as shareware is a marketing decision and does not change the legal requirements with respect to copyright.

3. FREEWARE - the conditions for freeware are in direct contrast to generally understood copyright restrictions. Although the software is covered by copyright, the license allows for free use, modification, and distribution of the software as long as the purposes are not for profit and credit for the original work is given to the copyright holder.

4. PUBLIC DOMAIN - software for which the copyright holder has explicitly relinquished all rights to the software. It must be clearly marked as "Public Domain." Since March 1, 1989, all works assume copyright protection unless the "Public Domain" notification is stated.

Back to Table of Contents

COMPUTER SCANNING

Computer scanning is the process of entering books, periodicals, art works, etc., into a computer by means of an optical scanner. Once a work is entered in the computer, it can be edited, manipulated, and reproduced. Scanning a text may be a fair use if it is used only for research (e.g., for textual analysis). **Except for research uses, any other scanning of copyrighted texts requires the permission of the copyright holder.** The Library will not put scanned text on electronic reserve without permission. Faculty should not scan text and mount it on their Web pages without permission unless the material is in the public domain. Art works should not be scanned without permission unless they are in the public domain. Scanning by students as a learning exercise may be permissible, but the copies should be promptly erased.

Back to Table of Contents

DATABASE DOWNLOADING

Downloading involves copying a data transmission from a database utility to a user's computer.

This shortens the "connect time," which is the basis for most user fees. It also enables the searcher to clean up the data before printing a copy. Databases are copyrightable, and copying from a database to a computer appears to be a copyright infringement. The copyright owners generally accept temporary downloading as a fair use as long as only one report is printed and the data is erased after printing the report. The problem centers on long-term retention of data to reuse or to combine to create a local database. Long-term retention for any purpose requires a downloading license. These licenses are offered by most database utilities.

"Most commercial databases, whether available on-line electronically or on CD-ROM, include a copyright notice on the terminal screen and on printouts and downloaded files. Further, license agreements include a notice of copyright and usually refer to the fair use provisions of the copyright law. **Virtually all of the basic license agreements forbid resale of data retrieved from on-line searching or any kind of commercial use without permission from the on-line vendor. Most on-line databases permit a disk copy to be made for a user, although some are beginning to restrict how many lines or entries can be downloaded.** Under the statute, if it is permissible to print information from the database for the user, it is permissible to give the user a disk containing the information unless the license agreement specifically prohibits downloading. There generally seems to be some understanding on the part of vendors that users can download 'insubstantial portions' of the database, but there is little information as to what particular vendors believe constitutes an insubstantial portion of a database. Virtually all vendors say that the data is for personal use only and may not be transmitted or sold." [Reprinted from *Libraries and Copyright: a Guide to Copyright Law in the 1990s*, Laura N. Gasaway and Sarah K. Wiant (Special Libraries Association, © 1994).]

Back to Table of Contents

REQUESTING PERMISSION TO USE COPYRIGHTED MATERIAL IN EXCESS OF FAIR USE

It is not difficult to request permission to duplicate, adapt, or perform copyrighted materials. Well-established procedures are available (see Appendix A for a sample letter). Email has made asking for permission incredibly easy and is often the fastest and surest way of getting a response. A letter requesting permission may be expedited by (1) enclosing a self-addressed, stamped envelope, (2) including lines at the bottom of the letter for the copyright owner to date, sign, and grant/deny permission (see Appendix A), and (3) mailing two copies of the letter so that the copyright owner can keep one and mail the other signed copy back to you in the SASE.

It is important to maintain orderly records of permissions sought, denied, or granted. Faculty and staff should keep copies of permission letters "forever" to defend against claims of infringement. In some cases royalty or copyright fees must be paid to agencies such as Copyright Clearance Center, ASCAP, BMI, Motion Picture Licensing Corporation, etc.

Back to Table of Contents

CONCLUSION

Keep in mind: the law provides for fair use; educators should exercise these rights. The law also guarantees owners' right; educators, many of whom are also creators and owners, must respect these rights. Individuals who disregard copyright law put themselves legally and financially at risk. For more information about topics in this handbook, please refer to the appendices and the complete copyright law, which may be consulted in the Library.

Back to Table of Contents

[1] Gasaway, Laura N., and Sarah K. Wiant, *Libraries and Copyright: A Guide to Copyright Law in the 1990s* (Washington, D.C.: Special Libraries Association, © 1994), p. 20.

[2] Gasaway and Wiant, *Libraries and Copyright: A Guide to Copyright Law in the 1990s* (Washington, D.C.: Special Libraries Association, © 1994), p. 239.

APPENDIX A

SAMPLE PERMISSION LETTER

Material Permission Department

Hypothetical Book Company

500 East Avenue

Chicago, Illinois 60601

Dear Madam or Sir:

I am requesting permission to copy the following for continued use in my classes in future semesters:

Title: *Learning Is Good*, Fourth Edition

Copyright: Hypothetical Book Co., 1989, 1994

Author: Frank Jones

Material to be duplicated: Chapters 10, 11, and 14

Number of Copies: 50

Distribution: The material will be distributed to students in my classes, and they will pay only the cost of photocopying.

Type of reprint: Photocopy

Use: Supplementary teaching materials.

I have enclosed a self-addressed, stamped envelope for your convenience in replying to this request.

Sincerely,

Faculty Member

Permission is granted _____ denied _____ with these conditions (if any):

_____

Signature(s)

_____

Date

Back to Table of Contents

APPENDIX B

AGREEMENT ON GUIDELINES

FOR CLASSROOM COPYING IN NOT-FOR PROFIT

EDUCATIONAL INSTITUTIONS

With Respect to Books and Periodicals

The purpose of the following guidelines is to state the minimum and not the maximum standards of educational fair use under Section 107 of H.R. 2223. The parties agree that the conditions determining the extent of permissible copying for educational purposes may change in the future; and conversely that in the future other types of copying not permitted under these guidelines may be permissible under revised guidelines.

Moreover, the following statement of guidelines is not intended to limit the types of copying permitted under the standards of fair use under judicial decision and which are stated in Section 107 of the Copyright Revision Bill. There may be instances in which copying which does not fall within the guidelines stated below may nonetheless be permitted under the criteria of fair use.

GUIDELINES

I. Single Copying for Teachers

A single copy may be made of any of the following by or for a teacher at his or her individual request for his or her scholarly research or use in teaching or preparation to teach a class:

> A. A chapter from a book;
>
> B. An article from a periodical or newspaper;
>
> C. A short story, short essay or short poem, whether or not from a collective work;
>
> D. A chart, graph, diagram, drawing, cartoon or picture from a book, periodicals, or newspaper.

II. Multiple Copies for Classroom Use

Multiple copies (not to exceed in any event more than one copy per pupil in a course) may be made by or for the teacher giving the course for classroom use or discussion, provided that:

> A. The copying meets the tests of brevity and spontaneity as defined below; and
>
> B. The copying meets the cumulative effect test as defined below; and
>
> C. Each copy includes a notice of copyright.

DEFINITIONS

Brevity

> (i) Poetry: a complete poem if less than 250 words and if printed on not more than two pages, or, from a longer poem, an excerpt of not more than 250 words.

> (ii) Prose: a complete article, story or essay of less than 2,500 words, or an excerpt from any prose work of not more than 1,000 words or 10 percent of the work, whichever is less, but in any event a minimum of 500 words.

[The numerical limits stated in (i) and (ii) above may be expanded to permit the completion of an unfinished line of a poem or of an unfinished prose paragraph.]

(iii) Illustration: One chart, graph, diagram, drawing, cartoon or picture per book or per periodical issue.

(iv) "Special" works: Certain works in poetry, prose or in "poetic prose" which often combine language with illustrations and which are intended sometimes for children and at other times for a more general audience fall short of 2,500 words in their entirety. Paragraph (ii) above notwithstanding, such "special works" may not be reproduced in their entirety; however, an excerpt comprising not more than two of the published pages of a special work and containing not more than 10 percent of the words found in the text thereof may be reproduced.

Spontaneity

(i) The copying is at the instance and inspiration of the individual teacher, and

(ii) The inspiration and decision to use the work and the moment of its use for maximum teaching effectiveness are so close in time that it would be unreasonable to expect a timely reply to a request for permission.

Cumulative Effect

(i) The copying of the material is for only one course in the school in which the copies are made.

(ii) Not more than one short poem, article, story, essay or two excerpts may be copied from the same author, nor more than three from the same collective work or periodicals volume during one class term.

(iii) There shall not be more than nine instances of such multiple copying for one course during one class term.

[The limitations stated in (ii) and (iii) above shall not apply to current news periodicals and newspapers and current news sections of other periodicals.]

III. Notwithstanding I and II above, the following shall be prohibited:

A. Copying shall not be used to create or to replace or substitute for anthologies, compilations or collective works. Such replacement or substitution may occur whether copies of various works or excerpts therefrom are accumulated or reproduced and used separately.

B. There shall be no copying of or from works intended to be "consumable" in the course of study or of teaching. These include workbooks, exercises, standardized tests and test booklets and answer sheets and like consumable material.

C. Copying shall not:

(a) substitute for the purchase of books, publishers' reprints and periodicals;

(b) be directed by higher authority;

(c) be repeated with respect to the same item by the same teacher from term to term.

D. No charge shall be made to the student beyond the actual cost of the photocopying.

Back to Table of Contents

APPENDIX C

AMERICAN LIBRARY ASSOCIATION LIBRARY RESERVE GUIDELINES:

SECTIONS A & B

LIBRARY RESERVES

A. *American Library Association Reserve Guidelines*

Although there are no congressional guidelines on library reserves, the American Library Association (ALA) has promulgated suggestions for libraries regarding photocopying for library reserve as a part of a model policy for colleges and universities. Since the reserve area is an extension of the classroom, the ALA views copying for reserve as permissible under conditions similar to the classroom guidelines, a position supported by the Association of American Law Schools but rejected by the Register of Copyrights. In particular, the Register maintains that since the guidelines require spontaneity, libraries may not place material on reserve for consecutive terms. Nonetheless, the reserve guidelines enjoy wide acceptance among libraries and presumably among publishers since they have not been litigated.

Single copies may be made for reserve use, the ALA believes, so long as the standards of the classroom guidelines are observed. When multiple copies are requested for reserve by a faculty member, the ALA makes the following recommendations.

1. The amount of material should be reasonable in relation to the total amount of material assigned for one term of a course. Matters such as the nature of the course, its subject matter and level should be taken into account. This statement makes it clear that library reserves are not to take the place of a purchased textbook or course pack on which royalties have been paid to the copyright holder. Materials photocopied for reserve generally are intended to supplement the other materials assigned for the course and not to serve in lieu of any other materials.

2. The number of copies should be reasonable in light of the number of students enrolled, the difficulty and timing of assignments, and the number of other courses which may assign the same materials. This likely means that the library rather than the faculty member should determine what number of copies is reasonable.

3. The material should contain a notice of copyright. If the article contains the notice of copyright on the first page of the article, the library need do nothing more than ensure that the notice is legible. If the notice is not printed on the article, then the library must write or stamp the notice.

4. The effect of photocopying the material should not be detrimental to the market for the work.

5. In general, the library should own at least one copy of the work. This does not mean that occasionally a library could not place on reserve a photocopy that belongs to a faculty member or one the library obtained through interlibrary loan. The library should not make a general practice of this, however, if it is to comply with the ALA model policy.

Some writers have said that a reasonable number of copies would be six, although other factors may permit more copies to be made, including the difficulty of the assignment, the number of students in the class and the length of time the students have to complete the assignment. If there is too little time for the professor to request permission from the copyright holder to make the copies, more copies may be placed on reserve than in the normal situation. A faculty member who is uncertain about placing copies on reserve should defer to the library's policy or obtain the copyright holder's permission.

A more puzzling part of the model policy is found in the materials that precede the requirements discussed above. As an introductory matter, the policy states that, in general, photocopying for reserve collections should follow the classroom guidelines. Then four specific requirements are listed: (a) the distribution of the same material does not occur every semester, (b) only one copy is distributed to each student, (c) the material contains a notice of copyright on the first page of the portion copied, and (d) students are not assessed any charge beyond the actual charge of making the copy. When one examines these four requirements, it is difficult to see their applicability to reserves.

Regarding requirement (b), for library reserve situations, the library would practically never reproduce a copy for each student in the class. In fact, the very reason for placing materials on reserve is that a few copies are made and not one per student. The last requirement concerning a charge to students for the copies is totally irrelevant to reserve practices. No library charges a fee for library reserve use! Thus, the cost per student limitation is unnecessary. The requirement concerning the inclusion of a notice of copyright on the photocopied material is important; in fact, it is so important that the requirement is repeated in the specific portion of the guidelines that relate to reserve copying.

Thus, the only requirement of the four that either has any relevance or is not repeated is (a), distribution of the same material does not occur every semester. Libraries have struggled with the meaning of this as it applies to reserve copying. Some libraries apply the requirement as if it were mandated by the law itself. Other libraries take a more liberal view and believe that when the model policy says that in general the classroom guidelines should be followed, that is what it means. Therefore, some libraries without written permission from the copyright owner. Libraries that follow this strict interpretation vary in whether they handle permission requests or whether they require faculty members who want the items placed on reserve to contact the copyright holder for permission. Some libraries go so far as to refuse a request to put an item on reserve the second semester without written permission from the owner which the faculty member must submit along with the request.

Among the libraries that apply a more liberal view of the policy, some encourage faculty to obtain permission to use photocopied material on reserve the second semester but stop short of an absolute requirement. Others take the tack of removing from reserve all materials each semester and returning them to the faculty member in the hopes that over time he will pare down the amount of material placed on reserve.

The course chosen by the library concerning this requirement may depend more on space management issues than on a literal reading of the guidelines. In other words, if the library is concerned about finite reserve space, it may decide to interpret strictly the meaning of the first general requirement. This relates not so much to copyright as to an important administrative issue for the library. Unfortunately, there is no general guidance on this issue. No library has been sued over its reserve collections nor have there been other interpretations from the ALA, the Copyright Office or others.

B. ELECTRONIC RESERVES

Some libraries have substituted electronic copies for traditional photocopy reserve collections and many others are considering doing so. Electronic reserves could solve space and staffing problems currently associated with reserve collections of photocopies of copyrighted articles, chapters, etc. Is it possible to comply with the ALA Reserve Guidelines and still develop and maintain an electronic reserve system? Perhaps, but the publisher community is very concerned about retention and repeated use of electronically stored copies. The *ALA Reserve Guidelines* state that the amount of material a faculty member requests be placed on reserve as well as the number of copies should be reasonable. In the photocopy reserve situation, the library determines what number of copies is reasonable based on the number of students in the class, level of the class, length of the assignment, length of time before the assigned material must be read and the like. For example, based on these factors, a college library might decide that eight copies on reserve are sufficient for a class of 25 students.

When one thinks of an electronic reserve collection, the usual situation envisioned is that materials would be scanned and stored on a central library computer which students could access from terminals in the library or even from remote locations. There are other ways this could be done. For example, the library could scan the items and put them on a floppy disk that is circulated just as hard copies are circulated. Another method is to put the scanned copies onto the central computer and then make a "copy" for each user by putting the copies into the electronic mailboxes for each student. For purposes of this chapter, however, assume that scanned copies are stored on a central computer in the library and that users access the material through terminals within the library and from remote locations.

Where libraries have initiated electronic reserves, there is no uniformity in what types of materials are available and whether the library considers the activity to be fair use or one on which royalties should be paid. Both Rice and Duke universities have experimental electronic reserve collections of copyrighted materials. Rice is paying royalties on every copy made (i.e., for every use) of material in the electronic reserve collection; Duke believes an electronic reserve collection is fair use and is not paying royalties. The University of Pittsburgh has created an electronic reserve collection that consists of heavily used but uncopyrighted works created by faculty such as reserve collections will be able to help answer some of the unanswered questions.

Electronic reserve collections present several copyright concerns. First, what is the number of copies that are made and does the number raise fair use concerns? Instead of any reserve collection photocopy that might be read by several students, one electronic copy is made includes whenever a copy is displayed on the screen in addition to when a copy is printed from the screen or downloaded to a disk. Second, will the library erase the scanned copy at the end of the class term? Third, is it necessary for the library to restrict access to the electronic copies to students enrolled in particular classes? If so, will it be done through access codes or some other mechanism? Fourth, must the library require the professor to obtain permission to place the item on reserve for subsequent terms? For the present, these and other considerations have meant that few libraries actually have created electronic reserve collections, although the numbers seem to be increasing. It is possible that because of these concerns electronic reserve collections are more closely akin to course packets than to traditional reserve collections. If they are analogous to course packets, then the *Guidelines on Multiple Copying for Classroom Use* must be met and royalties paid for copying in excess of fair use. The question then for the calculation of royalties becomes how many copies were made. For the library, an important question follow: who pays the royalty, the library or the student? Since the Copyright Clearance Center has not been authorized to collect royalties for electronic copies, if royalties are due, they must be paid directly to the publisher or copyright holder. This alone may discourage some libraries from converting traditional reserve collections to electronic format.

Another important concern arises under section 108(g) which states that the exemptions for the library copying extend to isolated and unrelated reproduction of a single copy. This applies to the reproduction of the same material on separate occasions but does not extend where the library engages in related or concrete reproduction and distribution of multiple copies of the same material, on one occasion or over a period of time. Section 108(g) applies whether the multiple copying is by aggregate use by one or more individuals or for separate use by the individual members of a group. The publisher community apparently does not object to reserve collections that carefully adhere to the ALA guidelines for photocopies as evidenced by the lack of complaints, articles challenging the guidelines, or litigation. Why the same acquiescence is not present for electronic reserve collections appears somewhat inconsistent to many in the library community.

Back to Table of Contents

APPENDIX D

CONTU GUIDELINES ON PHOTOCOPYING AND INTERLIBRARY ARRANGEMENTS

As part of the effort to revise the copyright laws, the U.S. National Commission on New Technological Uses of Copyrighted Works (CONTU) was created to provide recommendations on copyright law and procedure. The guidelines in the Commission's 1978 final report address section §108(g)(2) and attempt to clarify what was meant by "systematic reproduction." Libraries, in general, follow these guidelines:[1]

1. As used in the proviso of subsection 108(g)(2), the words "such aggregated quantities as to substitute for a subscription to or purchase of such work" shall mean:

    (a) with respect to any given periodical (as opposed to any given issue of a periodical), filled requests of a library or archives (a "requesting entity") within any calendar year for a total of six or more copies of an article or articles published within five years prior to the date of the request. These guidelines specifically shall not apply, directly or indirectly, to any request of a requesting entity for a copy or copies of an article or articles published in any issue of a periodical, the publication date of which is more than five years prior to the date when the request is made. These guidelines do not define the meaning, with respect to such a request, of "such aggregate quantities as to substitute for a subscription to [such periodical]."

    (b) with respect to any other material described in subsection 108(d) (including fiction and poetry), filled requests of a requesting entity within any calendar year for a total of six or more copies or phonorecords of or from any given work (including a collective work) during the entire period when such material shall be protected by copyright.

2. In the event that a requesting entity:

    (a) shall have in force or shall have entered an order for a subscription to a periodical, or

    (b) has within its collection, or shall have entered an order for, a copy or phonorecord of any other copyrighted work, material from either category of which it desires to obtain by copy from another library or archives (the "supplying entity"), because the material to be copied is not reasonably available for use by the requesting entity itself, then the fulfillment of such request shall be treated as though the requesting entity made such copy from its own collection. A library or archives may request a copy or phonorecord from a supplying entity only under those circumstances where the requesting entity would have been able, under the provisions of section 108, to supply such copy from materials in its own collection.

3. No request for a copy or phonorecord of any material to which these guidelines apply may be fulfilled by the supplying entity unless such request is accompanied by a representation by the requesting entity that the request was made in conformity with these guidelines.

4. The requesting entity shall maintain records of all requests made by it for copies or phonorecords of any materials to which these guidelines apply and shall maintain records of the fulfillment of such requests, which records shall be retained until the end of third complete calendar year after the end of the calendar year in which the respective request shall have been made.

5. As part of the review provided for in subsection 108(i), these guidelines shall be reviewed not later than five years from the effective date of this bill.

6.

[1] Reprinted from Virginia Boucher, *Interlibrary Loan Practices Handbook*, 2nd ed. (Chicago and London: American Library Association, © 1997).

Back to Table of Contents

APPENDIX E

FAIR USE GUIDELINES FOR EDUCATIONAL MULTIMEDIA

TABLE OF CONTENTS

1. Introduction

2. Preparation of Educational Multimedia Projects Under These Guidelines

3. Permitted Educational Uses for Multimedia Projects Under These Guidelines

4. Limitations

5. Examples of When Permission is Required

6. Important Reminders

1. INTRODUCTION

1.1 Preamble

Fair use is a legal principle that defines the limitations of the exclusive rights** of copyright holders. The purpose of these guidelines is to provide guidance on the application of fair use principles by educators, scholars and students who develop multimedia projects using portions of copyrighted works under fair use rather than by seeking authorization for non-commercial educational uses. These guidelines apply only to fair use in the context of copyright and to no other rights.

There is no simple test to determine what is fair use. Section 107 of the Copyright Act*** sets forth the four fair use factors which should be considered in each instance, based on particular facts of a given case, to determine whether a use is a "fair use": (1) the purpose and character of use, including whether such use is of a commercial nature or is for nonprofit educational purposes, (2) the nature of the copyrighted work, (3) the amount and substantiality of the portion used in relation to the copyrighted work as a whole, and (4) the effect of the use upon the potential market for or value of the copyrighted work.

While only the courts can authoritatively determine whether a particular use is fair use, these guidelines represent the endorsers' consensus of conditions under which fair use should generally apply and examples of when permission is required. Uses that exceed these guidelines may or may not be fair use. The participants also agree that the more one exceeds these guidelines, the greater the risk that fair use does not apply.

The limitations and conditions set forth in these guidelines do not apply to works in the public domain--such as U.S. Government works or works on which copyright has expired for which there are no copyright restrictions--or to works for which the individual or institution has obtained permission for the particular use. Also, license agreements may govern the uses of some works and users should refer to the applicable license terms for guidance.

The participants who developed these guidelines met for an extended period of time and the result represents their collective understanding in this complex area. Because digital technology is in a dynamic phase, there may come a time when it is necessary to review the guidelines. Nothing in these guidelines shall be construed to apply to the fair use privilege in any context outside of educational and scholarly uses of educational multimedia projects.

This Preamble is an integral part of these guidelines and should be included whenever the guidelines are reprinted or adopted by organizations and educational institutions. Users are encouraged to reproduce and distribute these guidelines freely without permission; no copyright protection of these guidelines is claimed by any person or entity.

Back to Table of Contents

* These Guidelines shall not be read to supersede other preexisting education fair use guidelines that deal with the Copyright Act of 1976.

** See Section 106 of the Copyright Act.

*** The Copyright Act of 1976, as amended, is codified at 17 U.S.C. Sec. 101 et seq. guidelines and clearly indicate the variety of interest groups involved, both from the standpoint of the users of copyrighted material and also from the standpoint of the copyright owners.

1.2 Background

These guidelines clarify the application of fair use of copyrighted works as teaching methods are adapted to new learning environments. Educators have traditionally brought copyrighted books, videos, slides, sound recordings and other media into the classroom, along with accompanying projection and playback equipment. Multimedia creators integrated these individual instructional resources with their own original works in a meaningful way, providing compact educational tools that allow great flexibility in teaching and learning. Material is stored so that it may be retrieved in a nonlinear fashion, depending on the needs or interests of learners. Educators can use multimedia projects to respond spontaneously to students' questions by referring quickly to relevant portions. In addition, students can use multimedia projects to pursue independent study according to their needs or at a pace appropriate to their capabilities. Educators and students want guidance about the application of fair use principles when creating their own multimedia projects to meet specific instructional objectives.

1.3 Applicability of These Guidelines

(Certain basic terms used throughout these guidelines are identified in bold and defined in this section.)

These guidelines apply to the use, without permission, of portions of lawfully acquired copyrighted works in educational multimedia projects which are created by educators or students as part of a systematic learning activity by nonprofit educational institutions. **Educational multimedia projects** created under these guidelines incorporate students' or educators' original material, such as course notes or commentary, together with various copyrighted media formats including, but not limited to, motion media, music, text material, graphics, illustrations, photographs and digital software which are combined into an integrated presentation. **Educational institutions** are defined as nonprofit organizations whose primary focus is supporting research and instructional activities of educators and students for noncommercial purposes.

For the purposes of the guidelines, **educators** include faculty, teachers, instructors, and others who engage in scholarly, research and instructional activities for educational institutions. The copyrighted works used under these guidelines are **lawfully acquired** if obtained by the institution or individual through lawful means such as purchase, gift, or license agreement but not pirated copies. Educational multimedia projects which incorporate portions of copyrighted works under these guidelines may be used only for **educational purposes** in systematic learning activities including use in connection with non-commercial curriculum-based learning and teaching activities by educators to students enrolled in courses at nonprofit or educational institutions or otherwise permitted under Section 3. While these guidelines refer to the creation and use of educational multimedia projects, readers are advised that in some instances other fair use guidelines such as those for off-air taping may be relevant.

2. PREPARATION OF EDUCATIONAL MULTIMEDIA PROJECTS USING PORTIONS OF COPYRIGHTED WORKS

These uses are subject to the Portion Limitations listed in Section 4. They should include proper attribution and citation as defined in Sections 6.2.

2.1 By students:

Students may incorporate portions of lawfully acquired copyrighted works when producing their own educational multimedia projects for a specific course.

2.2 By Educators for Curriculum-Based Instruction:

Educators may incorporate portions of lawfully acquired copyrighted works when producing their own educational multimedia programs for their own teaching tools in support of curriculum-based instructional activities at educational institutions.

3. PERMITTED USES OF EDUCATIONAL MULTIMEDIA PROGRAMS CREATED UNDER THESE GUIDELINES

Uses of educational multimedia projects created under these guidelines are subject to the Time, Portion, Copying and Distribution Limitations listed in Section 4.

3.1 Student Use:

Students may perform and display their own educational multimedia projects created under Section 2 of these guidelines for educational uses in the course for which they were created and may use them in their own portfolios as examples of their academic work for later personal uses such as job and graduate school interviews.

3.2 Educator Use for Curriculum-Based Instruction:

Educators may perform and display their own educational multimedia projects created under Section 2 for curriculum-based instruction to students in the following situations:

3.2.1 for face-to-face instruction,

3.2.2 assigned to students for directed self-study,

3.2.3 for remote instruction to students enrolled in curriculum-based courses and located at remote sites, provided over the educational institution's secure electronic network in real-time, or for after class review or directed self-study, provided there are technological limitations on access to the network and educational multimedia project (such as a password or PIN) and provided further that the technology prevents the making of copies of copyrighted material.

If the educational institution's network or technology used to access the educational multimedia project created under Section 2 of these guidelines cannot prevent duplication of copyrighted material, students or educators may use the multimedia educational projects over an otherwise secure network for a period of only 15 days after its initial real-time remote use in the course of instruction or 15 days after its assignment for directed self-study. After that period, one of the two used copies of the educational multimedia project may be placed on reserve in a learning resource center, library or similar facility for on-site use by students enrolled in the course. Students shall be advised that they are not permitted to make their own copies of the multimedia project.

3.3 Educator Use for Peer Conferences:

Educators may perform or display their own multimedia projects created under Section 2 of these guidelines in presentations to their peers, for example, at workshops and conferences.

3.4 Educator Use for Professional Portfolio:

Educators may retain educational multimedia projects created under Section 2 of these guidelines in their personal portfolios for later personal uses such as tenure review or job interviews.

4. LIMITATIONS—TIME, PORTION, COPYING AND DISTRIBUTION

The preparation of educational multimedia projects incorporating copyrighted works under Section 2, and the use of such projects under Section 3, are subject to the limitations noted below.

4.1 Time Limitations

Educators may use their educational multimedia projects for educational purposes under Section 2 of these guidelines for teaching courses, for a period of up to two years after the first instructional use with a class. Use beyond that time period, even for educational purposes, requires permission for each copyrighted portion incorporated in the production. Students may use their educational multimedia projects as noted in Section 3.1.

4.2 Portion Limitations

Portion limitations mean the amount of a copyrighted work that can reasonably be used in educational multimedia projects under these guidelines regardless of the original medium from which the copyrighted works are taken. **In the aggregate** means the total amount of copyrighted material from a single copyrighted work that is permitted to be used in an educational multimedia project without permission under these guidelines. These limits apply cumulatively to each educator's or student's multimedia project(s) for the same academic semester, cycle or term. All students should be instructed about the reasons for copyright protection and the need to follow these guidelines. It is understood, however, that students in kindergarten through grade six may not be able to adhere rigidly to the portion limitations in this section in their independent development of educational multimedia projects. In any event, each such project retained under Sections 3.1 and 4.3 should comply with the portion limitations in this section.

4.2.1 Motion Media

Up to 10% or 3 minutes, whichever is less, in the aggregate of a copyrighted motion media work may be reproduced or otherwise incorporated as part of a multimedia project created under Section 2 of these guidelines.

4.2.2 Text Material

Up to 10% or 1000 words, whichever is less, in the aggregate of a copyrighted work consisting of text material may be reproduced or otherwise incorporated as part of a multimedia project created under Section 2 of these guidelines. An entire poem of less than 250 words may be used, but no more than three poems by one poet, or five poems by different poets from any anthology may be used. For poems of greater length, 250 words may be used but no more than three excerpts by a poet, or five excerpts by different poets from a single anthology may be used.

4.2.3 Music, Lyrics, and Music Video

Up to 10%, but in no event more than 30 seconds, of the music and lyrics from an individual musical work (or in the aggregate of extracts from an individual work), whether the musical work is embodied in copies, or audio or audiovisual works, may be reproduced or otherwise incorporated as a part of a multimedia project created under Section 2. Any alterations to a musical work shall not change the basic melody or the fundamental character of the work.

4.2.4 Illustrations and Photographs

The reproduction or incorporation of photographs and illustrations is more difficult to define with regard to fair use because fair use usually precludes the use of an entire work. Under these guidelines a photograph or illustration may be used in its entirety but no more than 5 images by an artist or photographer may be reproduced or otherwise incorporated as part of an educational multimedia project created under Section 2. When using photographs and illustrations from a published collective work, not more than 10% or 15 images, whichever is less, may be reproduced or otherwise incorporated as part of an educational multimedia project created under Section 2.

4.2.5 Numerical Data Sets

Up to 10% or 2500 fields or cell entries, whichever is less, from a copyrighted database or data table may be reproduced or otherwise incorporated as part of an educational multimedia project created under Section 2 of these guidelines. A field entry is defined as a specific item of information, such as a name or Social Security number, in a record of a database file. A cell entry is defined as the intersection where a row and column meet on a spreadsheet.

4.3 Copying and Distribution Limitations

Only a limited number of copies, including the original, may be made of an educator's educational multimedia project. For all of the uses permitted by Section 3, there may be no more than two used copies, only one of which may be placed on reserve as described in Section 3.2.3.

An additional copy may be made for preservation purposes but may only be used or copied to replace a used copy that has been lost, stolen, or damaged. In the case of a jointly created educational multimedia project, each principal creator may retain one copy but only for the purposes described in Sections 3.3 and 3.4 for educators and Section 3.1 for students.

5. EXAMPLES OF WHEN PERMISSION IS REQUIRED

5.1 Using Multimedia Projects for Non-Educational or Commercial Purposes

Educators and students must seek individual permissions (licenses) before using copyrighted works in educational multimedia projects for commercial reproduction and distribution.

5.2 Duplication of Multimedia Projects Beyond Limitations Listed in These Guidelines

Even for educational uses, educators and students must seek individual permissions for all copyrighted works incorporated in their personally created educational multimedia projects before replicating or distributing beyond the limitations listed in Section 4.3.

5.3 Distribution of Multimedia Projects Beyond Limitations Listed in These Guidelines

Educators and students may not use their personally created educational multimedia projects over electronic networks, except for uses as described in Section 3.2.3, without obtaining permissions for all copyrighted works incorporated in the program.

6. IMPORTANT REMINDERS

6.1 Caution in Downloading Material from the Internet

Educators and students are advised to exercise caution in using digital material downloaded from the Internet in producing their own educational multimedia projects, because there is a mix of works protected by copyright and works in the public domain on the network. Access to works on the Internet does not automatically mean that these can be reproduced and reused without permission or royalty payment and, furthermore, some copyrighted works may have been posted to the Internet without authorization of the copyright holder.

6.2 Attribution and Acknowledgment

Educators and students are reminded to credit the sources and display the copyright notice © and copyright ownership information if this is shown in the original source, for all works incorporated as part of the educational multimedia projects prepared by educators and students, including those prepared under fair use. Crediting the source must adequately identify the source of the work, giving a full bibliographic description where available (including author, title, publisher, and place and date of publication). The copyright ownership information includes the copyright notice (©, year of first publication and name of the copyright holder).

The credit and copyright notice information may be combined and shown in a separate credit section of the educational multimedia project except for images incorporated into the project for the uses described in Section 3.2.3. In such cases, the copyright notice and the name of the creator of the image must be incorporated into the image when, and to the extent, such information is reasonably available; credit and copyright notice information is considered "incorporated" if it is attached to the image file and appears on the screen when the image is viewed. In those cases when displaying source credits and copyright ownership information on the screen with the image would be mutually exclusive with an instructional objective (e.g. during examinations in which the source credits and/or copyright information would be relevant to the examination questions), those images may be displayed without such information being simultaneously displayed on the screen. In such cases, this information should be linked to the image in a manner compatible with such instructional objectives.

6.3 Notice of Use Restrictions

Educators and students are advised that they must include on the opening screen of their multimedia program and any accompanying print material a notice that certain materials are included under the fair use exemption of the U.S. Copyright Law and have been prepared according to the multimedia fair use guidelines and are restricted from further use.

6.4 Future Uses Beyond Fair Use

Educators and students are advised to note that if there is a possibility that their own educational multimedia project incorporating copyrighted works under fair use could later result in broader dissemination, whether or not as commercial product, it is strongly recommended that they take steps to obtain permissions during the development process for all copyrighted portions rather than waiting until after completion of the project.

6.5 Integrity of Copyrighted Works: Alterations

Educators and students may make alterations in the portions of the copyrighted works they incorporate as part of an educational multimedia project only if the alterations support specific instructional objectives. Educators and students are advised to note that alterations have been made.

6.6 Reproduction or Decompilation of Copyrighted Computer Programs

Educators and students should be aware that reproduction or decompilation of copyrighted computer programs and portions thereof, such as the transfer of underlying code or control mechanisms, even for educational uses, is outside the scope of the guidelines.

6.7 Licenses and Contracts

Educators and students should determine whether specific copyrighted works or other data information are subject to a license or contract. Fair use and these guidelines shall not preempt or supersede licenses and contractual obligations.

APPENDIX F

GUIDELINES FOR OFF-AIR RECORDINGS OF BROADCAST PROGRAMMING FOR EDUCATIONAL PURPOSES

1. The guidelines were developed to apply only to off-air recording by non-profit educational institutions.

2. A broadcast program may be recorded off-air simultaneously with broadcast transmission (including simultaneous cable retransmission) and retained by a nonprofit educational institution for a period not to exceed the first forty-five (45) consecutive calendar days after date of recording. Upon conclusion of such retention period, all off-air recordings must be erased or destroyed immediately. "Broadcast programs" are television programs transmitted by television stations for reception by the general public without charge.

3. Off-air recordings may be used once by individual teachers in the course of relevant teaching activities, and repeated once only when instructional reinforcement is necessary, in classrooms and similar places devoted to instruction within a single building, cluster or campus, as well as in the homes of students receiving formalized home instruction, during the first ten (10) consecutive school days in the forty-five (45) day calendar day retention period. "School days" are school session days--not counting weekends, holidays, vacations, examination periods, or other scheduled interruptions--within the forty-five (45) calendar day retention period.

4. Off-air recordings may be made only at the request of and used by individual teachers, and may not be regularly recorded in anticipation of requests. No broadcast program may be recorded off-air more than once at the request of the same teacher, regardless of the number of times the program may be broadcast.

5. A limited number of copies may be reproduced from each off-air recording to meet the legitimate needs of teachers under these guidelines. Each such additional copy shall be subject to all provisions governing the original recording.

6. After the first ten (10) consecutive school days, off-air recordings may be used up to the end of the forty-five (45) calendar day retention period only for teacher evaluation purposes, i.e., to determine whether or not to include the broadcast program in the teaching curriculum, and may not be used in the recording institution for student exhibition or any other non-evaluation purposes without authorization.

7. Off-air recordings need not be used in their entirety, but the recorded programs may not be altered from their original content. Off-air recordings may not be physically or electronically combined or merged to constitute teaching anthologies or compilations.

8. All copies of off-air recordings must include the copyright notice on the broadcast program as recorded.

9. Educational institutions are expected to establish appropriate control procedures to maintain the integrity of these guidelines.

[Reprinted with permission from *The Copyright Primer for Librarians and Educators*, 2nd ed., Janis H. Bruwelheide (Chicago, American Library Association, © 1995).]

Back to Table of Contents

APPENDIX G

WEB ADDRESSES

SUL: Copyright & Fair Use: Library Copyright Guidelines	http://fairuse.stanford.edu/library
American Library Association: Copyright At A Glance	http://www.ala.org/washoff/copyrightataglance.html
THE UT System Crash Course in Copyright	http://www.utsystem.edu/OGC/IntellectualProperty/cprtindx.htm
U.S. Copyright Office Home Page	http://www.copyright.gov/
U.S. Copyright Office - Rulemaking on Exemptions from Prohibition on Circumvention of Technological Measures that Control Access to Copyrighted Works	http://www.copyright.gov/1201/
MEL: Laws Affecting Libraries	http://mel.org/libraries/LIBS-laws.html
Copyright Information for University of Michigan	http://www.lib.umich.edu/copyright/
MLC - Library Copyright Information	http://mlcnet.org/services/copylinks.php

:: Technology Guide

Policies
RESNET Use

Albion College Acceptable Use Policy for Use of the Residential Network (ResNet)

Purpose

Albion College grants permission to residential students for the academic and non-commercial use of the Albion College Residential Network Service (ResNet) in support of the educational mission of the College.

Implied Consent

This policy governs the relationship of Albion College and its ResNet users. ResNet use is also governed by the Merit Acceptable Use Policy (available at http://www.merit.edu/mn/about/policies.html), Albion College Acceptable Use Policy for Use of Information Technology Resources and the Albion College *Student Handbook*. Use of ResNet constitutes acknowledgment of the effect of those policies as well as this ResNet Acceptable Use Policy. ResNet users are responsible for informing themselves of changes in these policies as they occur.

In addition, all users of information networks generally are subject to an array of laws and regulations - local, state, federal and even international - which are rapidly developing as technology evolves. Each student is solely responsible for his/her lawful use of ResNet and for staying abreast of changes in laws applicable to information network users. Albion College does not undertake to provide comprehensive legal guidance to its users. However, these federal and state statutes are of particular importance to information network users:

· Federal Copyright Law prohibits the unauthorized copying of copyrighted materials, including, but not limited to electronic text, graphic files, commercial software, and audio and video files.

· Federal Wire Fraud Law prohibits the use of interstate communications systems for illegal or fraudulent purposes.

· Federal Computer Fraud and Abuse Law prohibits the unauthorized access to, or modification of information contained in national defense, banking or financial computers.

· Federal Child Pornography Law prohibits the creation, possession or distribution of graphic or computer graphic depictions of minors engaged in sexual activity.

· Michigan Computer Crime Law prohibits inappropriate access to computers and use of computers to commit crimes.

Open Expression

Albion College recognizes an individual's rights to freedom of thought, inquiry and expression specifically as they extend to the electronic information environment. Albion College respects the privacy of its students and considers personal information to be confidential. Furthermore, the privacy of student records is protected by the Family Educational Rights and Privacy Act of 1974. The College cannot ensure the total privacy or security of electronic documents, including but not limited to that information transmitted by electronic mail. Accidental access or access to electronic documents by hackers must always be considered as a possible risk. Albion College will take reasonable precautions to protect the privacy of electronic documents and will not endeavor to access student documents or messages except when necessary to:

· Comply with College policies.

· Comply with local, Michigan or federal laws.

· Protect the integrity of the College's information technology resources and/or the rights and property of the College.

· Allow the Department of Information Technology to perform system administration activities.

Waiver

When the restrictions of this policy interfere with the educational, research or service missions of the College, students may request a written waiver. Requests for waivers should be directed to the vice president for information technology (e-mail at infotech@albion.edu).

General Standards

Students are responsible for **any** use of their ResNet connections and may not extend or re-transmit ResNet services or wiring. Moreover, students may not use ResNet to provide Internet access or accounts to anyone outside the College community.

Students should further understand the following:

· Students are expected to use the College network in a manner that is safe, legal and does not interfere with the operation of the network (see Albion College Acceptable Use Policy for Use of Information Technology Resources for details).

· Albion College provides ResNet as a service to its students, but does not undertake to provide continuous or uninterrupted network service. Interruptions may occur in connection with maintenance or network infrastructure problems. Albion College, at its discretion, may discontinue the service or any feature of it, limit its availability or reconfigure the network.

· Albion College does not represent that the network will support all hardware and software configurations.

· ResNet users connect to the network at their sole risk. Albion College will not be responsible for damage to or loss of hardware, software or data stored in computers located on College property or connected to the network. Users are advised to insure against loss or damage resulting from connection to ResNet and use of network resources, as well as from breaches of computer security, fluctuations in electric power supply, fire, theft and other causes.

· Students should take appropriate measures in configuring and using their own computers to ensure security and backup of important data.

· ResNet users are restricted from all activities and behaviors prohibited by the Albion College Acceptable Use Policy for Use of Information Technology Resources.

Any misuse of the Albion College network or violation of ResNet policy may result in the loss of network privileges and referral to the Albion College Judicial Board for disciplinary action and/or to authorities for legal action. Violation of city, state or federal laws and regulations may also result in seizure of computer hardware and software, fines and/or imprisonment.

Albion College ? Albion, Michigan ? 517/629-1000
Home | Site Index | People Directory | Search | Contact Us
© 2008 All rights reserved.

:: Technology Guide

Policies
Acceptable Use

**Albion College Acceptable Use Policy for Use of Information
Technology Resources**

Purpose

Albion College grants permission to all students, faculty and staff for the
academic and non-commercial use of Albion College electronic resources
and services in support of the educational, research and service missions of
the College.

Implied Consent

Each user with access to the College's computing resources is personally
responsible to use these services appropriately and by their use agrees to
comply with all applicable Albion College policies, including, as applicable, the
Merit Acceptable Use Policy (available at
http://www.merit.edu/mn/about/policies.html), the Albion College Acceptable
Use Policy for Use of the Residential Network, the Albion College *Academic
Catalog*, the Albion College Employee Services Manual including Policies and
Procedures, the Albion College Faculty Handbook and the Albion College
Student Handbook. Users are responsible for informing themselves of
changes in those policies as they occur.

Each user with access to Albion College's computing resources is also
personally responsible to use the services only lawfully, and by their use
agrees to comply with all local, state, federal and applicable international
laws. Albion College does not undertake to provide comprehensive legal
guidance to its users. However, these federal and state statutes are of
particular importance to information network users:

· Federal Copyright Law prohibits the unauthorized copying of copyrighted
materials, including, but not limited to electronic text, graphic files, commercial
software, and audio and video files.

· Federal Wire Fraud Law prohibits the use of interstate communications
systems for illegal or fraudulent purposes.

· Federal Computer Fraud and Abuse Law prohibits the unauthorized access
to, or modification of information contained in national defense, banking or
financial computers.

· Federal Child Pornography Law prohibits the creation, possession or
distribution of graphic or computer graphic depictions of minors engaged in
sexual activity.

· Michigan Computer Crime Law prohibits inappropriate access to computers
and use of computers to commit crimes.

Open Expression

Albion College recognizes an individual's rights to freedom of thought, inquiry and expression specifically as they extend to the electronic information environment. Albion College does not monitor, review or endorse the creation of personal World Wide Web pages and is not responsible for their contents; the views and opinions expressed in such pages or in electronic mail are strictly those of the authors. The College cannot ensure the total privacy or security of electronic documents, including but not limited to that information transmitted by electronic mail. Accidental access or access to electronic documents by hackers must always be considered as a possible risk. Albion College will take reasonable precautions to protect the privacy of electronic documents and will not endeavor to access user documents or messages except when necessary to:

· Comply with College policies.

· Comply with local, Michigan or federal laws.

· Protect the integrity of the College's information technology resources and/or the rights and property of the College.

· Allow the Department of Information Technology to perform system administration activities.

Waiver

When the restrictions of this policy interfere with the educational, research or service missions of the College, members of the College community may request a written waiver. Requests for waivers should be directed to the vice president for information technology (e -mail at infotech@albion.edu).

General Standards for Acceptable Use of Computer Resources

Electronic resources and services are provided to users in support of the educational, research and service missions of the College. Uses that threaten or interfere with the mission of the College, the integrity of the network, the privacy or safety of others, or that are illegal, are prohibited.

The following activities and behaviors are prohibited:

User Identification

· Misrepresentation (including forgery) of the identity of the sender or source of an electronic communication.

· Searching for information about another user against his/her wishes.

· Acquiring or attempting to acquire computer accounts or e-mail accounts assigned to others.

· Lending of passwords, computer accounts or e-mail accounts to others.

· Alteration of the content of a message originating from another person or computer with the intent to deceive.

· Unauthorized use of, modification of, or deletion of another person's computer files, e-mail or newsgroup posting.

Access to Computer Resources

· Unauthorized use or attempted use of restricted -access computer resources, privileges or accounts.

· Intentional compromising of the privacy or security of electronic information including unauthorized access, possession or distribution, by any means, of information deemed confidential under the College's policies regarding individual privacy or confidentiality.

· Interception of or attempted interception of communications by parties not intended to receive them.

· Making available any materials of which the possession or distribution is illegal.

· Unauthorized duplicating or use of copyrighted computer software and materials including infringement of the intellectual property rights of others.

· Commercial, non-academic use of the College's electronic resources.

· Unlawful communications including threats of violence, obscenity, child pornography or harassment (as defined by the Albion College *Academic Catalog*, the Albion College Employee Services Manual including Policies and Procedures, the Albion College Faculty Handbook, the Albion College *Student Handbook* and/or the law).

Operational Integrity

· Deliberate attempts at compromising the integrity and functioning of network accounts, services or equipment, including but not limited to the propagation of viruses; repeated sending of unwanted e-mails; sending of spam e-mail, junk mail, or electronic chain letters; or other activities which interfere with the work of others.

· Any transmission of e-mail to the general student population without approval from the office of Campus Programs and Organizations.

· Any transmission of e-mail from students to the general faculty or staff populations without approval from the Office of Campus Programs and Organizations.

· Any transmission of e-mail from staff to the general faculty or staff populations without approval from the sender's Vice President. This does not apply to staff using the campus Electronic Bulletin Board system.

· Extension or re-transmission of network services or wiring including providing Internet access or accounts to anyone outside the College community.

·Hosting of external domains (those domains outside of Albion.edu) on the Albion College network unless written permission has been obtained from the user's vice president and the associate vice president for communications; domain forwarding, also called URL redirection, or redirecting Web requests for a domain name to content hosted on Albion College servers.

· Attempts to alter or damage in any way College computing or networking equipment, including but not limited to public laboratory computer hardware, ResNet ports, and network wiring, bridges, routers or hubs.

· Damage to the integrity of electronic information, or computer hardware or software.

· Attempts to disrupt, slow down or interfere with the function of the electronic network, information systems or the legitimate work of another user including attempts to circumvent network or system security.

· Intentional wasting of human or electronic resources.

· Negligence leading to damage of College electronic information, equipment and/or resources.

· File sharing of copyrighted information. Students found participating in copyright infringement activities (e.g., file sharing of copyrighted material via peer-to-peer applications such as Kazaa, Grokster, Imesh, WinMX, LimeWire, Bearshare, Aimster, Morpheus, and Gnutella) may be charged a minimum $200.00 fee for the first violation and may be subject to judicial action. Subsequent violations may result in a minimum $500.00 fee and subject to judicial action.

Other

· Running programs that overutilize network bandwidth during high network use hours, especially during workday hours (Monday through Friday, 8 a.m.- 5 p.m.).

· Eating, drinking or smoking in any College computer laboratories, including those in campus residences.

· Overuse of campus printing resources (see printing guidelines posted in public laboratories).

Any misuse of the Albion College network or violation of this policy may result in penalties for infractions up to and including the loss of network privileges, employment termination, referral to the Albion College Judicial Board, expulsion and/or legal action. Violation of city, state or federal laws and regulations may also result in seizure of computer hardware and software, fines and/or imprisonment.

This policy is subject to updates. Please view the most current version of this policy at http://www.albion.edu/it/policies.asp

---

Assumption College

Emmanuel d'Alzon Library
ASSUMPTION COLLEGE

Resources

Catalog

Databases/Indexes

Frequently Accessed
Databases

Print and Online
Journal Locator

Research Guides

Other Libraries

Information

About Us

Off Campus Access

Services

Staff Directory

d'Alzon Arts Series

Library Home

Assumption Home

e-Reserves - FAQs for Faculty

Click here to access the e-Reserves request form.

1. What are e-Reserves and how can they benefit my students?
2. How will my students access these e-Reserves?
3. Will all my students be able to access my e-Reserve materials?
4. What can be placed on e-Reserves?
5. How do I send materials to the Library so that they will be posted as e-Reserves, and how long will it take?
6. How long will my e-Reserve articles remain posted?
7. What do I do if I want the article to be available in future semesters?
8. What about Copyright?

1. What are e-Reserves and how can they benefit my students?

The e-Reserves system allows faculty to place course materials on the Web so that they are accessible to their students 24/7 to view, download and print.

The e-Reserves system accepts and displays documents that you provide in print or electronic format to staff at the d'Alzon Library. When submitting your e-Reserve materials to the library, you must indicate if you wish them placed on your Blackboard course site or made available via the library's online catalog. Assumption students can access these materials from any computer on campus or off campus. Depending on the location of your e-Reserve materials, students will be required to login to Blackboard or the library's catalog to view e-Reserves.

2. How will my students access these e-Reserves?

A. For e-Reserves placed on the Library site:

- Go to the Library home page: (http://www.assumption.edu/dept/library).
- Select CATALOG from the menu in the left-hand column. This will link to the full catalog search screen.
- Click on the Course Reserves tab, then select the name of the professor.
- Click on the Search button.
- All reserve items that meet the search criteria will be displayed. This includes items in print as well as online e-Reserves.
- e-Reserves are identified by the library location: Online.
- Click on the line number to display the catalog record, and then select the CLICK HERE FOR ARTICLE link.
- Log in using last name and the ID barcode number.

B. For e-Reserves placed on Blackboard:

- Log into your Blackboard account to access your course.
- Follow the instructions provided by your instructor.

3. Will all my students be able to access my e-Reserve materials?

Yes. All students enrolled in your course will be able to access e-Reserve materials on your Blackboard site and/or on the library site. If students encounter problems accessing Blackboard materials, they will need to contact the IT help desk at x7060 and if they have trouble accessing e-Reserve materials on the library's catalog, they will need to contact the Library Circulation desk at x7271.

4. What can be placed on e-Reserves?

Examples of items that can be placed on e-Reserves include: syllabi, exams, lecture notes, journal or book chapters, study materials, articles from databases, web sites, etc.

If any articles you wish to place on e-Reserve are already available in a database to which the library subscribes, we will create a direct link to the database article. Because we subscribe to these databases, copyright permission is not required to access these materials. If you have any questions about the full-text availability of your materials, please contact the Reference Department at x7273.

5. How do I send materials to the Library so that they will be posted as e-Reserves, and how long will it take?

- Attach a completed e-Reserve request form to each item you wish to place on reserve.
- Submit the e-Reserve material to Janice Wilbur as a clean photocopy or send to jwilbur@assumption.edu as an email attachment. Adobe PDF format is preferred for electronic files. No faxes please.
- When submitting photocopies, please keep these guidelines in mind:
   o Pages should have a ½" margin on all sides to prevent text from being cut off   during scanning.
   o Pages should be clean and free of dark edges.
   o Number each page
   o Do not staple pages; paperclips are okay
- Individual readings over 50 pages will not be scanned and made available for e-reserve. However, these readings will be placed on regular reserve and made available for check-out at the library's circulation desk.
- To ensure that materials will be available when your students need them, please submit your materials well before the start of the semester (at least two weeks) and at least one week in advance of an assignment during the semester.
- Readings can only remain on e-reserve for one semester before copyright permission is required. If you wish to use e-reserve materials more than once, you must notify the library at least 2 months in advance so copyright permission can be obtained. The library will cover costs at least until the end of academic year 2007-2008.
   PLEASE make sure that the title/author of your e-Reserve article matches the entry on your syllabus. It is frustrating for students, and the librarian helping them, to look through multiple articles trying to figure out what the professor wants them to read.

6. How long will my e-Reserve articles remain posted?

e-Reserves will remain posted until the end of the semester.

7. What do I do if I want the article to be available in future semesters?

Readings can only remain on e-Reserve for one semester before copyright permission is required. If you wish to use e-reserve materials more than once, you must notify the library at least 2 months in advance so copyright permission can be obtained. The library will cover costs at least until the end of academic year 2007-2008.

8. What about Copyright?

The Emmanuel d'Alzon Library has chosen to follow the *Fair-Use Guidelines for Electronic Reserve Systems* developed at CONFU: The

Conference on Fair Use. To view the full text of these guidelines, go to: http://www.utsystem.edu/OGC/IntellectualProperty/rsrvguid.htm.

These guidelines interpret fair use quite broadly, but they are clear in stating, "Permission from the copyright holder is required if the item is to be reused in a subsequent academic term for the same course offered by the same instructor." *Therefore, we will not re-activate e-Reserve materials unless permission has been sought and granted for their re-use.* The Library has worked with the Copyright Clearance Center in obtaining permissions in the past and will be happy to assist professors in applying for permission. The library will cover costs at least until the end of academic year 2007-2008.

If you have further questions, please contact Janice Wilbur (x7271) or Dawn Thistle (x7272).

Catalog | Databases/Indexes | Frequently Accessed Databases | Print and Online Journal Locator | Research Guides | Other Libraries | About Us | Off Campus Access | Services | Staff Directory | d'Alzon Arts Series | Library Home | Assumption Home

Assumption College
Emmanuel d'Alzon Library
500 Salisbury Street
Worcester, MA 01609

(508) 767-7273
TTY: (508) 767-1777
Email: library@assumption.edu

Page last updated: April 2, 2007

College of Mount St. Joseph

▶ **VI. Appendices**

Home • Departments • Human Resources • Employee Handbook • VI. Appendices • H. Policy on Copyright Compliance

Employee Handbook

H. Policy on Copyright Compliance

The College of Mount St. Joseph recognizes and respects intellectual property rights. As part of our mission to maintain the highest standards for ethical conduct, we are committed to fulfilling our moral and legal obligations with respect to our use of copyright-protected works.

Article I of the U.S. Constitution authorizes Congress to pass legislation "to promote the Progress Of Science and useful Arts by securing for limited Times to Authors and Inventors the exclusive Right to their respective Writings and Discoveries." On the basis of the Constitution, Congress has enacted the Copyright Act found at Title 17 of the US Code.

As a matter both of moral integrity and of adherence to US copyright law, the College of Mount St. Joseph sets forth these policies for all employees and students to demonstrate our respect for intellectual property and compliance with the law:

1. No employee or student of the College of Mount St. Joseph may reproduce any copyrighted work in print, video, or electronic form in violation of the law. The easiest way to ensure no violation is by receiving express written permission of the copyright holder. Works are protected by copyright laws in the US even if they are not registered with the US Copyright Office and even if they do not carry the copyright symbol ().

   Copyrighted works include, but are not limited to, printed articles from publications, TV and radio programs, videotapes, music performances, photographs, training materials, manuals, documentation, software programs, databases, and World Wide Web pages. In general, the laws that apply to printed materials are also applicable to visual and electronic media. Examples include diskettes, CD-ROMs, and World Wide Web pages.

2. The College of Mount St. Joseph has obtained a repertory license from the Copyright Clearance Center permitting it to make photocopies of portions of CCC's 1.75 million registered published works. The CCC license permits unlimited copies to be distributed to College of Mount St. Joseph employees for internal use only. The list of CCC registered works, including trade, newspaper, and magazine titles, is available at www.copyright.com.

3. For all other copyrighted works, the College of Mount St. Joseph directs its employees to obtain permission from copyright holders directly, or their licensing representative, when the reproduction or duplication exceeds fair use.

4. The College of Mount St. Joseph designates the Director of Library Services as the copyright officer to administer the College's copyright policy. The Director of Library Services can help you determine whether a work is covered by the CCC license and how to handle any special copyright issues. Questions concerning copyright procedures, including fair use, should be addressed to the attention of this officer.

   To obtain permission to reproduce copyrighted works not covered by the CCC license or other prior agreements, the employee should contact the Rights and Licensing Department of the copyright holder. Questions on specific procedures should be directed to the copyright officer named above.

Instructions for Handling an Incident of Copyright Infringement

The College of Mount St. Joseph encourages its employees to educate their peers and students on copyright compliance. If any employee witnesses or becomes aware of a potential copyright infringement, we encourage the employee to bring the matter to the attention of the individual as well as to our copyright officer named above. Employees who illegally duplicate copyrighted works may be subject to disciplinary action up to and including termination. Students who illegally duplicate copyrighted works are also subject to disciplinary action up to and including dismissal. Consult the Student Handbook under "Student Conduct and Disciplinary Procedures" for details.

Examples of copyrighted works include:

a. Literary Works (e.g., books, magazines, newspapers, cartoons, trade journals, training materials, newsletters, documentation)
b. Computer software
c. Pictures, graphics, and sculptures (e.g., maps, cartoon characters, photographs)

d. Sound recordings (e.g., MP3 files, compact discs, cassette tapes, and phonographic records)
e. Architectural works (e.g., blueprints)
f. Dramatic works (e.g. plays, screenplays)
g. Audiovisual works (e.g., videotapes)
h. Pantomimes and choreographic works

The principal rights of the copyright owner are:

a. to reproduce the work (e.g., photocopies, scans, CD-ROMs)
b. to prepare derivative works based on the original work
c. to distribute copies of the work for sale, rental or lease
d. to perform the work publicly (e.g., motion pictures, videos, plays)

For more information on copyright, consult the following web sites:

- American Society of Composers, Authors, and Publishers -- www.ascap.com

- American Society of Media Photographers www.asmp.org

- Association of American Publishers www.publishers.org

- Broadcast Music, Inc. www.bmi.com

- Graphic Artists Guild www.gag.org

- International Federation of Reproduction Rights Organizations www.ifrro.org/

- Media Photographers' Copyright Agency www.mpca.com

- Motion Picture Licensing Corporation www.mplc.com

- National Writers Union www.nwu.org/

- Software Publishers Association www.spa.org

- US Copyright Office lcweb.loc.gov/copyright/

This information is part of the College of Mount St. Joseph's Employee Handbook.

 PRINT PAGE

Home | Site Map | Feedback

College of Mount St. Joseph Intranet
5701 Delhi Road • Cincinnati, Ohio 45233-1670
513-244-4200 • 1-800-654-9314 • Fax: 513-244-4601
© Copyright 2008 All rights reserved

Earlham College

Copyright Policy for Earlham College[1]

As an increasing number of questions have been raised about electronic documents and the ability to copy and distribute them, it became clear the institution needed to develop a statement on copyright. While informal policies existed the institution has never formally developed and approved a policy through faculty and/or administrative action. As an extension of Earlham's "Principles and Practices"[2] and consistent with its philosophy, this document is intended to serve as a set of guidelines for students, faculty and staff of the college in their uses of copyrighted materials.

The purpose of the document is to provide a basis for guiding practice. The writers understand that the field of copyright law and interpretation of Fair Use is in great flux and we will not be able to write a definitive policy that will have much staying power. Instead, we have written what might be called guidelines that will need to be revised frequently as the legal landscape changes. As the appendix to this statement indicates, we believe that an educational program will be very important follow-up to the implementation of the guidelines.

The appropriate place for such a policy to be developed is the Information Technology Policy Committee (ITPC) –a faculty committee that includes representation from all segments of the on-campus community. In the summer of 2003 Information Services (IS) explored possible shapes for such a policy. Because so many institutions have developed such statements we did not want to start from scratch. In our exploration of other statements we were attracted to that of Princeton University. We liked the general approach the statement took and the statement was in many ways consonant with our own practices. Staff of IS created a version of the Princeton document that more accurately represented Earlham's current informal policies, was consistent with the authors' understanding of current law, and used language that is locally appropriate (e.g., college instead of university). The approach is to develop a document that focuses on the fair use provisions recognized in the law and vigorously apply them to our circumstances. ITPC revised the document during the fall semester 2003. What follows is the latest version to result from that revision process. ITPC expects that there will be further changes as the document is reviewed broadly on the campus. This introduction will be revised as the process goes forward.

–Mickey White and Tom Kirk, July 2005

---

[1] We wish to acknowledge Princeton University's "Guidelines for Instructional Use of Copyrighted Electronic and Multimedia Materials" [http://infoshare1.princeton.edu/reserves/libcitcopyright.html] that was the starting point for the development of this policy. Some language from the Princeton University Policy has been retained in this document. This version approved by ITPC on December 8, 2004.

[2] Principles and Practices. Richmond, IN: Earlham College, 2000. [http://www.earlham.edu/policies/p&p.html] "The *Community Principles and Practices* describes principles and practices that guide those of us who live and work at Earlham College and who form its campus community: students, teaching and administrative faculty, and staff. As well, College trustees, and many alumni and former employees of the College, feeling themselves still members of the community, choose to embrace these principles.

Introduction: Instructional Use of Copyrighted Materials

The staff members of Information Services support the basic objectives of Earlham College's policy for use of Intellectual Property as stated in Computing Resources Acceptable Use Policy (http://www.earlham.edu/ecs/html/policies/ecs-aup.html).

The staff members will follow college policy and U.S. copyright law related to the use of electronic and multimedia materials. This includes the recording, reproducing, storing, and distribution of media-based instructional materials, such as: audio, video, and multimedia (combinations of data, text, sounds, and still and moving images that may also be modified interactively). All members of the college community are governed by these regulations.

Members of the college community who engage in any activity that infringes on copyright law may be subject to disciplinary action. Under circumstances involving repeated instances of infringement through the use of the College's computing network, such disciplinary action may include the termination or suspension of network privileges.

Members who are accused of infringement but who are also able to demonstrate to the college that they acted based on a reasonable application of this policy, Fair Use and copyright law will receive support from the college in defending themselves.

Further information about appropriate uses of college technology may be found at (http://www.earlham.edu/ecs/html/policies/ecs-aup.html). More information regarding copyright may be viewed at the United States Copyright Office web site.

Why Should I Read These Guidelines?

Individuals are liable for their own actions. The copyright law (Title 17, United States Code) sets strict limits on making copies of copyrighted works. Willfully exceeding these limits may subject the copier to liability for infringement with damages up to $100,000 per work.

Earlham College is not required to defend an individual who knowingly fails to comply with the College's Policy on Copying, fair use guidelines, and any licenses that affect the rights to use others' works. Information Services will not permit the duplication or use of any material submitted which is known or suspected not to meet the requirements of the guidelines. The College expects those using the materials to be familiar with the guidelines and abide by them.

"Fair Use"

Information Services Staff will assist faculty in evaluating instructional materials to identify those that fall within the "fair use" clauses of the copyright law. The "fair use" exemptions incorporated into the copyright law describe permitted educational uses of certain categories of copyrighted materials.

Copyright Law and Electronic Materials

In some areas, particularly relating to electronic and multimedia materials, copyright law and fair use guidelines are unclear. As expected, challenges to the copyright law are being debated. Information Services staff will make every effort to provide common-sense interpretations of the existing law and guidelines.

Copyright Permission

When use of copyrighted material falls outside of the "fair use" guidelines or is more than quoting small sections of a source, permission must be obtained from the copyright holder. Electronic material supplied by the library must include a copyright statement. Other materials must contain a documented copyright permission statement or a "fair use" disclaimer statement as detailed in the specific guidelines below. Obtaining such permission is usually possible, if sufficient lead-time is allowed, although a fee may be involved. The length of this process varies and can take from a few days to many weeks, or can last for unexplained lengthy periods.

General Information about Fair Use

Copyright law protects certain exclusive rights of copyright holders for a set period of time, including the following rights: copying their works, making derivative works, distributing their works, and performing their works.

These rights exist from the moment a work is created, whether or not a copyright notice appears on the work. It is always best to assume that the provisions of copyright law protect materials being used for instructional purposes, unless the materials are explicitly identified as belonging in the public domain. In using copyrighted materials for instructional purposes, even under "fair use" guidelines, it is always wise to acknowledge the copyright owner in a very clear way. Academic honesty and its negative, plagiarism, are not issues of fair use. Academic honesty requires citing others' ideas.[*]

Fair use: a limited exemption
Copyright law does allow limited copying, distribution, and display of copyrighted works without the author's permission, *under certain conditions* known as "fair use."

---

[*] For more information on plagiarism see Robert A. Harris. The Plagiarism Handbook. (Los Angeles: Pyrczak Publisher, 2001).

The Fair Use Statute

The following is the full text of the fair use statute of the U. S. Copyright Act.

Section 107 of the Copyright Act of 1976. Limitations on exclusive rights: Fair Use

> *Notwithstanding the provisions of sections 106 and 106A, the fair use of a copyrighted work, including such use by reproduction in copies or phonorecords or by any other means specified in that section, for purposes such as criticism, comment, news reporting, teaching (including multiple copies for classroom use), scholarship, or research, is not an infringement of copyright.*

But note that the concept of "fair use" provides *limited* exemption, and does not encompass wholesale copying and distribution of copyrighted work for educational or any other purpose, without permission.

Copyright law does not specify the exact limitations of fair use. Instead, the law provides four interrelated standards or tests, which must be applied in each case to evaluate, whether the copying or distributing falls within the limited exemption of fair use.

Here are the four standards:

1. *The purpose and character of the use*.
   Duplicating and distributing selected portions of copyrighted materials for specific educational purposes falls within fair use.
2. *The nature of the copyrighted work*.
   The characteristics of the work help determine the application of fair use. For example, works built on facts and published materials may have a better claim to fair use than imaginative and unpublished works. Commercial audiovisual works and consumable "workbook" materials are subject to less fair use than many printed materials.
3. *The amount and substantiality of the portion used in relation to the copyrighted work as a whole*
   Copying extracts that are short relative to the whole work and distributing copyrighted segments that do not capture the "essence" of the work are more likely to be considered within fair use.
4. *The effect of use on the potential market for or value of the work*.
   If copying or distributing the work does not reduce sales of the work, then the use may be considered fair. Of the four standards, this is arguably the most important test for fair use.

Further material on Fair Use is available from the library, which maintains reference sources on copyright and its current legal status.

Currently the following Web sites provide up-to-date and useful information. (Additions and deletions will be made as these become inactive or new resources become available.)

> Fair-use guidelines from the Consortium for Educational Technology in University Systems (CETUS)
  http://www.cetus.org/fairindex.html
> Copyright and fair-use guidelines from IUPUI
  http://www.copyright.iupui.edu/
> Copyright and fair-use guidelines from Stanford
  http://fairuse.stanford.edu/
> University of Texas System. Crash Course in Copyright
  http://www.utsystem.edu/ogc/IntellectualProperty/cprtindx.htm
> U.S. Copyright Office
  http://www.copyright.gov/
> Creative Commons (creating works in the Public Domain)
  http://creativecommons.org/learn/aboutus/
> University System of Georgia
  http://www.usg.edu/admin/legal/copyright/
> © (Copyright) Primer (University of Maryland)
  http://www-apps.umuc.edu/primer/enter.php
  Tutorial introduction to copyright for the higher education community which includes a quiz on major concepts.

Guidelines for Using Copyrighted Materials In an Instructional Setting

1. **Copying**
   Following the "fair use" guidelines outlined above, segments of copyrighted electronic and multimedia materials may by captured, copied, digitized, transformed to another medium, or manipulated *for educational purposes only*, by members of the college community.
2. **Acknowledgement**
   The holder of the copyright to each segment must be clearly and prominently acknowledged on or next to the digitized material, even when "fair use" guidelines are observed. (Citing a source from which a quotation is taken is considered proper acknowledgment.)
3. **Incorporating materials into new works**
   Segments of material may be incorporated into studies and projects for instructional and scholarly purposes. Permission must be sought to use materials in works, other than small excerpts that are used as quotations, that are circulated beyond the original educational setting (e.g., a class, faculty seminar, some recognized group organized for educational purposes) or that may have commercial application.
4. **Building digitized collections.**
   Collections of digitized images or multimedia segments that are designed for instructional or study purposes are limited under "fair use" to items directly related to teaching, learning, or research at Earlham.
5. **Network access to digitized materials**
   Network access, including World Wide Web access, to Earlham

College-created digitized study collections that include copyrighted material, is restricted to the Earlham campus network and those authorized to use the network. Such digitized collections are accessible temporarily and for instructional purposes only by the group of Earlham students and faculty for whom the material is intended. These collections are removed at the end of the academic term in which they were being used. Prominent notice must be given that such study materials may not be downloaded, retained, printed, shared, or modified, except as needed temporarily for specific academic assignments.

6. **Personal and course Web pages**

    Faculty and students who create Web pages should respect the rights of copyright holders. Fair use exemptions to copyright law apply when personal or course Web pages are used exclusively for educational purposes. This may be done by acknowledging sources, restricting access through course management software or some other password-protected mechanism, obtaining permission or license for use, or some combination of all of these.

Student Use of Electronic Materials: What You Can and Cannot Do

For students enrolled in a course at Earlham College, here are guidelines to follow before using the electronic or multimedia materials[3] for study or for use in creating projects and writing papers.

Library Reserves / Electronic materials

The purpose of the Reserve Services of Lilly and Wildman libraries is to collect and maintain course-related materials for intensive student use. Both library-owned materials and those supplied by faculty members are processed for reserve by library staff. Policies on print reserves are below. The use of a course management system (e.g., Moodle) will provide the capability to provide controlled access to electronic forms of class material.

Copyright law

The U.S. copyright law grants to creators, such as authors and artists, the exclusive right to copy, distribute, and perform their work, as well as the right to create "derivative" works based on their original work.

But the law recognizes that scholarly work requires teachers, students, and researchers to reproduce and share pieces of original, copyrighted work for study and criticism. So, the law also allows a student to make limited use of copyrighted material for educational purposes. What follows provides guidelines for the legal use of electronic and multimedia materials:

---

[3] Multimedia materials are combinations of data, texts, still images, animations, moving images, and sounds. Multimedia materials may be found on videotapes, audiotapes, and laserdiscs. Digitized multimedia materials may reside on floppy disks, CD-ROMs, digital tapes, and the hard disks of networked computer servers, including World Wide Web servers.

Use of electronic and multimedia materials

In the course of study one must assume that copyright law protects all electronic and multimedia materials encountered, unless there is a specific reason to believe that they are in the public domain, the copyright holders will permit the item's use, or they are public domain government publications.

Students may read, examine, watch, and listen to electronic and/or multimedia materials in the library, classrooms, Instructional Technology and Media (ITAM) Center, on public computers and video monitors, and on personal equipment (television sets, computers) attached or authenticated to use the campus network. In general students may copy assigned multimedia materials for private study and/or research. However they may not actively distribute it or passively make it available for use by others without written permission of the copyright holder.

Students may copy small segments of electronic or multimedia material, and transfer the segments to another medium (e.g. from videotape to digitized form), if they use the materials in a project or paper that has been assigned to meet the requirements of an Earlham College course or that is part of an independent work project or paper for which Earlham College credit is received. There is no legal definition of "small," but the segments copied should represent only a fraction of the original work. The work must be given due credit through a citation to the source.

Students may manipulate these small segments (that is, change their look or sound) only for purposes of study or criticism. They must clearly state what changes have been made to the original.

Students must obtain permission from the copyright holder(s) to make extensive use of copyrighted material beyond the fair use guidelines on page 3, or to share the material beyond the class, or to create a new work.

Library Reserve Guidelines

1. The guidelines used to determine what is included in the Library's reserves system will include a fair use analysis using the four standards on a case-by-case basis. The four standards will allow us to make balanced decisions about what material is appropriate for consideration in the project. Reserves will be limited to copies of single articles or chapters, or other small portions of a work or originals of an entire work. The four standards are reviewed in detail earlier in this policy and include:

   a) The purpose and character of the use.
   b) The nature of the copyrighted work
   c) The amount and substantiality of the portion used in relation to the copyrighted work as a whole.
   d) The effect of use on the potential market for or value of the work.

2. When the material requested for reserve exceeds what might be permitted under fair use as defined on page 3, the faculty member should seek permission from the holder of the copyright or the Copyright Clearance Center to ensure compliance with the Copyright Law and retention of documentation.

3. Under fair use, students may make one copy for private study or research.

4. All copied material must carry the following statement: NOTICE: This material may be protected by copyright law. (Title 17 U.S. Code).

Instructional Technology & Media (ITAM)

Guideline #1: Audio and Video Materials

1. **Recording.** Instructional Technology & Media (ITAM) will audiotape or videotape live performances on campus (such as lectures, speeches, and cultural or public events) for which performance permissions and music clearances have been *obtained in advance and in writing.* ITAM will not audiotape or videotape any performance for which the producer or the performers do not have permission or the right to perform the copyrighted material except as permitted for archival and study purposes. Permission forms are available through ITAM.

2. **Reproducing.** ITAM may make copies of any video or audiotape that is in the public domain or that is provided directly by the copyright holder or with the written permission of the copyright holder. If the performers are not holders of the copyright to materials being performed, ITAM is obliged additionally to obtain the written permission of the performers to have their individual performances recorded and reproduced.

   ITAM is generally unable to make copies of any work that can be legitimately purchased. This includes transferring film to videotape, if a videotape version is commercially available, and foreign standards conversions, if an identical converted version can be purchased. Standards conversions of foreign language tapes without subtitles can be made for instructional purposes when the only available NTSC versions are subtitled. Standards conversions of an instructor's personal tapes can be made for convenient use in instructional settings (defined as face-to-face instruction and individual) when equipment to play the program is not available with the following provisions: that the original tape is a legal copy and that the converted copy is erased at the end of the semester.

3. **Storing and distributing.** The college maintains ITAM for educational purposes; it is not a recreational facility. The materials in the collection can be viewed in the ITAM Center for instructional purposes by faculty members and by registered undergraduate and graduate students only.

The ITAM staff will add legally obtained or original tapes to the audio and videotape library, and will also place such tapes in the reserve collection.

ITAM collects videos and other multimedia primarily in support of the curriculum. All multimedia in the collection may be shown to class groups outside the ITAM Center in the course of face-to-face instruction; but tapes that are not cleared for public performance (which includes most tapes in ITAM, and all those purchased with a "home use only" restriction) cannot be circulated for public performance.

Audiotapes can sometimes be legally duplicated for limited distribution to students enrolled in courses using the taped material. Unenrolled language learners with a valid college ID may listen to audiotapes in the ITAM, but may not receive duplicated tapes for home study purposes.

Undocumented tapes cannot be included in the audio and videotape library. ITAM staff cannot accept a tape made on a home VCR for inclusion in the college collections, because legally that tape was made for personal use only. Tapes made by ITAM staff from off-air recording of US television programs must be removed from the video tape library after the 10-day use period has expired (see the section, Televised Materials). ITAM staff will explore the cost of obtaining the right to acquire and display any tape that a faculty member would like to include in the collection.

Rented videotapes can be placed on reserve and/or shown to groups of students during face-to-face instruction.

ITAM Guideline #2: Televised Materials

1. **Recording commercial material**. ITAM will record off-air television programming (including broadcast, cable retransmission of broadcast materials, and satellite programming) when faculty members request this service in advance. Recording cable TV or satellite programming may require permission.

   Individuals may not use the TV-VCR machines in the ITAM lab for the purpose of duplicating televised programs.

2. **Retaining and distributing commercial material.** Use of off-air recordings of commercial material for general educational classroom purposes must be tested using the four guidelines of fair use. There is some period, of fairly short duration, in which the off-air recording can be used because it is more convenient or appropriate to the educational program. However at some point the retention of the recording may become a substitute for purchasing the material or conflict with one of the other three criteria for measuring appropriateness under fair use.

When such retention is in conflict with the fair use guidelines, retention is in violation of copyright.

Copyright and materials for people with disabilities

The Center for Academic Enrichment provides digital or audio recorded forms of texts required for college-related work or when a student or employee demonstrates ownership by presenting a print copy of the texts.

Copyright law provides specific rights to copy materials and distribute it to those with disabilities, for college related work. The person with disabilities is responsible for obtaining permission or ownership of the materials before any format conversion or duplication may begin.

Emmanuel College

EMMANUEL COLLEGE   CARDINAL CUSHING LIBRARY
400 The Fenway   Boston, MA 02115   617-735-9927

College Links:
Home | Departments | FirstClass

Library Home
About Us
Staff
Services &
Policies
  Circulation
  Interlibrary
  Loan/Storage
  × Reserves
  Media
Online Catalog
Finding Articles
E-Reference
Resources
Subject Guides
Tutorials
Blackboard
Vista Support
Site Map

Services and Policies: Reserves

> Course Reserve Policies for Faculty
> Reserve Circulation Policies for Students
> Course Reserve Forms
> Search for Reserves
> Contact the Head of Circulation

Course Reserve Policies for Faculty: Placing Items on Reserve:

Emmanuel faculty can place Library-owned or personally-owned original items on the reserve shelf for student use in support of course instruction.

Each item to be placed on reserve must be accompanied by a completed reserve request form and submitted at the circulation desk to be processed by the Head of Circulation. Forms are located at the circulation desk or through the above link.

New reserve forms must be submitted at the beginning of each semester for all reserve items. The Library will not retain permanent reserves.

By submitting materials for reserve, the instructor consents to adhere to the Emmanuel College reserve policies and rights.

All requests will be processed in the order in which they are received. The normal processing time is approximately two business days although this may vary. An email notification will be sent to the instructor once the item(s) have been processed and are available for student use.

PLEASE wait to inform students of an item's reserve status until after the receipt of the "availability" email.

To view the current status of a reserve item, select the Reserves link on the Library's online catalog.

The Library cannot accept photocopied materials. The instructor must provide an original work for the Library to photocopy according to copyright restrictions. The Library will only produce one copy from the original work for reserve. Photocopies may be placed on reserve **only once** unless written permission from the publisher is submitted to the library. If the above copyright restrictions are not followed, items will not be placed on reserve and will be returned to the faculty member immediately. Please refer to the copyright guidelines below for further information.

Library Rights:
Once an item has been placed on reserve, it is considered property of the Cardinal Cushing Library, and the library is not responsible for any theft or damage of personal items placed on reserve.

Returning Items:
A 24-hour notice period needs to be given to the Head of Circulation in order to remove an item from reserve. Otherwise, the items will be left on reserve until the date indicated on the reserve forms or until the end of each semester.

Copyright Guidelines:
Cardinal Cushing Library has developed Interim Guidelines for usage of its Reserve Shelf. They are based on the American Library Association's Model Policy Concerning College and University Photocopying for Classroom, Research, and Library Reserve Use (March 1982).

Please refer to: http://www.copyright.gov/fls/fl102.html for further information.

The library reserves the right to refuse an item for reserve if, in its judgment, acceptance of the item will result in copyright infringement.

The library will make one copy **without copyright permission** of any of the following items for **ONE SEMESTER ONLY**:

- an entire article;
- an entire chapter from a book; or
- an entire poem.

The library will not accept the following for reserve without permission from the copyright owner:

- **Repetitive copying:** The classroom or reserve use of photocopied materials in multiple courses or successive years will normally require advance permission from the owner of the copyright, 17 U.S.C. sec.107 (3). [THUS, permission must be obtained if a faculty member intends to use the material for more than one semester.]
- **Copying for profit:** Faculty should not charge students more than the actual cost of photocopying the material, 17U.S.C. sec. 107(1).
- **Consumable works:** The duplication of works that are consumed in the classroom, such as standardized tests, exercises and workbooks, normally requires permission from the copyright owner, 17 U.S.C.sec.107 (4).
- **Creation of anthologies as basic text material for a course:** This can be done through the College bookstore, which will obtain appropriate permissions. The Library will put one copy of such course material on reserve for one semester only.
- **Copies of entire entities:** The Library can only photocopy five chapters (or articles) from one source each calendar year. This is in addition to the "Repetitive Copying" restriction (see above). Recorded copies such as CD's or video tapes are strictly prohibited. Only commercial products are accepted for reserve.

Should a faculty member want to place on reserve a photocopy of material that exceeds these guidelines, he/she will need to obtain copyright permission. The faculty member must produce documentation of this permission to the library before the photocopied material will be made available through reserve.

Members of the Emmanuel College community are expected to be mindful of the restrictions imposed on them by copyright law and comply with copyright policies and laws.

For more information, please contact:
Jennifer Woodall
Head of Circulation and Interlibrary Loan Services
Emmanuel College – Cardinal Cushing Library
617-264-7653
(woodall@emmanuel.edu)

TOP

Last updated: 02/12/2008
Web site feedback: tuohyc@emmanuel.edu

Goucher College

GOUCHER COLLEGE

COPYRIGHT POLICY

Portions of this document were adapted from the Catholic University of America Copyright Policy, with the permission of Margaret O'Donnell, Esq. (http://counsel.cua.edu/Copyright/resources/Copyright_Policy.cfm). The drafters are also grateful to Georgia Harper, Esq., at the University of Texas, for permission to utilize excerpts of the *University of Texas Crash Course on Copyright*, and, in particular, the discussion of fair use and links to the "Rules of Thumb."

COPYRIGHT POLICY

It is the policy of Goucher College to comply with the United States Copyright Law of 1976, as amended (Title 17, United States Code). Thus, all faculty, staff, and students of Goucher College are required to respect the proprietary rights of owners of copyrights and to refrain from actions that infringe the rights of copyright owners.

The Goucher College Copyright Guidelines and Copyright Compliance Checklist were developed to assist members of the Goucher community in complying with federal copyright law and to enable them to distinguish between permitted and prohibited uses of copyrighted materials. Members of the Goucher College community are expected to familiarize themselves with these documents and to comply conscientiously with their requirements. The guidelines contain extensive information about copyright law as well as directions to resources on campus that will assist members of the community in complying with this policy and the law.

All departments are responsible for posting notices reflecting this policy at all photocopying stations that may be used for reproducing copyrighted materials (e.g., those in the library and in departmental copy rooms), and at or near all computer stations. Appendix I contains a suggested notice.

The penalties for violation of United States copyright law can be severe. Employees and students who willfully disregard copyright law place themselves at risk of civil and criminal legal action. Individuals who engage in infringing activities also place the college at risk of legal action. The college will defend any faculty or staff member against a civil action alleging copyright infringement:

> where the use is in accordance with the provisions of a valid software or database license agreement;
> where the use is within the Safe Harbor rules as detailed in these guidelines;
> where the permission of the copyright owner has been obtained; or
> where the Fair Use Committee has assisted in determining that the use was permissible.

Otherwise, the faculty or staff member will be personally responsible for the defense of a civil action for copyright infringement. Students who are sued for copyright infringement are generally not entitled to a defense provided by the college. In addition, members of the college community who willfully violate this Policy are subject to disciplinary action by the college up to and including termination, consistent with established college procedures.

Note: The full text of the guidelines, checklist, and Safe Harbor rules can be found on the Web at www.goucher.edu/it/index.cfm?page_id=123.

THIS POLICY IS EFFECTIVE AS OF OCTOBER 26, 2004.

Sanford J. Ungar
President

COPYRIGHT COMPLIANCE CHECKLIST

To determine whether your proposed use of copyrighted material conforms to this policy, analyze the proposed use according to the following checklist:

1. Determine whether the work is in the **public domain** or whether it is protected by copyright. To determine the copyright status of a work, see Library of Congress Copyright Office Circular 22 (available at http://lcweb.loc.gov/copyright/circs/circ22.pdf). If the work is not protected by copyright, you may use it as you wish.

2. Determine whether the work is already **licensed by the college** (e.g., an article from an electronic database licensed by the college). If so, determine whether your proposed use is permitted by the terms of the license. For example, you may be able to direct students to an electronic version of a journal article with a link, but not to download and copy the article and place it on reserve. If you need assistance in this process, contact the Reserve Desk in the library (sezell@goucher.edu; x6361). If the proposed use is permitted by the terms of the license, your analysis ends here.

3. Determine whether the proposed use falls within the **Safe Harbor** guidelines (link). If so, you can use the document as you propose.

4. If the proposed use goes **beyond** the Safe Harbor guidelines, you will have to apply the Fair Use Test (link). To receive assistance in determining whether the proposed use meets the fair use test, we strongly encourage you to contact the Fair Use Committee (link). If you choose not to consult the committee or to disregard the opinion of the committee, the college will not indemnify you in the event you are sued for copyright infringement.

5. If the proposed use involves a **coursepack** or **print or digital reserve**, ensure that you have complied with the requirements applicable to those documents.

   Is it a coursepack? See (link)

   Is it an item to be placed on print reserve in the library? See (link).

   Is it an item to be placed in the electronic learning environment? See (link).

   Consider whether it may be more efficient for you to direct your students to articles in an electronic database licensed by the college, rather than to create a coursepack.

6. If you need to request **permission**, you may ask for assistance (link) or obtain the permission on your own (link).

7. If you wish to use a copyrighted work in your **distance-learning** course, analyze the proposed use as you would for any other work. If your proposed use does not constitute Fair Use or fit within the Safe Harbor guidelines, you may still be able to use it. Contact the Fair Use Committee for assistance (link).

8. If you have any questions at any stage of the process, consult the Reserve Desk in the library (sezell@goucher.edu; x6361) or the bookstore (efranz@goucher.edu; x6089) (for permissions), the Information Technology Help Desk (for Blackboard questions), or the Fair Use Committee (your inquiry will be directed to the committee by the Office of General Counsel, lburtong@goucher.edu; x6032, or bstob@goucher.edu; x6011).

GOUCHER COLLEGE COPYRIGHT GUIDELINES

I.   What works are protected?

II.   When may copyrighted materials be copied or otherwise used without the
        copyright owner's permission?

        A. The Fair Use Doctrine
        B. Safe Harbor Rules
        C. Library and Archival Use
        D. The Composition and Role of the Fair Use Committee

III.   What if the work is licensed?

IV.   How can I obtain permission?

V.   What special rules apply to reserves and coursepacks?

VI.   What special rules apply to the use of copyrighted materials in distance
        learning courses?

VII.   What special rules apply to peer-to-peer file sharing?

VIII.   Whom should I contact if I have a question about the policy or guidelines?

GOUCHER COLLEGE COPYRIGHT GUIDELINES

I.   What works are protected?

Copyright protects "original works of authorship" that are fixed in a tangible form of expression. Copyrightable works include the following categories:

1. Literary works
2. Musical works, including any accompanying words
3. Dramatic works, including any accompanying music
4. Pantomimes and choreographic works
5. Pictorial, graphic, and sculptural works
6. Motion pictures and other audiovisual works
7. Sound recordings
8. Architectural works
9. Computer programs

It is best to assume that anything published after 1920 is protected by copyright, even if it does not contain a copyright notice. The Library of Congress Copyright Office Circular 22 explains how to determine the copyright status of a work, when you are in doubt (http://lcweb.loc.gov/copyright/circs/circ22.pdf). Helpful summaries of this publication can be found at counsel.cua.edu/copyright/resources/guidelines/Public_Domain.cfm and www.unc.edu/~unclng/public-d.htm.

II.   When may copyrighted materials be copied or otherwise used without the copyright owner's permission?

The Copyright Act grants copyright owners certain exclusive rights with respect to their work. These include the rights to reproduce the work, prepare derivative works based on the work, distribute copies of the work to the public, and perform and display the work publicly. If you intend to exercise any of these rights with respect to a copyrighted work, you must obtain the owner's permission to do so. For general information about copyright law, see www.copyright.gov/circs/circ1.html#wci.

A. The Fair Use Doctrine. There are certain circumstances under which it is permissible to exercise one of the exclusive rights of the copyright owner without first obtaining permission. You may use or copy copyrighted materials without the copyright owner's permission where such use or copying constitutes "fair use" under the Copyright Act. Determining whether a proposed use constitutes "fair use" involves applying a four-factor test established by copyright law. The four factors are:

1. The character of the use (e.g., educational vs. commercial);
2. The nature of the work to be used (e.g., factual vs. creative);

3. The amount of the work to be used (a lot or a little); and
4. The effect of such use, were it widespread, on the market for the original or for permissions.

It is not always easy to apply this test, and everyone does not always agree on the outcome in any given case. The University of Texas has posted an excellent webpage that contains an explanation of fair use written by Georgia Harper, a leading expert in copyright law (www.utsystem.edu/ogc/IntellectualProperty/copypol2.htm#test). Another good source of information is the discussion of fair use found at www.cetus.org/fair5.html.

B. Safe Harbor Rules. Because application of the fair use doctrine does not always yield a clear answer, educational organizations and copyright owners negotiated a set of guidelines to provide some certainty as to what constitutes fair use. Negotiators agreed upon and finalized the first three categories of guidelines below (Classroom Copying, Educational Use of Music, and Off-Air Recording of Broadcast Programming for Educational Purposes); these guidelines are part of the legislative history accompanying the Copyright Act of 1976.

As part of an attempt to introduce rules for the fair use of electronic materials, industry representatives developed, but did not ultimately agree upon, the remaining three categories of guidelines (Digital Images, Educational Multimedia, and Electronic Reserve Systems). These latter guidelines are not as persuasive as the first three regarding what constitutes fair use. Nevertheless, all six sets of guidelines probably represent the minimum limits of fair use and are intended in this policy to describe a "safe harbor" for users, not to define all possible practices of fair use. It is thus possible that a particular use may exceed these guidelines, yet still constitute fair use under the Copyright Act.

1. **Classroom Copying**
   (http://lcweb.loc.gov/copyright/circs/circ21.pdf, page 8**)**

   These guidelines are perhaps the most important, because they cover the use of traditional educational materials, such as articles and book excerpts, which are most often used in the classroom. They also apply to the use of reserve materials.

   The guidelines, which you should read, emphasize three general principles, summarized below (the summary also can be found at www.roanoke.edu/copyright/photocopies.htm):

   Brevity means your copies should not constitute a substantial portion of the total work. Acceptable examples include:

a chapter from a book.

an essay, poem, or story from a collected work.

an article, essay, poem, or story from a periodical or newspaper.

a cartoon, chart, diagram, drawing, graph, or picture from a book, newspaper, or periodical.

excerpts of sheet music if they do not constitute a performable unit and do not exceed 10% of the work.

Cumulative effect means copies should not have a detrimental effect on the market. You should avoid, for example:

copying an item for more than one course in the college.

copying more than one work from the same author.

making more than three copies from the same collective work or periodical volume during one class term.

Spontaneity means you lack adequate time between the decision to use a work and the time needed to gain permission for its scheduled use. Reusing material cannot be considered spontaneous.

2. **Educational Use of Music** (http://lcweb.loc.gov/copyright/circs/circ21.pdf, page 9);

3. **Off-Air Recording of Broadcast Programming for Educational Purposes** (http://lcweb.loc.gov/copyright/circs/circ21.pdf; page 22);

4. **Digital Images** (These guidelines were proposed but not adopted ; www.utsystem.edu/ogc/intellectualproperty/imagguid.htm#5);

5. **Educational Multimedia** (These guidelines were proposed but not adopted ; www.utsystem.edu/ogc/intellectualproperty/ccmcguid.htm);

6. **Electronic Reserve Systems** (These guidelines were proposed but not adopted; www.utsystem.edu/ogc/intellectualproperty/rsrvguid.htm).

NOTE: The University of Texas has summarized these guidelines in plain English for seven categories of materials, including reserves and coursepacks, and adopted them as "Rules of Thumb" (see www.utsystem.edu/ogc/intellectualproperty/copypol2.htm#course). We suggest that you consult these "Rules of Thumb" for further guidance; they are shorter and easier to read than the corresponding guidelines. **Use of materials that falls within these "Rules of Thumb" will be**

considered to fall within the Safe Harbor guidelines for purposes of this policy.

    C. <u>Library and Archival Use</u>. Goucher College's Julia Rogers Library is authorized to exercise special rights in addition to fair use. These rights are described in Section 108 of the copyright law and include:

        1. Archiving lost, stolen, damaged, or deteriorating works (see www.utsystem.edu/ogc/intellectualproperty/l-108abc.htm);

        2. Making copies for library patrons (see www.utsystem.edu/ogc/intellectualproperty/l-108de.htm); and

        3. Making copies for other libraries' patrons (interlibrary loan) (see www.utsystem.edu/ogc/intellectualproperty/l-108g.htm).

    D. <u>The Composition and Role of the Fair Use Committee</u>.

The president shall annually appoint three individuals to serve on the Fair Use Committee. The committee shall consist of two representatives from the faculty and one representative from the administration. A representative from the Office of General Counsel shall serve the committee in an advisory role.

If you wish to obtain assistance in determining whether your proposed use of copyrighted material constitutes fair use within the meaning of the Copyright Act, you should contact the Fair Use Committee for an opinion by sending your inquiry to the General Counsel's Office (lburtong@goucher.edu; x6032 or bstob@goucher.edu; x6011), from which it will be directed to the committee. If the committee determines that the proposed use constitutes fair use, and you use the material in the proposed way, you will be defended by the college in the event that a copyright infringement action is brought against you. In the event the committee determines that your proposed use does not constitute fair use, and you decide to use the material anyway, or if you choose not to consult with the committee, the college will not indemnify you in the event that you are sued for copyright infringement.

III.   <u>What if the work is licensed?</u>

When the work is licensed, any use of the work must be in accordance with the terms of the license. This will apply most often to software, but may have application to electronic and other databases acquired through license. If in doubt whether particular software that you wish to copy or use is licensed, consult with the chief technology officer (bleimbach@goucher.edu; x6138). Questions about electronic databases available through the Julia Rogers Library should be addressed to the access services librarian (x6361).

IV.   How can I obtain permission?

If you need to obtain permission to use a copyrighted work, contact the Reserve Desk in the library (sezell@goucher.edu; x6361) or the bookstore (efranz@goucher.edu; x6089) for assistance. Allow at least six weeks prior to the beginning of the term to obtain the necessary permissions. The cost of obtaining permission will be charged to your department.

Alternatively, if you wish to obtain permission to use a copyrighted work on your own, consult www.utsystem.edu/ogc/intellectualproperty/permissn.htm for an extensive listing of organizations that can be contacted to obtain permission to use a variety of works. The site will refer you to both domestic and foreign collective rights organizations (which provide permission for images, authors, music, and movies) as well as sources that can assist in locating copyright owners directly. You should ensure that the individual giving you permission is in fact authorized to do so and should obtain written evidence of the scope of the permission. See Appendix II for a sample permission letter.

If the owner of the copyright cannot be located or is not responsive, you should not use the work, unless it meets the Fair Use test or Safe Harbor guidelines.

V.   What special rules apply to reserves and coursepacks?

Much has been written about the implications, under copyright law, of placing course materials on reserve and, in particular, about the practice of placing coursepacks on electronic reserve. Several high-profile court cases have addressed the practice of commercial copyshops reproducing copyrighted materials for use in coursepacks. Copyright owners will pay increasing attention to these practices, particularly as more of these materials are digitized and available for loading into electronic networks. The ease with which students can download, reproduce, and circulate electronic reserve materials is a matter of great concern to publishers and copyright owners, because they view this practice as potentially having a significant impact on the market for these works.

In order to assist the college community in complying with copyright law with respect to these types of materials, the following guidelines will apply to reserves and coursepacks, whether in print or electronic form. For purposes of this policy, a "coursepack" is a collection of readings and other academic materials that is put together by an instructor for use as primary or supplementary course material.

The rationale for these guidelines is derived primarily from the **Guidelines for Classroom Copying**, mentioned above, because the reserve "shelf" in these circumstances functions as an extension of classroom readings. (See http://lcweb.loc.gov/copyright/circs/circ21.pdf, page 8).

1. If you wish to create and distribute a **print or digital coursepack** for use in your class, you must utilize the services of the Goucher College Bookstore (unless you want to make the coursepack yourself).

    The college's subcontractor will obtain all required permissions to produce the coursepack and offers full indemnification for compliance with copyright law for any coursepack it produces. The turn-around time for coursepacks is approximately 4 to 6 weeks. [Link to coursepack request form]. If you want to create the coursepack yourself, you must obtain all required permissions. You also assume all responsibility for compliance with copyright law and must comply with the additional conditions listed in paragraph four below.

2. If you wish to make materials available **electronically** to your students, the college recommends that you load the document(s) to the college's electronic courseware environment. You may contact the IT Help Desk (x6322) for assistance with this process.

    Materials should <u>not</u> be posted to a faculty member's web page, unless you are able to restrict access to the web page to the students enrolled in your course, as required by these Guidelines (see below).
    Permission is required in order to place "digital coursepacks," out-of-print material, or more than the amount allowed under the **Classroom Guidelines** (above) into the electronic learning environment. See http://lcweb.loc.gov/copyright/circs/circ21.pdf, page 8).

3. If you wish to place a **non-coursepack item on print reserve** (i.e., ad hoc or supplemental readings used for no more than one semester) in the library, the following steps must be taken:

    Permission is required in order to place out-of-print material or more than the amount allowed under the **Classroom Guidelines** (above) on reserve. See http://lcweb.loc.gov/copyright/circs/circ21.pdf, page 8).
    Library staff may consult with the Fair Use Committee to seek advice regarding whether the proposed use constitutes fair use. If the committee determines that the proposed use exceeds fair use, library staff will assist you in obtaining permission.

4. After determining that a work may be placed on print reserve, or in the electronic learning environment, you must follow these **additional guidelines**:

> The number of copies should be limited or, in an electronic environment, passwords or some other authentication method should be used to ensure that only students enrolled in that class have access to the copyrighted material;
>
> Duplicated, distributed, or displayed material should always include available bibliographic information;
>
> Each item placed on reserve must include a notice of copyright (e.g., "Copyright 1990 by Academic Books, Inc.") if the material falls within the Safe Harbor or Fair Use Analysis, but not if the material is in the public domain;
>
> Students should not be charged more than the actual cost of copying, producing, or otherwise making the material available; and
>
> **Permission must be obtained for materials that will be used more than one semester by the same instructor for the same course.**

VI.   What special rules apply to the use of copyrighted materials in distance learning courses?

Congress recently updated the Copyright Law to provide exemptions for the use of certain works in distance education courses. The TEACH (Technology, Education and, Copyright Harmonization) Act allows the incorporation of certain kinds of materials into distance-education materials without the permission of the copyright holder. This exemption is fairly narrow, however. For an excellent discussion of this act and the types of uses it authorizes, see www.lib.ncsu.edu/scc/legislative/teachkit/background.html.

If you would like to use copyrighted work in your distance education course, you should first conduct the analysis described above to determine if your proposed use constitutes Fair Use or fits within the Safe Harbor guidelines. If your proposed use would not be in compliance with those guidelines or Fair Use, you should contact the Fair Use Committee for guidance as to whether the TEACH Act would authorize your proposed use. The TEACH Act does **not** apply to your use of reserve or other materials in your non-distance-learning courses.

VII.   What special rules apply to Peer-to-Peer File Sharing?

Recently, the Recording Industry Association of America (RIAA) filed civil suits against students at several universities, including Michigan Technical University and Princeton University, seeking damages from them for copyright infringement resulting from peer-to-peer (P2P) file sharing. In addition, the RIAA has placed increasing pressure on institutions of higher learning to take action against copyright violations attributable to such conduct. Some uses of the P2P technologies are perfectly legitimate, but conduct such as copying and sharing of music files without the authorization of the copyright owner, for example, is not. For more information about the application of copyright law to these types of activities, see www.dartmouth.edu/copyright/peer2peer/index.html.

Pursuant to the Digital Millennium Copyright Act, the college has designated an agent to receive notices of copyright infringement from copyright owners. [link]. If the college receives notification from a copyright owner that you have engaged in infringing activity, such as P2P file sharing, it will investigate such complaint, and, if appropriate, notify you to take down the offending material and cease from engaging in such conduct. In addition, if you violate copyright law by engaging in unauthorized file sharing, you may be subject to discipline under the college's copyright policy, computer use policies, and other applicable policies. Violations of copyright law may also subject you to civil and criminal prosecution. See www.dartmouth.edu/copyright/peer2peer/question7.html.

VIII.   <u>Whom should I contact if I have a question about the policy or guidelines?</u>

Questions about Permissions. If you need assistance obtaining permissions, contact the Reserve Desk in the library (sezell@goucher.edu; x6361) or the bookstore (efranz@goucher.edu; x6089).

Questions about Fair Use. Questions about fair use should be addressed to the Fair Use Committee by sending an inquiry to the General Counsel's Office (lburtong@goucher.edu; x6032; or bstob@goucher.edu; x6011). Your inquiry will be referred to the committee.

To report an incident of infringing activity. If you become aware of infringing activity that you believe may place the college at risk of liability, notify the chief technology officer (bleimbach@goucher.edu; x6138).

APPENDIX I

SUGGESTED COPYRIGHT NOTICE

Copyright Notice

Copying, displaying, and distributing copyrighted works may infringe the owner's copyright. Goucher College's Copyright Guidelines can help you determine whether your use of a copyrighted work is a fair use or requires permission. Any use of computer or duplicating facilities by students, faculty, or staff for infringing use of copyrighted works is subject to appropriate disciplinary action as well as those civil remedies and criminal penalties provided by federal law.

APPENDIX II

SAMPLE PERMISSION LETTER*

Return Address
Date of Request

Copyright and Permissions Department
[Name of Publisher]
[Number Street Address]
[City, State Zip Code]

To Whom It May Concern:

I would like permission to copy the following for continued use in my classes in future seminars:

> Title: *Education is the Key to Our Future*, third edition
> Copyright: Your Company, 1995, 1996, 1998
>
> Author: Learned B. Sure
> Material to be copied: Chapter 3
> Pages: 45-60
> Number of copies: 20
> Distribution: This copy will be distributed to students in my classes, and they will pay only the costs for photocopying.
> Type of reprint: Photocopy
> Use: The chapter will supplement teaching materials.

I have enclosed a copy of the copyright page to assist you in evaluating my request. Please inform me if there are any fees for this permission.

I have also enclosed a stamped, self-addressed envelope for your convenience in responding to my request. Please also note my e-mail address and fax number below.

Sincerely,

[Your Name]
[Phone number]
[E-mail address]
[Fax number]

*(Source: www.macalester.edu/~library/copyright/formlet.html)

Middlebury College

Middlebury

Copyright and Fair Use Guidelines

U.S. law provides protection to authors, creators and publishers of works. It also grants privileges *(fair use)* that do not infringe copyright, for purposes such as criticism, comment, news reporting, teaching, scholarship or research. Middlebury College values and respects intellectual property rights, even as it recognizes an equivalent responsibility to advance the needs of scholarship and teaching within the framework of the law.

The following are Guidelines only and do constitute legal advice that can be assumed to be applicable to every situation. In some instances, federal court cases result in interpretation of copyright law that pertains to specific acts of copying or to particular media; also, contract law (such as license and purchase agreements) takes precedence over fair use.

Basic rules of thumb for fair use copying

On a case-by-case basis, consider these four factors together for each item you desire to copy.
(see also Appendix A: Applying the Fair Use Factors)

1. The copy is for **nonprofit educational purpose**
- multiple copies for classroom use are permitted, if the material is an excerpt and does not infringe on the market place
- a copy for "scholarship or research" is permitted, if the other factors below are met

2. Consider the **nature of the work**
- the more creative and less factual a work, the more it is protected by copyright law
some examples of degrees of protection under the law:

More protection
                        Less protection
fiction   factual works
original movies   news broadcasts
                        compilations
creative works

for creative works only small portions should be copied unless permission has been acquired, whereas greater portions of purely factual items may be copied under fair use

3. Only a **limited portion** of a work may be copied
- it is not permitted to copy an *entire or significant portion* of a publication or work that is still under copyright without permission of the copyright holder.

4. Sales of original materials (**"the market"**) should not be affected by copies being made
- consider copies for classroom use on case-by-case basis:
--- *the student would not normally be a potential purchaser of the work unless enrolled in the course*
--- *since the student uses the excerpts as a member of the class, the use probably has very little, if any, effect on the actual or potential market for the work*

CLASSROOM HANDOUTS

Copyrighted material can be provided to students in a class if:

1. The instructor is the copyright owner of the material, *or*
2. The copyright owner of the material grants permission, *or*
3. The material is in the public domain, *or*
4. The use of the material is a "fair use" under the law *(see above)*

COURSE PACKS

The College Store prepares and sells course packs that include photocopied readings.

1. Because copyrighted material is packaged for re-sale, permissions are required for all items included in a course pack, unless the item is in the public domain.

2. Copyright fees are built into the selling price of the compilation.

COURSE MANAGEMENT SYSTEMS

Copyright issues must be considered when placing protected materials in an online setting, applying the same factors as for classroom handouts, or seeking permission.

1. Materials must be limited by password access to those currently enrolled in College courses.

2. Materials can be distributed outside the class or posted on publicly accessible internet sites if and only if copyright permission has been secured.

COURSE WEB PAGES

Consider all the following for fair use of copyrighted material:

1. Access
- ensure web page is accessible *only* to students currently enrolled in your course
- at end of semester, take down web page with digitized materials, or remove copyrighted materials

2. Attribution
- include copyright attribution and citations to original works

3. Brevity
- keep portions of copied materials brief/minimal
- number of digitized texts and audiovisual images/clips should be few and brief

4. Effect on market
- text, images, etc., on a course webpage should never be extensive enough to substitute for the purchase of an issue of a journal, a book, recording, or a course pack

Freely permitted on a course web page:

1. Links to others' works
- links from your webpage to another image, document, table, etc., on the Web

2. Your own work
- your own problem sets, sample exams, class and lecture notes, photographs, video, audio, etc.
- *note*: you may not hold copyright to your own work if, for example, it has been published and you have assigned rights to the publisher

3. Works in the public domain
- in general, works copyrighted before 1923 may be freely copied
- see separate chart for an up-to-date table of different types of materials and when they fall into public domain

4. U.S. govt. publications
- Federal documents published through the Government Printing Office are not protected by copyright and may be freely copied

LIBRARY COURSE RESERVE AND ELECTRONIC RESERVES

Library course reserves are an extension of the classroom. Copies provided via library reserves and electronic reserves (ERes) are considered equivalent to multiple copies for classroom use, limited to use by those enrolled in the course.

1. The library applies fair use principles when making materials available on reserve, whether print or online.

2. All reserve materials are either library-owned or provided by the faculty member.

3. Copyright permissions may be required by the library in instances where a significant number of excerpts from the same publication are included on reserve, or the use of items is repeated from semester to semester (hence, potentially affecting the market place), or a copy of an entire work not owned by the College or library is placed on reserve.

LIBRARY ONLINE CONTENT

Licenses governing the use of library full text databases, electronic journals, e-books, and other digital resources may follow fair use or may have more or less liberal use restrictions.[1] The terms of a license will generally prevail over copyright law. By making use of licensed material, you inherently agree to its license terms, even if those terms limit your fair use rights. LIS staff can assist in determining what uses are permissible under each license.

PHOTOCOPYING, SCANNING, DIGITIZATION

Copyright law limits the reproduction of copyrighted material.[2]

> 1. Usually, only a small portion of a copyrighted work may be legally copied unless special permission has been secured.
> - *Reprographics and the Library will not copy or digitize an entire book, journal, CD, DVD or film for individual use unless the item is in the public domain, or copyright permission has been acquired*
> - *Individuals should be aware that copyright restrictions may apply in making their own copies of entire items, particularly if the item is currently copyrighted and available for purchase. Copies should remain for private use, and never be redistributed or resold.*
>
> 2. Based on Court cases, Congressional hearings, and agreements between publishers and the academic community, this typically means the following may be copied for books and journals:
> - a single chapter chapter of a book
> - a small portion of a copyrighted book
> - a single article from a journal
>
> 3. Libraries may be permitted to make copies of entire works for archival purposes
>
> 4. Particular restrictions apply to media such as music and video *(see sections below)*.
> - Use of copyrighted films, videos, recordings, and software generally requires permission, purchase or licensing.
> - Only legally acquired copies should be used in classroom presentations

WEB PAGE CONTENT

College policy does not permit the posting of copyrighted material on its publicly accessible web servers without permission of the copyright holder.

> 1. You must have the written permission of the copyright holder copy to distribute any materials of a third party (including software, database files, documentation, articles, graphics files, audio or video files) via the web or other College internet servers.
>
> 2. For course web pages, see above guidelines.
> - Copyright permission must be secured if course web pages are made publicly accessible and they include any copyrighted material.

VIDEO

The display (screening) of films, broadcasts, videos and DVDs is affected by copyright law and licensing agreements.

> 1. Films, broadcasts, videos, and DVDs may be shown in a face-to-face classroom setting during the regular course of instruction. The item used in the classroom or placed on reserve must be one of the following:
>
> - A legally purchased copy acquired by the College or the course instructor (copyright law explicitly prohibits the presentation of unlawfully made copies of films in educational settings)
> - A copy made by the College/Library under copyright law for preservation/archival purposes
> - A rental copy, which may legally be used or placed on reserve as well.
>
> 2. Use of materials borrowed from the library is limited to private viewing, with the exception of classroom screenings and viewings directly related to a current College course by students enrolled in that course. Most other showing and viewing of films, videos or DVDs constitute a public performance and permission for the showing must be obtained by paying a licensing fee to the copyright holder or licensing agent.
>
> 3. Students who need to obtain public performance licensing for an event should contact the Center for Campus Activities and Leadership (CCAL) in McCullough Hall, ext. 3108.
> LIS staff can provide information about purchase or licensing of films and broadcasts for curricular use.
>
> 4. Students and faculty members who plan to schedule screenings should be mindful of the following guidelines:

- Screenings of films or videos for which we hold no non-theatrical public performance rights may only be listed in the calendar if the screening is for a specific course and the number and/or name of the course is also listed in the calendar.

- Films or videos screened for entertainment purposes, or for which the College has non-theatrical public performance rights, may be advertised and promoted only on campus (which includes WRMC-FM, the Campus, and the alumni magazine). None of this promotion may say that the public is invited, nor will there be separate admission prices for ID and non-ID card holders. In general, all off-campus promotion is prohibited, including posters and flyers, unless for those specific titles for which the College has obtained rights.

5. Presentations viewed through ERes or a course web/server site must be restricted to those registered in the course. Access to the materials via ERes or the web shall be removed following the terms in which they are viewed as part of the curriculum.

MUSIC

Only portions of printed musical works should be copied for study purposes, as with other printed matter: the law indicates that multiple copies of a "performable unit" should not be provided to all members of a class. Entire works may be copied for emergency rehearsal and performance purposes, provided purchased copies will be substituted in due course.

Commercially distributed and copyrighted recordings (LPs, CDs, licensed downloads) may be played in a face-to-face classroom setting during the regular course of instruction, and may be made available via library reserves as an extension of the classroom.

1. Copyright law indicates an entire recording may be presented ("performed") in a face-to-face teaching situation. Otherwise, only portions of a work are permitted to be copied.

2. Presentations viewed through ERes or a course web/server site must be restricted to those registered in the course. The complete contents of a recording may not be digitized, downloaded and redistributed without copyright permission or licensing fees being paid.

3. Middlebury College agrees with the the Music Library Association's *Statement on the Digital Transmission of Electronic Reserves*, excerpted below:

The Music Library Association fully supports ...[the] view that students enrolled in a class have the educational right to aurally access its assigned musical works both in the classroom and through class reserves. The MLA also believes that the dubbing or digital copying of musical works for class reserves falls within the spirit of the fair use provision of the copyright law.

In light of the above, the Music Library Association supports the creation and transmission of digital audio file copies of copyrighted recordings of musical works for course reserves purposes, under the following conditions:

- Access to such digital copies must be through library-controlled equipment and campus-restricted networks.
- Access to digital copies from outside of the campus should be limited to individuals who have been authenticated: namely, students enrolled either in a course or in formal independent study with an instructor in the institution.
- Digital copies should be made only of works that are being taught in the course or study.
- Digital copies may be made of whole movements or whole works.
- Either the institution or the course instructor should own the original that is used to make the digital file. The Library should make a good faith effort to purchase a commercially available copy of anything that is provided by the instructor.
- The library should remove access to the files at the completion of the course.
- The library may store course files for future re-use. This includes the digital copy made from an instructor's original if the library has made a good faith effort to purchase its own copy commercially.

ART WORKS

Art works may be viewed in a face-to-face classroom setting during the regular course of instruction, and may be made available via library reserves and restricted-access databases such as MDID as an extension of the classroom for the purpose of research and study.

1. Art works photocopied, photographed, digitized or otherwise reproduced as part of a course assignment must be restricted to members of the course.

2. Multimedia presentations that are made public and that include art works must receive copyright permissions/licensing.

3. Contact the Visual Resources Curator for additional information.

APPENDIX A.

APPLYING THE FAIR USE FACTORS.

According to an opinion of the Attorney General of the State of Georgia issued in 1996:

Teachers should always act in good faith in copying excerpts for classroom use; and his or her conduct in copying must be such that an objective observer would conclude that the teacher acted in good faith. Therefore, it would be appropriate for teachers to comply with the following factors:

> *1. Limit the size of the excerpt copied to pedagogical needs.*
> *2. Limit the sale of the copies to members of the class.*
> *3. Limit the student's cost to the cost of reproducing the materials.*

In summary, notwithstanding broad copyright notices that may purport to prohibit any copying without written permission, copying for classroom use is a legitimate activity and a legal right under the fair use doctrine of 17 U.S.C. § 107. Moreover, where a teacher or librarian or other employee of a non-profit institution infringes a copyright with a good faith belief that the copying was a fair use, the Copyright Act requires courts to remit statutory damages if there is an infringement action.[3]

PERMISSIONS

In cases where the fair use analysis weighs against using any particular item, the user should seek permission from the copyright holder.

---

[1] *adopted from* **Common Academic Uses of Copyrighted Material.** Syracuse University Library. http://library.syr.edu/copyright/materials.html [accessed 10-October-2005]

[2] In good faith application of fair use, only *portions* of works will be copied by College staff for research purposes, library reserve or classroom use, unless a work is in the public domain. Some statements/agreements between publishers, libraries, and educational institutions suggest guidelines that provide a "safe harbor" by limiting the quantity and frequency of copies made for educational purposes. These guidelines are not actual law, and following them assumes (but does not guarantee) that *limited* classroom use of copies is protected from a copyright suit.

[3] Department of Law, State of Georgia, UNOFFICIAL OPINION. Re: The Scope of the Fair Use Doctrine, 17 USC §107, for making copies for classroom use, for teachers who make copies for research and scholarship, and the potential liability of teachers, librarians and employees of non-profit institutions for exceeding the parameters of fair use. Issued 14-February-1996.

Moravian College

Moravian College and Moravian Theological Seminary

Guidelines for the
Academic Use of Copyrighted Material

Moravian College and Moravian Theological Seminary recognize the moral and ethical imperative and the legal necessity of compliance with copyright laws by faculty, administrators, staff, and students. All members of the Moravian College and Moravian Theological Seminary community are encouraged to become knowledgeable about copyright.

This document outlines Moravian College and Moravian Theological Seminary copyright guidelines. It provides basic copyright information and gives instructions for finding fuller information. The Copyright Act of 1976 and amendments including the Digital Millennium Copyright Act plus additional information are available through links in this document and in Reeves Library.

These copyright guidelines are not a legal document but, if followed carefully, you will be less likely to be sued for copyright infringement. Please note that anyone who initiates a request which will result in copyright infringement or who actually commits copyright infringement is liable for legal action. Members of the Moravian College and Moravian Theological Seminary community who knowingly infringe on copyright do so at their own risk.

Additional copyright related policies:
- Seminary's *Student Handbook* found at http://www.moravianseminary.edu/handbook/Policies/POLWWW.htm
- *The Moravian College Student Handbook, Academic Honesty* found at http://www.moravian.edu/studentLife/handbook/academic2.htm
- Center for Information Technology's *Policy for Acceptable Use of Computing Resources* found at http://home.moravian.edu/public/cit/_policies/aup.doc

What is a Copyrightable Work?

To be copyrightable, the law stipulates that the work must 1) be an *original work of authorship* and 2) be *fixed in a tangible medium of expression by or under the authority of the creator.*

Original work of authorship means that the author must be the creator of the work and not have copied it from someone else. 'Create' is interpreted very loosely and needs only a minimum effort. Not included are ideas, facts like phone listings or news events, exact photographs of art works, titles, short phrases, etc. However, these items may be copyrightable if the expression, layout, and/or arrangement use them in a creative way.

A *tangible medium of expression* includes, print, tape, and other physical means. It also means saving the work on a computer's hard drive or to a disk or posting works on the Internet. *By or under the authority of the creator* excludes the unauthorized (bootleg) taping of a concert, speech, etc.; the copying (pirating) of a film or CD; or unauthorized off-air or Internet copying.

These categories of works are covered: literary, musical, dramatic works, pantomimes and choreographic works, pictorial graphic and sculptural works, movies and other audio-visual works including sound recordings. Architectural works were added in 1990. These categories are very broadly interpreted and cover almost everything.

If a work meets the two stipulations, copyright is *immediate and automatic.* Works do not have to be published nor do they have to have a copyright notice attached. This is a change in the law; previously, works did have to be published with a printed copyright notice. Works no longer have to be registered with the Copyright Office though doing so will provide protection in the event of a copyright infringement case.

The creator of the original work is the *copyright owner.* Copyright can be transferred to another party (i.e. a publisher) with the signing of a legal document. Authors should not sign away all rights in the standard publisher's contract without question because there is often room for negotiation. E.g. a time limit can be set at which time copyright reverts to the creator, or the creator can reserve the right to make copies for his/her own use.

Works for hire are different – copyright belongs to the employer if the work was done by an employee acting within the scope of his/her employment. Faculty members are employees of the institution and works produced belong to the employer unless specifically stated otherwise in their employment contract. This includes published works, unpublished teaching materials, websites, etc.

In order for the copyright of works done for hire by independent outside contractors (photographers, programmers, etc.) to belong to the employer, there needs to be a signed contract which specifies the work to be done and which includes transfer of copyright. A verbal agreement does not have legal standing.

Works produced by the U.S. government are not copyrightable (Section 105) when produced by government employees as part of their official duties. This includes laws, reports, court decisions, speeches, pamphlets, etc. Some exceptions do apply; e.g. work done under a federal grant is copyrightable.

Copyright owners' rights
The copyright owner's rights are called the "bundle of rights" and only the copyright holder has them:
1. Right to reproduce or to authorize reproduction including photocopying, microfilming, scanning, or any other fixed method
2. Right to prepare derivative works
3. Right to distribute by sale, lease, or lending
4. Right to perform publicly a literary, musical, dramatic, choreographic, motion picture or other audiovisual work
5. Right to display publicly any of the above plus pictorial, graphic, or sculptural works

Anyone else must have the copyright holder's permission unless the copying falls under the fair use proviso, one of the other exceptions, or the work is in the public domain. Infringement occurs when any one of the rights is violated.

Public Domain

After a period of time copyrights expire and works go into the public domain. The Copyright Act of 1976 and amendments extended the period of time that copyright remains in effect; with some exceptions, works are covered during the life of the author and for 70 years afterwards. For specific information go to "When works pass into the public domain" at http://www.unc.edu/~unclng/public-d.htm

New editions, critical editions, reprints, etc. are not in the public domain if they contain new material. However, the actual text of a reprint may be in the public domain depending on whether it was changed or improved in a significant way, e.g. reformatted for design purposes.

Exceptions

There are several exceptions built into the law. The most familiar of these is fair use (Section 107); another one is the library copying exception (Section 108).

Fair use

Fair use must take into consideration these four factors: 1) **Purpose** of the use; 2) **Nature** of the original work; 3) **Amount** used; and 4) **Effect** on the market or value of the original. They do not have to all be present but preponderance "on the whole" is used to determine whether the use is fair use or not.

Is the **purpose** commercial (no) or educational (yes)?
What is the **nature** of the original work? Use of nonfiction is more likely to be fair use than use of a work of fiction or other literary work.
What **amount** of the original is being used? The law is vague on this point and depends on usage. The 5-10% number we hear is not in the law but just a guideline.
What is the **effect** on the market or value of the original? Will the copying mean fewer copies sold by the publisher? This is also vague, difficult to ascertain, and can change as circumstances change.

Prof. Kenneth Crews has a Checklist for Fair Use at www.copyright.iupui.edu/checklist.htm to help faculty members and others determine if a proposed use is fair use or not. It is also in his book **COPYRIGHT LAW FOR LIBRARIANS AND EDUCATORS** on page 124.

The University of Minnesota has a "Fair Use Analysis Tool" at
www.lib.umn.edu/copyright/checklist.phtml

Guidelines for Classroom Copying in Not-for-Profit Institutions
Section 107 allows copying for educational purposes to be considered fair use, but there are restrictions depending on the circumstances. This is not a blanket exemption and educational institutions must adhere to the guidelines. See Circular 21 of the Copyright Office www.copyright.gov for details.

Copyright Office guidelines:
A single copy may be made of the following for the teacher's own use:
- One chapter from a book
- One article from a periodical or newspaper
- Short story, short essay, short poem
- A chart, graph, diagram, drawing, cartoon, or picture from a book, periodical, or newspaper

Multiple copies may be made for classroom use:
- Not more than one copy per student
- Amount copied is brief (one chapter, one article, one excerpt from a collective work, one chart, graph, diagram, etc.)
- Each copy has to include the copyright notice from the original work

In general, the law is broad, vague, and subject to interpretation. The stronger the case can be made for an educational purpose, the more likely the use will be fair use.

Library exception
Section 108 covers reproduction by libraries and archives. It is also vague but essentially it allows libraries to make copies under certain circumstances such as reserves, preservation, replacement, interlibrary loan, and for the personal use of library users.

Resources in Reeves Library

Alpern, Andrew. *101 Questions about Copyright Law.* 2nd edition. Mineola, NY: Dover Publications, Inc., 2002. (Ref KF2995 .A427 2002)

Crews, Kenneth D*. Copyright Law for Librarians and Educators: Creative Strategies and Practical Solutions.* Chicago: American Library Association, 2006. (Ref KF2995 .C74 2006)

Heller, James S. *The Librarian's Copyright Companion.* Buffalo, NY: William S. Hein & Co., Inc., 2004. (Ref KF2995 .H45 2004)

Russell, Carrie. *Complete Copyright: An Everyday Guide for Librarians.* Chicago: American Library Association, 2004. (Ref KF2995 .C57 2004)

Talab, R.S. *Commonsense Copyright: A Guide for Educators and Librarians.* 2d Ed. Jefferson, NC: McFarland & Company, Inc., Publishers, 1999. (Ref KF2994 .T36 1999)

Search for the subject keyword 'copyright' for additional works in Reeves. Use EZBorrow or WorldCat to find books not in Reeves. The booklet, *Questions & Answers on Copyright for the Campus Community,* 6th edition, Association of American Publishers, 2003, is a guide to helping faculty and other academic users conform to the copyright laws. Copies are available at Reeves' Reference Desk or from department chairs.

Fair Use Resources

U.S. Copyright Office. http://www.copyright.gov/circs/circ21.pdf
Circular 21, **Reproduction of Copyrighted Works by Educators and Librarians**

American Library Association. **Fair Use and Electronic Reserves**.
http://www.ala.org/ala/washoff/WOissues/copyrightb/Default1964.htm#pages
Click on **Fair Use and Electronic Reserves**. This site has other information as well.

Crews, Kenneth D. **Copyright Law for Librarians and Educators: Creative Strategies and Practical Solutions**. Chicago: American Library Association, 2006.

Harper, Georgia K. "Copyright Endurance and Change." *Educause Review* 35:6 (2000).
http://www.educause.edu/apps/er/erm00/erm006.asp

Harper, Georgia. "Fair Use of Copyrighted Materials"
http://www.utsystem.edu/OGC/IntellectualProperty/copypol2.htm

Indiana University. Checklist for Fair Use. http://copyright.iupui.edu
Click on **Fair Use Checklist**. This site has other information as well.

<u>**How to Request Permission**</u>:

If the proposed use does not fall under fair use, works may used with permission of the copyright owner. It is sometimes difficult to determine who that is but a good faith effort must be made. You still have to make an effort for so-called "orphan works" for which the copyright owner is not stated or cannot be found. To protect yourself in case of an infringement suit, keep a log and paper records of attempts to find and contact the copyright owner. Go to www.copyright.gov/orphan for help on orphan works.

Permission is usually granted for educational purposes. It may be granted for a one time use or perpetual use and it is important for that to be clearly stated in the agreement.

See Kenneth Crews' *Copyright* Law for *Librarians and Educators* (in Reeves, Ref KF2995 .C74 2006) for further information on permission. See "Dead End," page 111-2 for advice on what to do if you cannot find the copyright holder, are denied permission, get no response to your request, or permission is going to be too costly. The Indiana University-Purdue University, Indianapolis has an excellent Copyright Management Center site, directed by Prof. Crews: www.copyright.iupui.edu/permhome.htm
--Click on "Permissions Information"

Sample letters for requesting permission are available in:

Bruwelheide, Janis H. *The Copyright Primer for Librarians and Educators*. 2d. Ed. Chicago: American Library Association and The National Education Association, 1995, (in Reeves, Ref KF2989.5 .B78 1995), p. 93-95, "Requesting Permission for Academic Copying."

Crews, Kenneth D. *Copyright Law and Graduate Research: New Media, New Rights, and Your New Dissertation*. 2d. Ed. Ann Arbor, MI: Bell & Howell Information and learning, 2000. Available from http://www.umi.com/umi/dissertations/copyright Click on: "Appendix A: Sample Permission Letter"

Dukelow, Ruth H. *The Library Copyright Guide*. Washington, DC: Association for Educational Communications and Technology, 1992, (in Reeves, Ref KF2989.5 .D85 1992), p. 123, "Sample Permission Letter."

Talab, R.S. *Commonsense Copyright: A Guide for Educators and Librarians*. 2d Ed. Jefferson, NC: McFarland & Company, Inc., Publishers, 1999, (in Reeves, Ref KF2994 .T36 1999), p. 142-145.

Links to Copyright Web Sites

U.S. Copyright Office. www.copyright.gov

U.S. Copyright Office. *The Copyright Act of 1976* http://www.copyright.gov/title17/

U.S. Copyright Office. **Summary of the 1998 Digital Millennium Copyright Act** http://www.copyright.gov/legislation/dmca.pdf

U.S. Copyright Office. *Copyright Basics, Circular 1*. Washington, D.C., 1998. www.copyright.gov/circs/circ01.pdf
Excellent primer on copyright. See other circulars for other topics.

The Indiana University-Purdue University, Indianapolis has an excellent Copyright Management Center site, directed by Prof. Kenneth Crews: www.copyright.iupui.edu/permhome.htm

Templeton, Brad. *10 Big Myths about Copyright Explained*. www.templetons.com/brad/copymyths.html

This web site gives excellent explanations of copyright issues, including the issue of displaying links to web sites without the author's permission.

When Works Pass into the Public Domain www.unc.edu/~unclng/public-d.htm
The law changes, depending on the year the work was published.

Copyright Clearance Center www.copyright.com/default.asp
Fee-based service which gets permission for faculty to reproduce copyrighted works for class use.

Wellesley College Copyright Policy
www.wellesley.edu/Library/copyright.html
Scroll down the policy page to find frequently asked questions and answers about classroom and library reserves copyright issues.

University of Georgia Regents Guide to Understanding Copyright and Educational Fair Use www.usg.edu/legal/copyright
More excellent frequently asked questions and answers, including those on non-print media, provided by University System of Georgia.

Harper, Georgia. ***Crash Course in Copyright***.
www.utsystem.edu/OGC/IntellectualProperty/cprtindx.htm
Courtesy of the University of Texas System, Office of General Counsel: Intellectual Property.

Gasaway, Laura N. ***Copyright Law in the Digital Age: Course Materials***.
www.unc.edu/~unclng/gasaway.htm   A print version of this document is also available in Reeves. (Ref KF2995 .G38 2000).

Two additional library documents contain guidelines for use of Blackboard and media:
COPYRIGHT GUIDELINES FOR ELECTRONIC RESOURCES IN BACKBOARD
COPYRIGHT GUIDELINES FOR MEDIA

Rita Berk and Bonnie Falla
10/26/06 revised

COPYRIGHT GUIDELINES FOR
ELECTRONIC RESOURCES
IN BLACKBOARD

Moravian College and Moravian Theological Seminary

- **Considerations** for scanning material for Blackboard:
  - Is the material covered under copyright law?
  - If so, is the intended use permissible under the fair use guidelines (Section 107)?
  - If it is copyrighted but the use is not permissible, how do you get permission to use?
- **FAIR USE (Section 107) GUIDELINES**
  - Under copyright law, making of electronic copies for classroom use without permission is allowed under certain circumstances provided that the four factors governing fair use are followed:
    - 1. **Purpose and character** of the use – Non-commercial and not-for-profit educational use -- Electronic/Scanned copies must be initiated by a faculty member and intended only for the education of students
    - 2. **Nature** of the copyrighted work – Factual or imaginative? -- Use of factual works is more likely to be permissible under fair use than is use of fiction or poetry
    - 3. **Amount** of the portion used in relation to the work as a whole -- No more than 10% is the usual guideline
    - 4. **Effect** of its use on the potential market -- cannot be used in place of expecting students to purchase course material
    - Go to www.copyright.iupui.edu for a fair use checklist developed by Kenneth Crews, Associate Dean of the Faculties for Copyright Management, Indiana University/Purdue University at Indianapolis. Use the checklist to determine if a preponderance of the factors favors fair use. If not, permission must be obtained.
  - Permission may be required even if
    - It is posted elsewhere on the Internet
    - It is being used for the first time
    - It is characterized as supplemental or optional reading, rather than required
  - Materials scanned must be in the legal possession of the library, faculty member, or the institution; or legally obtained.
  - A general copyright notice should appear on the opening screen of Blackboard. *COPYRIGHT RESTRICTION: Title 17, United States Code, governs the making of photocopies or other reproductions of copyrighted material. Under certain fair use circumstances specified in the law, libraries and educational institutions are allowed to furnish copies to students. The copies may not be used for any purpose other than private study, scholarship or research. Electronic copies should not be shared with unauthorized users. If a user fails to comply with fair use restrictions, he/she may be liable for copyright infringement.*
  - A second copyright notice (*NOTICE: This material may be protected by copyright law. Title 17 US Code*) should appear on all individual items along with appropriate citation and/or attribution to the source including the original copyright information from the source.
  - Access to Blackboard must be limited to the teacher and students registered in the class (and personnel administering the system) and must be password protected.
  - All files must be removed at the end of the semester unless they are free from copyright restriction or if permission has been granted for continued use.
  - If it is going to be used for subsequent semesters, or if it is used in more than one section of a course taught by different professors, permission is required. Different professors may scan and post the same article if they are teaching different courses.
  - A small portion (the guideline is approximately 10%) of a work may be scanned (e.g., one chapter from a book, one article from a journal, one poem from an anthology). Scanning of a larger portion requires permission from the copyright holder.

- **PERMISSION TO COPY**
  - Copyright holders are usually publishers. Occasionally copyright reverts to the author after a certain amount of time or when the item goes out of print (determined by the publisher/author contract). Determining copyright holders and locating them are sometimes very difficult and time-consuming procedures.
  - Material for which permission is being sought may be scanned and retained temporarily

148 - Moravian College

- o Entire works may not be scanned without permission from the copyright holder. Such works might be put on Reserve in Reeves Library instead.
- o More than one article from any one journal title (not just an issue) should not be scanned without permission.
- o Follow this link for information on requesting permission: http://home.moravian.edu/public/reeves/about/Policies/RICYCopyright_1011.pdf
- o Fees are often charged for permission. Check with Copyright Clearance Center for their fee structure. http://www.copyright.com
- o Out-of-print titles are not necessarily in the public domain and may still be covered by copyright. If they are, classroom use must come under the fair use guidelines or permission must be obtained before scanning.
- o When in doubt, it is best to request permission from the copyright holder. When permission is granted, use is no longer restricted to the fair use guidelines. Permission may be granted for a one-time use or in perpetuity; it is important to be specific in your request.

- **EXCEPTIONS WHICH DO NOT NEED PERMISSION**
  - o Works in the public domain (a good rule of thumb is that a work with a publication date before 1923 is usually in the public domain). New editions, critical editions, reprints, etc. containing new material are not in the public domain although the actual text may be public domain depending on whether it was changed or improved in any way (e.g., reformatted for design purposes).
  - o Most government publications
  - o Works by the faculty member (his/her publications, lecture notes, past exams, assignments, syllabi, and other material created by the faculty member for which he/she is the copyright holder)
  - o Works clearly marked with blanket permission to reproduce
  - o Links to full text material found in the library's online databases may be used without permission; copyright permission for the use of these links is included in the library's licenses. Please contact one of the Reference Librarians for assistance in finding links. When links are available, they should be used instead of scanning or posting a digital copy.
  - o CIT will provide assistance in creating and maintaining links and in posting digital copies.

- **MISCELLANEOUS**
  - o All current and former student work must have written permission before it can be scanned. Removing names is not sufficient, permission must be obtained. (FERPA - Federal Educational Right to Privacy Act)
  - o It is not permissible to charge students for access.
  - o Students must not forward copies of copyrighted material by email.

- **For further information** http://home.moravian.edu/public/reeves/about/Policies/RICYCopyright_1011.pdf for "Guidelines for the Academic Use of Copyrighted Material, Moravian College and Moravian Theological Seminary." This document includes lists of reference books and websites which define fair use, public domain, and other copyright concepts. These sources also include information on how to request permission for the use of copyrighted material.

These guidelines are not to be construed as legal advice nor should they be considered a legal document but, if followed carefully, it will be less likely that you will be sued for copyright infringement. It is important to document your actions. The existence of this and the other copyright guideline and proof of a "Good Faith Effort" will provide protection against a monetary judgment even if you are sued and judged guilty of copyright infringement. Remember, anyone who initiates a request which will result in copyright infringement or who actually commits copyright infringement is liable for legal action.

11/17/06 rev
Rita Berk and Bonnie Falla

REEVES LIBRARY
COPYRIGHT GUIDELINES
FOR MEDIA

- Media includes videocassettes, DVDs, audiocassettes, and CDs (music or spoken word)
- The library's media collection does not include public performance rights except in those cases in which public performance rights come with the purchase.
- In all other cases, public performance is owned exclusively by the copyright holder.
- Videos and DVDs may be shown without the copyright holder's permission in classrooms under certain restrictions
  - Must be a non-profit educational institution
  - Use must occur in a space devoted to instruction
  - Use must be part of regular curriculum
  - Use must be only for the instructor and class members
  - Library Reserves constitute an extension of classroom teaching
    1. Such use is educational, not personal or recreational, and is part of the regular curriculum
    2. Such viewing comes under the classroom exemption of the copyright law which allows viewing in a classroom or other area used as a classroom including library carrels
    3. Students who are watching reserve videos and DVDs are doing so at the direction of their instructors
    4. Viewing is not timed, scheduled, promoted or otherwise advertised
- Private viewing in homes or dorm rooms is allowable under "fair use."
- All other showings must have the copyright holder's permission. Exceptions may be allowed if the showing has an educational purpose; e.g. if it is accompanied by a professor's introduction or Q&A session. However, the law is unclear on this point and obtaining permission is the safest way to go.

- The copyright holder's permission must be obtained before any media can be copied for the library collection.
- "Off-air" copies will not be added to the library collection without proof of permission to copy.
- The library will add recordings of in-class lectures, demonstrations, speeches, etc. since the copyright holder is the professor, student, or the institution.
- The library will add recordings of college or seminary programs if the participants are college or seminary personnel.
- The library will not add recordings of paid programs without proof of the performer's permission for the taping.

10/06

Oberlin College

Oberlin College Library

	Home	Art	Conservatory	Science	The Academic Commons

Search OBIS TITLE ▼ [   ] Search

Quick Links ▼

Library Home » **Reserve** » Copyright Policy for Library Course Reserves

Copyright Policy for Library Course Reserves

Introduction

Faculty are responsible for complying with copyright law for their reserve materials. Items that fall under fair use as well as those that are not covered by copyright, as explained below, may be placed on reserve without obtaining copyright permission or paying copyright royalties. The library will not place any items on either print or electronic reserve that it knows are not in compliance with copyright law.

Library Collections

The collections of the Oberlin College Library are purchased for the nonprofit educational use of students and faculty. All library materials are acquired with the understanding that there will be multiple uses of a limited number of puchased copies. Libraries frequently pay a premium institutional subscription price for journals that is many times the individual subscription price for the purpose of supporting multiple academic users.

Fair Use

The United States Copyright Act of 1976 (§107) expressly permits the making of multiple copies for classroom use. Such classroom copying is one of the specific examples of uses that do not require the payment of a royalty or the permission of the copyright owners provided that the circumstances of the use are fair as assessed by four factors:

1. The purpose or character of the use, including whether such use is of a commercial nature or is for nonprofit educational purposes;
2. The nature of the copyrighted work;
3. The amount and substantiality of the portion used in relation to the copyrighted work as a whole; and
4. The effect of the use upon the potential market for or value of the copyrighted work.

Oberlin College Library reserves services are used solely for non-profit educational purposes. Copies may be made for reserve without securing copyright permission if the copying is related directly to the educational objectives of a specific course and if the copyrighted material is limited to brief works, or brief excerpts from longer works. Examples include a single chapter from a book, a single article from a journal, or unrelated news articles.

Public Domain Materials

Many materials, such as government documents and older publications, are in the public domain and not protected by copyright. Items in both of these categories may be photocopied for reserve without permission. Refer to Cornell University's *Copyright Term and the Public Domain in the United States* Web page for details regarding older publications.

When are Permissions or Fees Required?

Faculty must obtain permission or pay appropriate royalty fees in order to place the following types of materials on either print reserve or ERes:

- Originals, photocopies, or digitized copies of standardized tests, exercises, or workbooks.
- Photocopies or digitized copies of an entire book or musical score, or substantial portions of a book or score.

General Guidelines for Print Reserve and ERes

- All materials placed on print reserve and ERes will be at the initiative of faculty for the non-commercial, educational usage of students.

- All copies, whether in print or digitized form, must include a notice of copyright: i.e.: © year of first publication (if known), name of copyright holder (if known), and a full bibliographic reference (author, title, journal title or book publisher, and date). Materials submitted for reserve without a full citation may be returned to the faculty member for the addition of the required information
- The copyright notice, "The copyright law of the United States (Title 17, United States Code) governs the making of photocopies or other reproductions of copyrighted materials. Users may be liable for copyright infringement." will appear on course access screen in the ERes system and individual users will accept this liability prior to being allowed to access ERes materials.
- Whenever possible, materials to be used for print reserve and ERes will be those purchased or licensed by the library.
- The library will not place materials on reserve without permission if the nature, scope, or extent of copying is judged by the library to exceed the reasonable limits of fair use. Faculty must obtain permission or pay appropriate royalties in order to place copies of longer works (or substantial portions of longer works), such as complete books and performance scores.
- Access to the ERes system is limited by password to students enrolled in a particular course. There is no charge for access to either print reserve or ERes.
- Users may make one copy for private study, personal reading, research, scholarship, or education.
- Electronic files will be removed from ERes when they are no longer used for reserve services.

Further Information

The electronic scanning of copyright-protected works for library reserve services is an unsettled area of the law which may be addressed in future revisions of the copyright law or through adjudication. Oberlin College will monitor legal developments which may affect the fair use analysis of electronic reserve services to ensure that library services are in compliance with the letter and spirit of the United States Copyright Law.

Further information on the copyright law as it pertains to fair use, seeking permissions, and the placement of items on reserve is available in the Main Reserve Room or from the Art, Science, and Conservatory reserve staff. Please contact the main reserve room at 775-5036 or e-mail *reserve.main@oberlin.edu* if you have any further questions.

Staff   Hours   Ask a Librarian

Search Library Web Site

Powered by Google

Last updated:
November 12, 2007

Oberlin Online

Oberlin College Library
148 West College Street · Oberlin, OH 44074-1532
tel (440) 775-8285 · fax (440) 775-6586
Library.Webmaster@oberlin.edu · © 2008 Oberlin College Library

Oberlin Archives

Randolph-Macon College

Copyright Guidelines for McGraw-Page Library
Randolph-Macon College
Ashland, Virginia
2/20/01

These guidelines summarize uses of copyrighted works permitted by the U.S. Copyright Act. If a proposed use does not fall within a permitted activity described here, you should obtain permission from the copyright owner before using the work. It is important to remember that the copyright owner is the only party permitted to:
- reproduce
- distribute
- adapt/create new works from
- perform and/or
- display

a work for any reason, monetary or otherwise.

TABLE OF CONTENTS

I.   Guidelines for Library Use
                Copies Made in Response to User Requests
                Library Reserve
                Interlibrary Loan
                Replenishment of Library Collections
                Unsupervised Copying
II.   Guidelines for Faculty
                Photocopying of Copyrighted Works
                Activities that Require Permission
                Use of Videotapes in the Classroom
III.   All Other Uses
                Use of any Work in the Public Domain
                Use of a Copyrighted Work that is Deemed to be "Fair Use"
IV.   Helpful Web-Sites
                Copyright Law and Guidelines
                Copyright Policies from Selected Universities and Libraries
                Sites to Help You Obtain Copyright Permission

Guidelines for Library Use

A library is permitted to engage in the activities described in this section if it meets the following three conditions:
1. no copies or distributions are made for commercial purposes;
2. the library is open to the public or to researchers unaffiliated with the library; and
3. copies or distributions of a work must include a copyright notice.[1]

Copies Made in Response to User Requests

A library may make and provide to a user one copy of an *article* from a periodical (or other collection) or a *small part* of any copyright work that it or another library (pursuant to interlibrary loan networks) owns, if it abides by all of the following requirements:[2]
1. the copy becomes the property of the user;
2. the library has no notice that the user will use it for any purpose other than private study, scholarship or research;
3. the copies are not made repeatedly or systematically;
4. the library does not believe that the user is requesting copies of the same work multiple times or that multiple users from a single group are requesting copies of the same work; and
5. the library prominently displays the following copyright warning (at the place where requests are accepted):[3]

NOTICE
WARNING CONCERNING COPYRIGHT RESTRICTIONS

The copyright law of the United States (Title 17, United States Code) governs the making of photocopies or other reproductions of copyrighted material.

Under certain conditions specified in the law, libraries and archives are authorized to furnish a photocopy or other reproduction. One of these specific conditions is that the photocopy or reproduction is not to be "used for any purpose other than private study, scholarship or research." If a user makes a request for, or later uses, a photocopy or reproduction for purposed in excess of "fair use," that user may be liable for copyright infringement.

This institution reserves the right to refuse to accept a copying order if, in its judgment, fulfillment of the order would involve violation of copyright law.

A library may make and provide to a user a copy of an *entire work* that it or another library (pursuant to interlibrary loan networks) owns if the work cannot otherwise be obtained at a reasonable price (e.g., if it is out-of-print).[4]

This permission to make and provide copies to users does not apply to musical, pictorial, graphical, or sculptural works and motion pictures or other audio-visual works,[5] except that a library may make and loan to users a small number of videotape recordings of daily news broadcasts.[6]

---

1 17 U.S.C. § 108(a).
[2] 17 U.S.C. § 108(d) and (g); Nimmer, § 8.03[D] and [E][2].
[3] 37 C.F.R. § 201.14; Nimmer, § 8.03[E][2].
[4] 17 U.S.C. § 108(e); Nimmer, § 8.03[E][2].
[5] 17 U.S.C. § 108(i); Nimmer § 8.03[B][1].
[6] 17 U.S.C. § 108(f)(3); Nimmer § 8.03[F].

Library Reserve[7]

The library will place on reserve:

1. a single copy of an article, chapter of a book, or a poem; and
2. multiple copies of a work if the library owns the work and the amount of material copied and the number of copies made are reasonable in comparison to the original work and the extent of student demand for the work.

Any materials placed on reserve will be removed at the end of the term.

At the request of a faculty member, the library may photocopy and place on reserve excerpts from copyrighted works in its collection in accordance with guidelines similar to those governing formal classroom distribution for face-to-face teaching discussed above. This College believes that these guidelines apply to the library reserve shelf to the extent it functions as an extension of classroom readings or reflects an individual student's right to photocopy for his personal scholastic use under the doctrine of fair use. In general, librarians may photocopy materials for reserve room use for the convenience of students both in preparing class assignments and in pursuing informal educational activities which higher education requires, such as advance independent study and research.

If the request calls for only one copy to be placed on reserve, the library may photocopy an entire article, or an entire chapter from a book, or an entire poem. Requests for multiple copies on reserve should meet the following guidelines:

1. the amount of material should be reasonable in relation to the total amount of material assigned for one term of a course taking into account the nature of the course, its subject matter and level;
2. the number of copies should be reasonable in light of the number of students enrolled, the difficulty and timing of assignments, and the number of other courses which may assign the same material;
3. the material should contain a notice of copyright; and
4. the effect of photocopying the material should not be detrimental to the market for the work. In general, the library should own at least one copy of the work.

For example, a professor may place on reserve as a supplement to the course textbook a reasonable number of copies of articles from academic journals or chapters from trade books. A reasonable number of copies will in most instances be less than six, but factors such as the length or difficulty of the assignment, the number of enrolled students and the length of time allowed for completion of the assignment may permit more in unusual circumstances.

In addition, a faculty member may also request that multiple copies of photocopied, copyrighted material be place on the reserve shelf if there is insufficient time to obtain permission from the copyright owner. For example, a professor may place on reserve several photocopies of an entire article from a recent issue of Time magazine in lieu of distributing a copy to each member of the class.

Interlibrary Loan

If the library requests, from another library, copies from a periodical or copyrighted work that it does not own, it may not request so many copies that such copies substitute for a subscription

---

7 Adapted from "Model Policy Concerning College and University Photocopying for Classroom, Research and Library Reserve, found at: http://www.cni.org/docs/infopols/ALA.html#mpup citing 17 U.S.C. §§ 107(1), (3) and (4) and 17 U.S.C. §401.

of the periodical or a purchase of the work. To stay within this rule, the library should abide by the following guidelines:[8]

1. Within any calendar year, the library may not request more than 5 copies of one or more articles from one periodical published within the previous five years.[9]
2. Within any calendar year, the library may not request more than 5 copies of material from any one work.
3. The library fulfilling a request for copies may not fulfill the request unless the requesting library provides a written statement that the request conforms with these guidelines.
4. The requesting library must maintain records of all requests it has made during the current calendar year and the three previous years, and must include a copyright notice.

From the National Commission on New Technological Uses of Copyrighted Works (CONTU) guidelines governing copying and interlibrary arrangements, CONTU Guidelines on Photocopying under Interlibrary Loan Arrangements, http://www.cni.org/docs/infopols/CONTU.html written in conjunction with Section 108 of the copyright law.

Replenishment of Library Collections

A library may make up to three copies of:

1. a *published* work that it owns, solely to replace that copy when it is damaged, deteriorating, lost or stolen, if it cannot obtain a replacement copy at a fair price, [10]
2. an *unpublished* work that it owns solely for the purposes of preservation and security. [11]

Unsupervised Copying

A library that permits users to make unsupervised copying of library materials much post a notice that the making of a copy may be subject to copyright law. Generally, the library should use the same notice as provided above under "Copies Made in Response to User Requests".

Guidelines for Faculty

Photocopying of Copyrighted Works

For your own research or use in teaching, you may make a single copy of:

- a chapter from a book
- an article from a periodical or newspaper
- one short story, essay or short poem, or
- one chart, graph, diagram, drawing, cartoon, or picture from one book or periodical. [12]

You may make multiple copies of a work for one-time distribution in class if:

1. you make no more than one copy per student;

---

[8] 17 U.S.C. § 108(g); Nimmer § 8.03[E][2][f].
[9] The law is unclear as to how many copies may be made from periodicals more than five years old. Generally, the library should not make so many copies that it substitutes such copies for a subscription. *See* Nimmer § 8.03[E][2][f].
[10] 17 U.S.C. § 108(c); Nimmer § 8.03[E][1].
[11] 17 U.S.C. § 108(b); Nimmer § 8.03[E][1].
[12] Nimmer § 13.05[E][3][b].

2. you include the copyright notice;
3. you do not charge the student for more than the actual cost of copying;
4. the copying does not create, replace or substitute for a book, anthology or compilation; and
5. the copying meets the following tests for brevity, spontaneity and cumulative effect: [13]

Brevity-

You may copy:

Poetry- a complete poem if less than 250 words and on no more than two pages, or an excerpt of 250 words from a longer poem

Prose – a complete article, story or essay of less than 2,500 words or an excerpt of not more than 1,000 words (or 10% of the work)

Illustration – one chart, graph, diagram, picture per book or periodical issue

Spontaneity-

The copying is at the inspiration of the individual teacher and the decision to use the work is so immediate that it is unreasonable to expect a timely reply to a request for permission (i.e., it may not be a part of a pre-planned curriculum).

Cumulative Effect-

- The copying is for only one course
- Not more than one short poem, article, story or essay may be copied from the same author during one class term
- No more than 9 instances of multiple copying for one course during one class term.

For additional information see the "Agreement on Guidelines for Classroom Copying in Not-For-Profit Educational Institutions, http://www.cni.org/docs/infopols/NACS.html

Activities that Require Permission

The following activities are not permitted and will require advance permission from the copyright owner: [14]

1. *Repetitive copying.* The classroom or reserve use of photocopied materials in multiple courses or successive years will normally require advance permission from the owner of the copyright.
2. *Copying for profit.* Faculty should not charge students more than the actual cost of photocopying the material.
3. *Consumable works.* The duplication of works that are consumed in the classroom, such as standardized tests, exercises, and workbooks, normally requires permission from the copyright owner.
4. *Creation of anthologies as basic text material for a course.* Creation of a collective work or anthology by photocopying a number of copyrighted articles and excerpts to be purchased and used together as the basic text for a course will in most instances require the permission of the copyrighted owners.

Use of Videotapes in the Classroom

Faculty may show a videotape in a classroom for educational purposes, provided the videotape is lawfully purchased or made. [15]

---

[13] Nimmer § 13.05[E][3][d].

[14] Adapted from "Model Policy Concerning College and University Photocopying for Classroom, Research and Library Reserve, found at: http://www.cni.org/docs/infopols/ALA.html#mpup citing 17 U.S.C. §§ 107(1), (3) and (4).

You may lawfully record and show for a class only television programs broadcast by a public or non-profit broadcasting entity.[16] If you do so, you must show the program and then erase the recording within 7 days of the date the program was broadcast.[17] You may not record and show television programs from for-profit entities without their permission.

Videos are covered in Section 110 (1) of the Copyright Act and Guidelines for Off-the-Air Recording of Broadcast Programming for Educational Purposes,
http://www.musiclibraryassoc.org/Copyright/guiderec.htm.

All Other Uses

If a proposed copy or other use of a work does not fall within one of the permitted activities described above, it does not mean that such use is necessarily unlawful. Other lawful uses include:

Use of any Work in the Public Domain

Works in the "public domain" are works that either were never copyrighted or works for which copyright has expired. There is no single clear-cut rule for determining what works were never copyrighted or for determining what copyrights have expired. The maximum copyright term is 95 years from December 31 of the year in which copyright was originally procured.[18]

For a detailed explanation of when a copyright enters the public domain, see the U.S. Copyright Office's Information Circulars No. 1, "Copyright Basics" and No. 15a, "Duration of copyright," which can be found at http://www.loc.gov/copyright/circs.

For the chart "When Works Pass into the Public Domain", created by Lolly Gasaway at UNC, see http://www.unc.edu/~unclng/public-d.htm.

As a general rule, almost all U.S. government publications are also in the public domain.[19] However, government publications may contain copyrighted materials in them. U.S. government publications are documents prepared by an official or employee of the U.S. government in an official capacity.[20]

Use of a Copyrighted Work that is Deemed to be "Fair Use"

Unfortunately, there are also no clear-cut lines for determining what kinds of uses are deemed to be fair. A use of a copyrighted work may be deemed to be fair use, and therefore lawful, upon a balancing of the following four factors:

(1) the purpose and character of the use, including whether such use is of a commercial nature or is for nonprofit educational purposes;
- If use of the work is not for profit and is for criticism, comment, news reporting, teaching, scholarship or research, it is more likely to be lawful.

(2) the nature of the copyrighted work;

---

[15] 17 U.S.C. § 110(1); Nimmer §8.15[B].
[16] 17 U.S.C. § 118(d)(3); Nimmer § 8.06[D].
[17] 17 U.S.C. §118(d)(3); Nimmer § 8.06[D].
[18] 17 U.S.C. § 304(b)
[19] 17 U.S.C. §105.
[20] 17 U.S.C. § 101.

- If the work is a factual one and has been published, use of the work is more likely to be lawful than if the work is imaginative and unpublished.

(3) the amount and substantiality of the portion used in relation to the copyrighted work as a whole; and
- The smaller the percentage of the work you use, the more likely the use will be lawful.

(4) the effect of the use upon the potential market for or value of the copyrighted work.
- If your use of the work is likely to compete with sales of the work or avoids payment of royalties where permission can be obtained, then the use is more likely to be unlawful.

For more information on fair use, consult the University of Texas web-site, "Fair Use of Copyrighted Materials" at http://www.utsystem.edu/ogc/IntellectualProperty/copypol2.htm.

Helpful Web-Sites

Copyright Law and Guidelines

LAW

Copyright Law of the United States of America
Title 17 of the United State Code, Revised to April 2000
http://www.loc.gov/copyright/title17

CONGRESSIONAL GUIDELINES

Agreement on Guidelines for Classroom Copying in Not-For-Profit Educational Institutions With Respect To Books and Periodicals
National Association of College Stores and the Association of American Publishers, 1976
http://www.cni.org/docs/infopols/NACS.html
Guidelines for Educational Uses of Music
Music Publishers' Association of the United States, et al., 1976
http://www.musiclibraryassoc.org/Copyright/guidemus.htm
Guidelines for Off-the-Air Recording of Broadcast Programming for Educational Purposes
1979
http://www.musiclibraryassoc.org/Copyright/guiderec.htm

LIBRARY GUIDELINES

Model Policy Concerning College and University Photocopying for Classroom, Research and Library Reserve Use
American Library Association, March 1982
http://www.cni.org/docs/infopols/ALA.html#mpup
CONTU (TU- Technological Uses) Guidelines on Photocopying under Interlibrary Loan Arrangements
Library of Congress, 1979
http://www.cni.org/docs/infopols/CONTU.html

CONFERENCE GUIDELINES

CONFU (FU- Fair Use)
    1997
    http://www.utsystem.edu/ogc/intellectualproperty/ccmcguid.htm

Copyright Policies from Selected Universities and Libraries

- American Library Association, "Copyright and Intellectual Property"
  http://www.ala.org/washoff/property.html

- Groton Public Schools, "Copyright Implementation Manual"
  http://www.groton.k12.ct.us/mts/cimhp01.htm

- Stanford University Libraries, "Copyright and Fair Use"
  http://fairuse.stanford.edu/library/

- University of Texas Libraries, "Copyright Tutorial"
  http://www.lib.utsystem.edu/copyright/

- University of Virginia Libraries, "Copyright"
  http://www.lib.virginia.edu/acqpres/copyright/copy.html

- Virginia Tech Libraries, "Copyright Policies"
  http://scholar.lib.vt.edu/copyright/

- Washington & Lee University, ""Policy for the Use of Copyrighted Works:
  http://www.wlu.edu/library/copyrighttoc.html

Sites to Help You Obtain Copyright Permission

For authors, use WATCH: Writers, Artists and their Copyright Holders, at the University of Texas:
http://www.hrc.utexas.edu/watch/watch.html

For copyright clearance on recent articles or books,
- check with the Copyright Clearance Center: http://www.copyright.com
- contact the permission department of the publisher, or
- pay an automated copyright permission clearinghouse, such as iCopyright.com:
  http://www.icopyright.com

Virginia E. Young
2/20/01

Smith College

Need Help ?

you are here: Services > Faculty Services > Copyright & the Classroom

Copyright & the Classroom

This page will help guide you through copyright issues to consider when you are using copies of any kind of material for your classes. Each section shows contacts for questions. For general questions, please contact Chris Hannon, Neilson Library, x2911.

For more information, please also consult:

- Smith College Copyright Policies
- Policy for Acceptable Use of Computer Resources

What do you want to do?

Copy print materials for distribution in class or for library reserves.	click here
Copy/scan print materials for e-reserves and/or Moodle.	click here
Create a course pack of readings for students to purchase.	click here
Copy images to show in class, to mount on Moodle, etc.	click here
Copy media (e.g., film clips, audio clips, music).	click here

COPYING PRINT MATERIAL FOR DISTRIBUTION OR LIBRARY RESERVES

Step One: Determine the copyright holder.

- For books, examine both sides of the title page for the © statement.
- For journal articles, look at the article itself or the front matter of the journal for a copyright statement.
- The copyright holder is usually either the publisher or the author.

Step Two: Determine the copyright status of the work.

- Check the web site Copyright Term and the Public Domain (University of Minnesota)
- If the work is in the public domain (not protected by copyright), there are no restrictions on your use.
- If the work is still protected by copyright, consult the fair use worksheet (University of Minnesota) to determine if you need permission.

Step Three: Request permission if needed.

- Administrative Assistants in each department can request permissions through the Copyright Clearance Center (CCC) or directly from the publisher. For more information, see How to Obtain Permissions.

Step Four: Make copies or send copying request to Central Services.

Questions? Contact Chris Hannon, channon@email.smith.edu, 585-2911, Neilson Library.

Return to Top

COPYING/SCANNING PRINT MATERIAL FOR E-RESERVES/MOODLE

Note: These procedures apply whether you're using the Libraries' e-reserve service or doing the work yourself.

Step One: Determine if an online copy is available.

- For journal articles, link to an online version whenever possible. Then you do not need to worry about copyright. Check the Libraries' journal locator for availability.
- If you're submitting an e-reserves list to the Libraries, note all items available online. Do not provide copies of these items for scanning.
- If you're linking to articles yourself, put the links on your Moodle site so they are password protected. Look for a **persistent link** to use; this may be called a durable or stable link. Otherwise your link may be only temporary. For help, please contact the Neilson Library reference desk, x2966.
- You may also link to other websites if you acknowledge them at the link.
- If you need to scan items (or have them scanned), follow the steps below.

Step Two: Determine the copyright holder.

- For books, examine both sides of the title page for the © statement.
- For journal articles, look at the article itself or the front matter of the journal for a copyright statement.
- The copyright holder is usually either the publisher or the author.

Step Three: Determine the copyright status.

- Determine the copyright holder and year by examining both sides of the title page for a book and the actual article or front matter for a journal.
- Check the web site Copyright Term and the Public Domain (University of Minnesota)
- If the work is in the public domain (not protected by copyright), there are no restrictions on your use.
- If the work is still protected by copyright, consult the fair use worksheet (University of Minnesota) to determine if you need permission.

Step Four: Request permissions if needed.

- Administrative Assistants in each department can request permissions through the Copyright Clearance Center or directly from the publisher. For more information, see How to Obtain Permissions.

Step Five: Submit materials to the Libraries or link items to your Moodle course.

- Consult the Libraries' procedures.

Questions? Contact Chris Hannon, channon@email.smith.edu, 585-2911, Neilson Library.

Return to Top

CREATING COURSE PACKS

- Submit materials to Central Services, in accordance with their <u>procedures and deadlines</u>.
- Central Services will seek permissions for use and copy, bind and send course packs to the Grecourt Book Shop for sale.

Questions? Contact Chris Gentes, <u>cgentes@email.smith.edu</u>, 585-2600, Central Services.

Return to Top

COPYING IMAGES TO SHOW IN CLASS OR PUT ON MOODLE

[under construction]

Return to Top

COPY MEDIA

[under constructions]

Return to Top

Terms of Use | Return to Top

<u>Home</u> | <u>Research</u> | <u>Library Services</u> | <u>General Information</u> | <u>Smith Libraries & Collections</u> | <u>Need Help?</u>

Smith College Libraries, Northampton, MA 01063 | [413] 585-2902
<u>TheLibraries'Webmaster@smith.edu</u>
Copyright © 2006 Smith College Libraries. All Rights Reserved.

Last Updated: November 20, 2006

SMITH COLLEGE   Admission | Academics | Student Life | About Smith | Offices

Home > Copyright Information

Copyright Information

**PROCEDURES FOR NOTIFICATION OF COPYRIGHT INFRINGEMENT
UNDER THE DIGITAL MILLENNIUM COPYRIGHT ACT**

Digital Millennium Copyright Act >

Smith College Policy on the Acceptable Use of Computer Resources >

Form downloads
require Acrobat Reader
(free).

Download Acrobat
Reader >

Designated Agent to Receive Notices
Smith College has registered the following agent with the Copyright Office:

Herbert Nickles
Executive Director for Information Technology Services
Stoddard Hall Room 12
Smith College
Northampton, MA 01063
Phone: 413-585-3770
Fax: 413-585-3073
Email: hnickles@smith.edu

Notice and Take-down Procedure
Written notification of allegedly infringing work must be sent to the college's agent at
the above address. The notice must include ALL of the following:

1. A physical or digital signature of the owner of an exclusive copyright
right (i.e., the copyright owner himself or the owner's exclusive licensee
of the right(s) to reproduce, distribute, display, perform or create
derivatives) or the owner's authorized agent;

2. A description of the works claimed to be infringed;

3. A description of the allegedly infringing works, sufficient to enable the
agent to find them;

4. Sufficient information to enable the agent to contact the complainer;

5. A statement that the complainer believes in good faith that the use of
the material is not authorized by the owner, the owner's agent or the
law; and

6. A statement that the information in the notice is accurate and, under
penalty of perjury, that the complainer is authorized to act on behalf of
the owner of one or more exclusive copyright rights.

*Individuals who wish to submit a notice are referred to the Digital Millennium
Copyright Act Section 512 (c) (3) (A) (for notices alleging that content infringes) or
Section 512 (d) (3) (for notices that allege that information location tools such as links
contribute to infringement of a work).*

The college's agent will review the notification to be sure it substantially conforms to
the statutory requirements. If the notice substantially conforms, the agent will take
reasonable steps to notify the page owner of the allegation of infringement and secure
voluntary take-down of the work or disable access to the work.

If the notice fails substantially to conform, but the problems are with requirements 1,
5 or 6 above, the agent will contact the complainer and try to obtain the missing
information. If the complainer provides substantially conforming information, the
agent will notify the page owner of the allegation of infringement and secure voluntary
take-down of the work or disable access to the work.

If the notice is nonconforming with respect to requirements 2, 3 or 4, or if the
complainer does not respond to the agent's request for additional information, the
agent will ignore the notice. The agent will archive the notice along with a copy of any

correspondence attempting to obtain additional information.

Counter-notification Procedure
After the page owner voluntarily takes down the page or the college's agent disables access to it, the college or the page owner may decide to proceed to counter-notification.

Counter-notices can only claim: (1) that the copyright owner is mistaken and that the work is lawfully posted or (2) that the work has been misidentified. A page owner may assert that a use of another's work qualifies as a fair use and so the copyright owner is "mistaken" in characterizing it as infringing.

Counter-notices must contain ALL of the following:

   1. A physical or digital signature of the page owner;

   2. A description of the material removed and its location before it was removed;

   3. A statement that the page owner believes in good faith that the material was removed by mistake or because it was misidentified;

   4. The page owner's name, address and phone number and his or her consent to jurisdiction of the Federal District Court for that address or any Federal District Court if the address is foreign; and

   5. A statement that the page owner will accept service of process from the complainer.

The page owner must send the counter notification to the college's agent who will:

   1. Promptly send a copy of any substantially conforming counter-notice to the complainer indicating that the college will restore access in 10 business days; and

   2. Restore access to the allegedly infringing work within 10 to 14 business days after the day the agent receives the counter-notice, unless the agent first receives a notice from the complainer that he or she has filed an action seeking a court order to restrain the page owner.

If the agent receives notice that the complainer has filed an action seeking a court order to restrain the page owner, the agent will:

   1. Not repost the allegedly infringing work while court action is pending;

   2. Forward the notice to the page owner; and

   3. Forward the notice to the appropriate College administrator (the Provost/Dean of the Faculty if the page owner is a faculty member, the Dean of the College if the page owner is a student, or the Vice President for Finance and Administration if the page owner is a staff member).

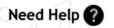

Need Help ?

SMITH COLLEGE
L i b r a r i e s

| Home | Research | Library Services | General Information | Smith Libraries & Collections |

you are here: Services > Faculty Services > **Smith College Copyright Policy**

Smith College Copyright Policies

USE OF COPYRIGHTED WORKS FOR EDUCATION AND RESEARCH

I. Introduction

II. Policy of the Use of Copyrighted Works for Education and Research

III. Copyright Protections and Fair Use Principles

IV. Practical Assistance: Frequently Asked Questions about Copyright

V. How to Obtain Copyright Permission

VI. Smith College Copyright Contacts

VII. Copyright Resources on the Web

I. INTRODUCTION

The purpose of copyright, as articulated in the in the United States Constitution, is to "promote the Progress of Science and useful Arts." As Smith College realizes its mission to educate its students, and to conduct research in the arts and sciences or engage in the performing and creative arts, the Smith College community has a special responsibility towards the use of copyrighted works. As creators of copyrighted works, we appreciate the incentive that copyright holds for the dissemination and preservation of our creative efforts in order to advance and expand general knowledge. As users of copyrighted works, we honor both the opportunities for and limitations to using the intellectual property of others. We also act as significant role models for our students for the responsible use of copyrighted work in teaching, learning, research and scholarship. We are acutely aware of the importance of striking an appropriate balance, as US law does, between the rights of intellectual property owners to govern the dissemination and use of their works and our need to use information quickly and efficiently in our teaching, learning and scholarship.

II. POLICY ON THE USE OF COPYRIGHTED WORKS FOR EDUCATION AND RESEARCH

Smith College will take appropriate measures to ensure that its students, faculty and staff are aware of copyright laws, regulations and agreements and can act responsibly as they use information that is owned by others in the course of teaching, learning, research or administration of the College. All members of the Smith College community are required to comply with copyright laws. Federal copyright laws provide valuable protection to the authors of original works, and Smith College expects all members of the Smith community to respect those rights. Copyright laws also permit users of copyrighted works to make fair use of copyrighted materials under some limited circumstances. Smith College is committed to full support of the fair use of copyrighted works by the Smith College community under the provisions of applicable laws. The Smith College community are expected to have knowledge of, and make reasonable application of, the four factors of fair use. Failure to comply with copyright laws and to act in good faith in the fair use of copyrighted material will result in a Smith College community member assuming liability for his or her actions and may result in disciplinary action.

Return to Top

III. COPYRIGHT PROTECTIONS AND FAIR USE PRINCIPLIES

To help members of the Smith community understand and comply with copyright laws, this document summarizes basic principles of copyright law including the application of the fair use balancing test. References (links) to appropriate sections of the Practical Assistance are also made to explain concepts included in these principles.

Copyright law is inherently complex. A fair use of a copyrighted work depends upon a specific determination based upon the circumstances of the use. New information technologies, e.g., digital information and networked environments, have introduced a wholly new, and in many ways transformed, working environment for the application of copyright. These principles are intended to provide an initial context for complying with the law.

Principle 1: The copyright holder has important and exclusive rights. Copyright law protects original works such as writings, music, visual arts, and films by giving the copyright holder a set of exclusive rights in that work. These rights include the right to copy, distribute, adapt, perform, display, and create derivative or collected works. In general, any use of copyrighted materials requires permission from, and potentially payment of royalties to, the copyright holder unless the use falls within an exemption in the law, such as the fair use exemption.

Principle 2: Responsible decision making means that Smith College community members must make demonstrable good faith efforts to understand the fundamentals of copyright law and the reasonable application of fair use. When Smith College community members plan to use a copyrighted work in their teaching or research, they must examine the specifics of their use within the context of the law in order to determine whether they should seek permission for the use or depend instead upon the fair use exemption.

Principle 3: An appropriate exercise of fair use depends on a case-by-case application and balancing of four factors as set forth in a statute enacted by Congress. A proper determination of fair use--in daily practice and in the courts--requires applying these four factors to the specific circumstances of the use:

> **Four Factors Used to Determine "Fair Use"**
>
> | | |
> |---|---|
> | Purpose or character of the use | Nature of the copyrighted work being used |
> | Amount and substantiality of the work being used | Effect of the use on the market for or value of the original |

These factors must be evaluated to determine whether most of them weigh in favor of or against fair use.

Principle 4: Nonprofit educational purposes are generally favored in the application of the four factors of fair use, but an educational use does not by itself make the use a "fair use." One must always consider and weigh all four factors of fair use together. The educational purpose of Smith College will usually weight the first of the four factors, the purpose or character of the use, in favor of fair use. However, an educational use does not mean that the use is, by that factor alone, a fair use. All four factors must be weighed in making a decision.

Principle 5: Reasonable people--including judges and legislators--can and will differ in their understanding of fair use. Copyright law rarely offers a definitive meaning of fair use for any specific application. Thus, the real meaning of fair use depends on a reasoned and responsible application of the four factors. One person's judgment and situation may not match the next, and the differences may be based on variations in facts and circumstances.

Principle 6: By acting responsibly and by making considered and intentional decisions, you can limit your potential liability; document your reasoning for a fair use. Because of the flexible and interpretive nature of fair use, Congress provided significant protection for educators. Not only does the fair use exception apply particularly to educational purposes, but additional laws may limit the monetary liability that educators may potentially face. In any event, however, educators must hold a reasonable and good-faith belief that their activities are fair use in light of the four factors. By documenting your application of the four factors of fair use to your specific use, you will be better able to demonstrate your activities were done in good faith.

Principle 7: Guidelines, while sometimes helpful, do not determine the entire breadth and scope of fair use protection. In an attempt to clarify the meaning of fair use for common situations, various private parties have negotiated guidelines, but those externally developed guidelines are sometimes inappropriate for the realistic application of fair use to higher education. Such guidelines may be consulted by courts in making fair use determinations, but the guidelines are not binding either as limiting permissible activity or as providing safe harbors. Fair use must be determined according to the circumstances of each situation.

Return to Top

IV. PRACTICAL ASSISTANCE: FREQUENTLY ASKED QUESTIONS

Determining the copyright status of a work

The four factors of Fair Use

Guidelines for using copyrighted works

Mounting course materials on the web

Obtaining copyright permission

Copyrighting your own materials

Special situations (out of print works, video & film, visual images, performance, software)

More information (websites and guidelines)

DETERMINING THE COPYRIGHT STATUS OF A WORK

Q. How do I know if a work is under copyright or in the public domain?

A. First examine the work for a copyright statement. Then consult the table Copyright Term and the Public Domain from the University of Minnesota.

THE FOUR FACTORS OF FAIR USE

Q. Can you provide more detail about the four factors that determine fair use?

A. Fair use (Section 107 of the Copyright Act of 1976) balances the rights of copyright holders with the needs of scholars to promote teaching, research and the free exchange of ideas. Fair use defines particular circumstances in which it is permissible to use copyrighted material, free from permissions and royalties. The four factors considered in weighing fair use are:

1. The purpose and character of the use. Use in nonprofit, educational teaching and research, or for criticism, commentary or news reporting, makes a finding of fair use more likely; commerical use makes a finding of fair use less likely. However, not all educational uses are fair uses.

2. The nature of the copyrighted work. Using works that are factual (e.g., historical data, scientific information, etc.) tends to weigh in favor of a finding of fair use; creative or unpublished works tend to indicate the need for copyright permission.

3. The amount and substantiality of the portion used. Use of small portions of a work usually favors a finding of fair use as long as the portion does not constitute "the heart of the work". The more material used the greater the balance away from fair use.

4. The effect of the use upon the potential market for the work. Use that substitutes for the purchase of a book, reprint or subscription weighs against a finding of fair use.

Clearly these factors are subject to varying interpretations and applications. For further guidance, see a Fair Use Analysis Worksheet from the University of Minnesota.

Q. Isn't any use in an educational setting considered fair use?

A. Unfortunately, not. Purpose and character of the use (i.e., educational) is only one of four factors determining fair use. Educational use does favor fair use but other factors may weigh against fair use (e.g., nature of the work, amount copied, effect on the market).

GUIDELINES FOR USING COPYRIGHTED WORKS

Q. Where can I find guidelines or rules of thumb to help determine fair use practices?

A. Look at the following sites for help with

Print materials for class use and library reserves
Multimedia
Music for class use, library reserves, performance
Visual Images for class use, library reserves, slide collections, etc.

MOUNTING COURSE MATERIALS ON THE WEB

Q. May I put electronic copies of course readings on my home page or Moodle site without copyright permission?

A. Yes, in accordance with these guidelines:

- Use materials in the public domain freely.
- Use material freely if you own the copyright (e.g., exams, syllabi, notes).
- Follow the classroom guidelines for use of other copyrighted materials.
- Whenever possible, point to documents available on other websites rather than downloading them onto your own site.
- If you mount copyrighted materials under fair use (i.e., without securing permission) keep them up only one semester AND restrict your website to class members only.
- When in doubt, seek permission!

Remember: more stringent guidelines may apply to images, graphics, video, sound, etc.

Q. I want to put several articles and book chapters that I wrote up on my website. Can I do this?

A. Yes, but only under fair use or if you retained the appropriate copyright privileges. Otherwise, check with the publisher or rightsholder.

Q. May I link to other websites from my home page or from Moodle?

A. Generally, this is permitted. Include an acknowledgement to the author if possible.

Q. What about other kinds of materials for my home page or Moodle (e.g., video, audio, images)?

A. Consult the multimedia guidelines, the music guidelines, or the visual images guidelines.

OBTAINING COPYRIGHT PERMISSION

Q. How do I get copyright permission when needed?

A. Click here for information.

COPYRIGHTING YOUR OWN MATERIALS

Q. How do I copyright my own materials?

A. Copyright protection is automatic for materials "fixed in a tangible medium" (i.e., written, recorded, etc.). If you wish to register your copyright, go to the U.S. Copyright Office website.

This is not required but may help if you wish to file a complaint about copyright violation.

Return to Top

SPECIAL SITUATIONS
(out of print works, video & film, visual images, performance, software)

Out of print works

Q. Is it okay to photocopy a book that is out of print?

A. No, many out of print books are still protected by copyright. Check with the Libraries about buying a copy through the out of print market or borrowing a copy through interlibrary loan.

Q. If an item is not available on the out of print market, is there any way to make a copy?

A. Yes, the Libraries may make up to three copies if a thorough search shows that a copy cannot be obtained at a reasonable price. This also pertains to works in obsolete formats (e.g., 8 track tapes, beta videocassettes).

Video & Film

Q. May I show a video labeled "Home Use Only" to my class?

A. Yes, this is considered permissible in face-to-face teaching for instruction (but not entertainment).

Q. May I show a video labeled "Home Use Only" in a campus auditorium?

A. Yes, as long as the performance is not open to the public and is for instructional purposes.

Q. May I show videos owned by the Libraries for a film series?

A. Yes, if the library purchased public performance rights for each video.

Q. May I copy a rental video or a preview copy to use later?

A. No!

Q. Some of our older films and videos are deteriorating badly and are now out of print. Can we make copies?

A. Yes, but only if you secure permission from the copyright owner.

Visual Images

Q. May I make slides, photographs or digital copies of images (plates, drawings, maps, charts, etc.) from a book?

A. Whenever possible, these must be purchased (or licensed) rather than photographed or scanned. If unavailable commercially or in a timely manner, one copy of an image may be made for classroom use - see Smith College Art Department Image Collections' Copyright Guidelines for more information.

Q. Can these copies be added to a slide collection for future use?

A. No, not without securing permission.

Performance (music, dance, drama)

Q. Because Smith is a nonprofit educational institution, aren't performances of music, dance and drama allowable under fair use?

A. This is a complex area of the law. In general, performances in the classroom are permitted; any kind of public performance requires permission and/or payment of royalties. Smith contracts with major services such as ASCAP, to handle payment of performance royalties. Consult with the Music, Theatre and Dance departments for more information.

Software

Q. Do fair use provisions also apply to software?

A. No, software is almost always licensed and the license stipulates use. Fair use does not apply.

Q. I often make a back-up copy of software. Is this okay?

A. Generally, yes, as long as you retain the copy as a true back-up and only use it when the original fails.

Q. Is it all right to load single-user license software on several computers?

A. No, you need to buy multiple copies or be licensed for multiple users.

Q. May I borrow software to download on my home/office pc?

A. No, unless the software license specifically permits this. (You could download it for use and immediately delete it afterward.)

Return to Top

V. HOW TO OBTAIN COPYRIGHT PERMISSION

Class handouts, photocopies for library reserves, online posting (e.g. Moodle)

Each faculty member is responsible for obtaining or arranging to obtain copyright permissions for classroom handouts, photocopies for library reserve use or online posting of materials (e.g., on Moodle). Please submit requests for permissions at least six weeks before the material is needed as the process can be slow, especially when dealing directly with a publisher. If permission is denied, or cannot be obtained in time, alternate material must be found.

In general, costs of securing copyright permission are charged to Smith's copyright compliance fund, managed by the Purchasing Office. Department administrative assistants have the account numbers.

Whenever possible, use the Copyright Clearance Center (CCC), a centralized service for requesting permissions and paying royalties. Department administrative assistants will process requests on the CCC website. CCC sets limits of 25% of a book and two articles per periodical issue. For further information about CCC services, contact Chris Hannon in Neilson Library (x2911 or channon@email.smith.edu) or consult the CCC website.

For items not listed with the CCC, contact the publisher or copyright holder directly. Many publishers now grant permissions via phone, fax, e-mail, website, etc. For assistance identifying and locating publishers, search AcqWeb's Directory of Publishers and Vendors or contact the Neilson Library reference desk, x2966, or the branch libraries

Course packs

If you wish to use a course pack, you may make arrangements through Central Services. The Central Services staff will request permissions for materials to be used, copy, bind and send the course packs to the Grecourt Bookshop. Please see the Central Services website for procedures.

Return to Top

VI. SMITH COLLEGE COPYRIGHT CONTACTS

General and policy questions, DMCA questions
Herb Nickles, x3770, Information Technology Services

Questions about copyright law, fair use, reserves, or the Copyright Clearance Center
Christine Hannon, x2911, Neilson Library

Questions about course packs
Chris Gentes, x2600, Central Services

Questions about use of other materials:

Art and images

Barbara Polowy, x2941, Hillyer Art Library or
Elisa Lanzi, x3106, Director of Image Collections

Audiovisuals
Information Technology Services

Manuscripts, etc
Nanci Young, x2976, College Archivist, Alumnae Gym

Music
Marlene Wong, x2931, Josten Library for the Performing Arts,

Software, Multimedia, Internet
Tom Laughner, x3079, Information Technology Services

Theatre
Alicia Guidotti, x3204, Theatre Department

Return to Top

VII. COPYRIGHT RESOURCES ON THE WEB

Website	Access
Crash Course in Copyright (University of Texas)	http://www.utsystem.edu/OGC/IntellectualProperty/
Copyright Management Center (Indiana University/Purdue University Indianapolis)	http://www.copyright.iupui.edu/
Copyright and Fair Use (Stanford University)	http://fairuse.stanford.edu/
Copyright: An Overview (Cornell Law School, Legal Information Institute)	http://www.law.cornell.edu:80/topics/copyright.html
Copyright Information & Education (University of Minnesota)	http://www.lib.umn.edu/copyright/
U.S. Copyright Office	http://lcweb.loc.gov:80/copyright/
Copyright and Intellectual Property (Association of Research Libraries)	http://www.arl.org/info/frn/copy/copytoc.html

Guidelines

Classroom guidelines for copying

Multimedia Guidelines

Smith College Art Department Image Collections' Copyright Guidelines

Music Guidelines

Return to Top

Home | Research | Library Services | General Information | Smith Libraries & Collections | Need Help?

 SMITH COLLEGE

SUNY @ Plattsburgh

Policy on Computer Software Copyright Observance

It is the policy of the SUNY College of Arts and Science at Plattsburgh that no person shall use or cause to be used on the college's computers (particularly microcomputers) any software which does not fall into one of the following categories:

1. It is in the public domain.
2. It is covered by a licensing agreement with the software author, vendor, or developer, whichever is applicable.
3. It has been donated to the college and a written record of a bona fide contribution exists.
4. It has been purchased by the college and a record of a bona fide purchase exists and can be produced by the user upon demand.
5. It is being reviewed or demonstrated by the users in order to reach a decision about possible future purchase or request for contribution or licensing.
6. It has been written or developed by a college employee or a student for the specific purpose of being used on a college-owned computer.
7. It has been written or developed by the user.

It is also the policy of the college that there be no copying of copyrighted or proprietary software which was acquired under the standard, single-use permit except for legitimate copying for archival backup purposes. These copies shall not be used on another machine while the originals or a working copy are in use.

Software acquired under a site or universal license shall only be copied and distributed in accordance with the agreement terms and only when the licensee has issued local serial numbers for the copies, unless the license permits unlimited copies. If there are any questions about campus rights to copy software under site or universal license, the licensee should be consulted.

Approved 10/31/88

This is an official publication of Plattsburgh State

Digital Millennium Copyright Act (DMCA)

What You Don't Know *Can* Harm You

The Digital Millennium Copyright Act (DMCA) allows the Recording Industry Association of America (RIAA) to target individuals who are illegally downloading copyrighted material, such as music, movies, and games.

The RIAA also can force Internet Service Providers to reveal the identities of these illegal file traders. Individual violators and their Internet Service Providers can be held liable and hit with heavy fines.

SUNY Plattsburgh and its students have become targets of the RIAA. Civil suits have been filed seeking compensation for damages. Fines of up to $150,000 per offence are possible.

Act Responsibly. Be Safe.

Illegal file-sharing places both the college and its students at risk. Students can't afford fines and colleges can't afford to have their networks compromised or threatened by legal actions.

The bottom line is that Plattsburgh students are expected to abide by the law and not engage in illegal file trading.

Make no mistake: major copyright holders, including software companies, video distributors, game producers, and the RIAA, have the resources, the technology, and the legal authority to find and prosecute anyone who shares copyrighted materials over campus network connections.

It's a situation in which you don't want to find yourself.

Learn More About the DMCA

- Download full text of the DMCA (.pdf file size 71kb) Note: this file requires the latest version of Adobe Acrobat, which is available as a free download
- Educause's Analysis of the impact of the DMCA on Colleges
- The Electronic Frontier Foundation's "Let the Music Play" Site

Contact Information

SUNY Plattsburgh's designated agent is:

Holly Heller-Ross
Interim Associate Dean of Library & Information Services
SUNY Plattsburgh
101 Broad Street
Plattsburgh, NY 12901
Telephone: (518) 564-5192
Fax: (518) 564-5100
E-mail: hellerhb@plattsburgh.edu

This is an official publication of Plattsburgh State

Responsible Use of Technology Resources at Plattsburgh State University of New York

Use of technology resources is a privilege granted by the College. Use of any information technology implicitly affirms that you will abide by all applicable federal, state and College policies that govern technology and information resources. The information technology facilities of PSUNY (computer hardware, software, networks, data, video, and other information facilities) are shared resources that directly support and facilitate teaching, research, public service, and administrative functions of the College.

The College strives to provide the most current and useful information technology, resources, and networks to faculty, students, and staff. The excellence of our system is dependent on the integrity of our users. Individuals are accountable for their actions and all activity involving the accounts for which they have responsibility. Therefore, users are expected to:

- Respect the rights of others; for example, users will comply with all College policies regarding sexual, racial, and other forms of harassment and disorderly conduct;
- Respect the intended usage of resources; for example, users will use only the unique account assigned, users will not share their account with others, and users will abstain from any activity that abuses system resources such as chain letters, flooding/spamming, etc;
- Respect the legal protection provided by copyright and licensing of programs and data; for example, users shall not make copies of a licensed software program or make multiple copies of information that is protected under copyright law;
- Respect the integrity of system and network resources; for example, users will try not to breach system security through any means, including hacking, viruses, Trojan horses, password grabbing, and disk scavenging;
- Respect the intended usage of computer systems and networks for electronic exchange (such as e-mail, Internet, World Wide Web, etc.); for example, users will not send forged or anonymous e-mail, read another person's electronic mail, send chain letters, conduct commercial activities, violate copyright, etc.

Network and system administrators will do their best to maintain a robust and responsive network and ensure privacy to all users.

Please know, however, that privacy cannot be guaranteed. Network troubleshooting sometimes requires the capture and analysis of data packs, so no privacy should be assumed. Right to privacy is forfeited by engaging in an activity outlined above. The administrator of the system will employ any means necessary to prevent a breach of system security including disabling an account or collecting evidence by scanning the content files.

Violations to the responsible use guidelines will be pursued in accordance with established College practices, policies, and procedures. Such violation may result in loss of technology privileges and campus judicial charges.

This is an official publication of Plattsburgh State

Trinity University

COATES LIBRARY

TRINITY UNIVERSITY

Home > **Access Services** > **Copyright/Reserves Policy and Procedures Statement**

Copyright / Reserves Policy and Procedures Statement

Contents:

> **Statement Of Guiding Principles**
> **Statement of Policy**
> **When Is Copyright Permission Not Necessary?**
> **Procedures for securing copyright permission**
> **Royalty Payments**
> **Related Issues**

Statement Of Guiding Principles

The Library seeks to encourage Fair Use of copyrighted materials, balancing the research needs of faculty, students, staff, and other patrons, while respecting the intellectual property rights of copyright holders and abiding by the pertinent laws governing usage of copyrighted materials.

Statement of Policy

OUR POLICY:
THE TRINITY UNIVERSITY LIBRARY WILL ABIDE BY U.S. COPYRIGHT LAW

Copyright addresses the right to make *copies*. The creator of a work usually gives that authority to his or her publisher, allowing for the work to be published in the first place. It is when that published work (an authorized original copy) is reproduced by the consumer that issues of copyright are introduced.

There may be restrictions imposed upon using "non-original" items as reserves.

The applicable laws, 17 U.S.C. Sec. 107 and the Digital Millennium Copyright Act, provide for a "Fair Use" defense of the reproduction of copyrighted material for research purposes. The Library will place reproductions of copyrighted material on reserve based on the instructor's assertion that the usage falls under "Fair Use" requirements in copyright law. The University will support and defend the faculty member's interpretation to that effect, where legally defensible. Copyrighted material reproduced and placed on Blackboard or in course packs is not covered by this policy. "Legally defensible" assumes, for example, that said reproductions do not constitute an excessive portion of the original work, nor are they excerpts from works explicitly commercial in nature (e.g., textbooks, workbooks, popular films/magazines, etc.). Circulation staff may refuse to place on reserve any material when doing so obviously fails to meet the Fair Use criteria. Copyright permissions purchases are available upon request through the Circulation department.

At present, a "four factors" test is used to determine if a proposed use is fair or not. These factors are:

1. **Purpose of the usage** -- Academic uses (criticism, commentary, etc.) are easier to defend as 'fair' than commercial uses.

2. **Nature of the copyrighted work** -- Nonfiction, fact-based works (information) are more understandably used fairly than creative fiction (entertainment).

3. **Amount and content of the portion of the work used** -- An academic work could conceivably use large portions of a work for critical or analytical purposes. But there comes a point when too much of the original work has been copied, at which time the use is no longer 'fair.'

4. **Impact on the market value of the work** -- Would the proposed usage damage the market value of the copyrighted item? Does the proposed usage compete with sales of the work? Is the proposed usage simply a way to avoid buying the book or journal?

An important note about factor #1: The use of the material for academic purposes is not by itself a sufficient justification of "fair use." The four factors interact with each other and must be considered together; no single one of them "trumps" the other three. However, recent court decisions have tended to give more weight to factor #4.

Faculty are reminded that copyright protections have expanded greatly in both scope and duration in recent years, as have statutory and punitive penalties for non-compliance. The Library will assist any instructor seeking guidance about copyright issues.

When is it *not* necessary to secure copyright permission?

1. If the item in question is an original, authorized copy, purchased from the rightsholder, distributor, or other consumer.

2. If the faculty member can demonstrate that the material is in the public domain, or that the faculty member is the copyright holder.

3. If the proposed usage of the item can be considered "fair use" in accordance with the provisions of the Copyright Act and its amendments.

Procedures for securing copyright permission

If the library determines that a document may not be used without having first secured copyright permission, how is such permission obtained?

Faculty members are welcome to secure copyright permissions for prospective reserves materials themselves. Faculty members who have done so should provide the pertinent documentation with their reserve submissions.

The library will assist faculty members to obtain copyright permissions for an item placed on reserve but they should be aware that the library's budget for copyright fee payments is limited.

1. Reserve items that are submitted with proof of copyright compliance will be placed on reserve as quickly as possible.

2. Materials that are submitted *without* proof of copyright compliance will *not* be placed on reserve immediately. **A processing period of two weeks is required to obtain copyright permission, if necessary.** Faculty are reminded to take this two-week delay into account when submitting reserves.

In order to expedite the copyright permissions process, all instructors submitting materials for reserves should provide complete bibliographic citations for all items, to include the items' ISBN or ISSN numbers, if possible.

Royalty Payments

Obtaining copyright permission usually entails the payment of a royalty fee. The Library has a small budget for royalty payments, which is allocated on a "first-come, first-serve" basis. **As a result, instructors are strongly encouraged to submit reserve lists as far in advance as possible to ensure the availability of funds to purchase required permissions.**

Once the Library's permissions budget is exhausted, permissions purchases may still be made, provided the associated academic departments assume all costs for such purchases.

Related Issues

http://lib.trinity.edu/servcols/circ/copyright.shtml

2/22/2008

192 - Trinity University

How else does copyright law pertain to reserves?

Copyright Notice: US copyright law requires copies made for reserve and ILL use to be marked to indicate that the original material may be copyrighted. The proprietary electronic reserves system the library has adopted has a built-in copyright notice to satisfy this requirement. Traditional reserve items will be stamped to satisfy this requirement.

Password Protection: Copyright laws require copyrighted materials on electronic reserves to be password protected to prevent unauthorized access to the material. The proprietary e-res system used by the library provides for protecting documents this way.

All instructor are required to list a password for each of their classes.

Instructors are responsible for providing password information to their students!

Library staff will not be privy to this information, so they will not be able to assist students in this regard. Instructors are cautioned to be discreet when disseminating their passwords.

Any questions, comments, or suggestions should be directed to **Mary González**, the Library's Copyrights and Reserves Manager, ext. 8189; or **Jason Hardin**, Manager of (Library) Access Services, ext. 8181.

Trinity University, Elizabeth Huth Coates Library
One Trinity Place, San Antonio, TX 78212-7200
Phone (210) 999-8126 / Fax (210) 999-8182
Contact us and/or send us your feedback here.

http://lib.trinity.edu/servcols/circ/copyright.shtml   Last update Monday, 25 Sep 2006

http://lib.trinity.edu/servcols/circ/copyright.shtml   2/22/2008

Washington and Lee University

| *Washington & Lee University* | *Leyburn Library* | *Copyright Policy* | *Table of Contents* |

Washington and Lee University
Policy for the Use of Copyrighted Works

I. Introduction

A. PURPOSE

It is the intent of Washington and Lee University that all members of the University community adhere to the provisions of the United States Copyright Law. Each member of the University community must take some individual responsibility for copyright compliance, and these extensive guidelines flow from this premise. Conforming to this policy may in some cases result in additional costs to the student for course materials and some additional inconvenience and time delay in the preparation procedure of those materials. Members of the University community who willfully disregard the copyright policy do so at their own risk and assume all liability.

B. WHAT IS A COPYRIGHT?

A copyright grants to its owner the right to control an intellectual or artistic creation, to prohibit others from using the work in specific ways without permission, and to profit from the sale and performance of the work. Under the current statute, copyright protection extends to not only copies of the written word and recordings of sound, but visual images such as photographs or illustration or animated images such as motion pictures or videotapes. It also extends to live performances that are taped as they are broadcast.

No protection is available for an idea/procedure, process, system, method of operation, concept, principle, or discovery, no matter how unique. Copyright protection is available only for an expression of the idea.

The owner of the copyright is granted five exclusive rights to ensure the opportunity to exploit the work for profit. These rights are: reproduction, distribution, adaptation, performance, and display.

The right to reproduce and distribute the work refers to the act of copying and distributing copies publicly. The adaptation right is the right to prepare derivative works such as new editions, translations, and condensation or new arrangements of musical composition. The right to perform the work publicly means to recite, render a play, or dance the work. Display is defined as the showing of a copy of work directly or by means of a television image. The performance and display right is limited to public performance and display.

The copyright law is violated whenever a third party exercises any of the above rights without authorization of the copyright owner or without having express permission to do so under the law. Even if a copyright owner is able to prove infringement, there are a number of limitations and exceptions to the exclusive rights granted under the copyright act. The statutory limitations cover a wide variety of uses but generally serve one of several purposes: scholarly inquiry which includes instruction, research criticism and newsworthiness; and performance and displays by educational, charitable, religious or government groups. Be aware that not all educational uses are fair uses. The limitation on the copyright owner's rights which provides the widest public exploitation of copyrighted work is known as the fair use exception. This is described in Section I.C.

C. FAIR USE

Fair use is a legal principle that provides certain limitations on the exclusive right of copyright owners. The purpose of this policy is to provide guidance on the application of the fair use principle to faculty, staff, and students, who wish to copy copyrighted works under fair use rather than by seeking authorization from the copyright owners for non-commercial educational purposes. NOT ALL EDUCATIONAL USES ARE FAIR USES.

There is no simple test to determine what is fair use. Section 107 of the Copyright Act sets forth the four fair use factors which should be assessed in each instance, based on the particular facts of a given case to determine whether a use is fair use:

1) What is the character of the use?
2) What is the nature of the work to be used?
3) How much of the work will you use?
4) What effect would this use have on the market for the original or for permissions if the use were widespread?

All four factors must be weighed equally.

Factor 1: What is the character of the use?
Uses for non-profit, educational purposes, or single copies for non-profit educational or personal use are more likely to be a fair use. On the other hand, uses which are predominantly commercial are more likely to require permission and/or the payment of royalties.

Factor 2: What is the nature of the work to be used?
Materials that are primarily factual such as scientific information, mathematical equations, or historical data tip the balance in favor of fair use. When the work is creative or unpublished, the balance is tipped in favor of seeking permission.

Factors 3: How much of the work will you use?
Generally, if you use a small amount of the whole work, the balance is more likely tipped in favor of fair use. If you use a significant amount, the balance is tipped in favor of seeking permission.

Factor 4: What effect would this use have on the market for the original or for permission?
If the use tips the balance in favor of fair use after considering the first three factors, the fourth factor should not effect the results even if there is a market. On the other hand, the fourth factor may tip the balance, if the copy becomes the substitute for the original.

D. REVIEW OF COPYRIGHT POLICY

The Copyright Committee will meet annually to review this policy.

Washington & Lee University | *Leyburn Library* | *Table of Contents* | *Top*

II. Photocopying Guidelines for Teaching and Research

Ordinarily, copying copyrighted material without the permission of the copyright owner is a violation of the exclusive rights of the copyright owner. The copyright act balances users rights by creating limited exemptions from these exclusive rights, such as allowing copying for face-to-face teaching or fair use. Under fair use, a teacher or researcher is allowed a rather limited amount of copying without the copyright owner's permission for purposes such as criticism, comment, news reporting, or teaching. Furthermore, there are some works of which copying is completely unrestricted, and other types of materials of which unauthorized copying is always forbidden.

A. COPYING WHICH IS COMPLETELY UNRESTRICTED

1. Published Works Which Were Never Copyrighted

Anyone may photocopy, without restriction, works published prior to 1989 which do not contain a notice of copyright.

A notice of copyright consists of the copyright symbol or the word "copyright," plus the first year of publication and the name of the copyright owner. Writings published without copyright notices prior to January 1, 1978 are not protected. Publication is defined to mean the distribution of copies of a work to the public by sale or other transfer of ownership, or by rental, lease, or loan.

Notice requirements for works published between January 1, 1978, and February 28, 1989, were relaxed somewhat with respect to both the position of notices and the inadvertent omission of them. Effective March 1, 1989, the requirement that a work have a notice of copyright was abolished. Thus, any work created or published after March 1, 1989 is protected by copyright even if no notice of copyright is affixed.

2. Published Works Whose Copyrights Have Expired

Anyone may photocopy, without restriction, published works on which the copyright term and any renewals have expired.

Copyrights dated 1920 (75 years prior to the current year) or later may or may not have expired, depending up on whether its owner renewed the copyright after the first term of protection. Thus it is recommended that copiers either assume the protection is still in effect, or ask the copyright owner or U.S. Copyright Office whether the work is still subject to copyright protection. Usually a publisher owns the copyright or knows the owner's location. If not, an owner can be located through the U.S. Copyright Office, Library of Congress, Washington, D.C., 20559, (202) 707-8350, http://lcweb.loc.gov/copyright.

3. U.S. Government Publications

U.S. government publications may be copied without constraint, except to the extent that they contain copyrighted work from other sources. When using copyrighted portions of U.S. government document, follow these guidelines.

4. State Documents

Unlike Federal documents, state documents may be copyrighted.

5. C-SPAN

C-SPAN grants educators and degree granting educational institutions the right to tape any C-SPAN programs without receiving prior permission from the network, as long as taping is for school use and not for commercial sale or political purposes. This liberal copyright policy allows teachers to air C-SPAN live, record programs (at school or at home) for later use, assign students to watch a program, or to create their own videotapes for classroom use.

Taped C-SPAN programs may be retained in perpetuity for future school use.

B. COPYING WHICH IS PERMITTED AS FAIR USE

The concept of fair use is described in Section I.C.

In an effort to further clarify the limits of fair use, an ad hoc committee of publishers, authors, and educational institutions prepared an **Agreement on Guidelines for Classroom Copying in Not-For-Profit Educational Institutions**. Higher education recognizes that these guidelines are inadequate and are generally considered to establish minimum permissible conduct under the fair use doctrine for unauthorized copying; however, these guidelines are not binding on the courts.

1. Single Copies

For teaching, including preparation for teaching, and for scholarly research, an instructor may make, or have made at his or her individual request, a single copy of:

> one chapter from a book;
> one article from a periodical or newspaper;
> one short story, essay, or short poem;
> one chart, graph, diagram, drawing, cartoon, or picture from one book or periodical.

2. Multiple Copies

For one-time distribution in class to students, an instructor may make, or have made, multiple copies if he or she:

> makes no more than one for each student;
> includes the notice of copyright;
> makes no charge to the student beyond actual cost of

photocopying;
the copying meets the tests of "brevity" and "spontaneity" and "cumulative effect" as defined below:

a. The copying meets the test of "brevity":

Poetry: a complete poem of fewer than 250 words printed on no more than two pages, or an excerpt from a longer poem not to exceed 250 words;

Prose: a complete article, story or essay of less than 2500 words, or an excerpt from any prose work of not more than 1000 words or 10% of the work, whichever is LESS, but in any event a minimum of 500 words;

Illustrations: one per book or periodical issue;

"Special" works (poetry and/or prose that combines language and illustration, such as a children's book): the work may not be reproduced in its entirety; however, excerpts may be reproduced of no more than two pages, totaling less than 10% of the work.

AND

b. The copying meets the test of "spontaneity":

The copying is at the instance and inspiration of the individual teacher;

The inspiration and decision to use the work and the moment of its use for maximum teaching effectiveness are so close in time that it would be unreasonable to expect a timely reply to a request for permission;

Faculty members are expected to apply the test of spontaneity in good faith, and not use procrastination or poor planning as an excuse to claim fair use.

AND

c. The copying meets the "cumulative effect" test:

The material copied is for use in one course;

Not more than one short poem, article, story or essay or two excerpts of the above may be copied from the same author, nor more than three copies from the same collective work or periodical volume during one class term;

There shall be no more than nine instances of such multiple

copying for one course during one class term.

In any case of photocopying that meets the above requirements for multiple copies, the original copyright notice must appear on all copies of the work.

C. COPYING FOR WHICH PERMISSION MUST BE OBTAINED

The guidelines prohibit the following:

1. Course Packs - Primary Course Materials

Copying shall not be used to create, replace, or substitute for, anthologies, compilations, or collective works. Such substitution copying is prohibited unless permission is obtained whether copies or various excerpts are accumulated as course packs or reproduced and handed out separately. Copying shall not be a substitute for the purchase of books or periodicals.

2. Consumable Works

There shall be no copying of or from works intended to be "consumable" in the course of studying or teaching. These include workbooks, exercises, standardized tests, test booklets and answer sheets, and similar consumable material.

3. Repetitive Copying

Copying of the same material by the same teacher from term to term is not legal without explicit permission.

Washington & Lee University | *Leyburn Library* | *Table of Contents* | *Top*

III. Guidelines for University Libraries and Archives

Section 108 of the copyright law provides certain conditions under which libraries may reproduce copyrighted works upon the request of library patrons. It specifically addresses instances of allowable copying, reserve room use, and interlibrary loan.

A. REPRODUCTION BY LIBRARIES AND ARCHIVES

1. Photocopy and Document Delivery Services to University Clientele

Although the University libraries do not provide any organized copying services for its clientele, it occasionally is necessary to reproduce copyrighted works to support the research and educational pursuits of the W&L community. The Copyright Act allows libraries or archives to reproduce or distribute no more than one copy of a work, provided the following conditions are met:

the reproduction or distribution is made without any purpose of direct or indirect commercial advantage;

the collections of the library or archives are open to the public;

the reproduction of the work includes a notice of copyright. All copies generated by the libraries must include formal notice, if it is available:

    a. the word "copyright," or the abbreviation "copr."
    b. the year of first publication
    c. the name of the copyright holder.

If notice of copyright is unavailable, the library staff should use "This material may be protected by copyright law (Title 17, U.S. Code)."

a. Articles and Small Excerpts

The University libraries are authorized to reproduce and/or distribute a copy of not more than one article or other contribution to a copyrighted collection or periodical issue, or of a small part of any other copyrighted work. The copy may be made by the library where the patron makes the request, or by another library pursuant to an interlibrary loan.

The copy must become the property of the user, and the library or archives must have had no indication that the copy would be used for any purpose other than private study, scholarship, or research.

b. Out-of-Print Works

The libraries may reproduce and/or distribute a copy of an entire work, if it has been established that the library has made a reasonable effort to obtain an unused replacement and if one is found it cannot be obtained at a fair price. Such a determination will require inquiries to commonly-known trade sources in the United States, and ordinarily also to the publisher or other copyright holder.

c. Multiple Copies and Systematic Reproduction

The rights of reproduction and distribution under Section 108 extend to the isolated and unrelated production of a single copy of the same material on separate occasions, but do not extend to cases where the library or archives is aware or has substantial reason to believe that it is engaging in related or concerted reproduction of multiple copies of the same material, whether made on one occasion or over a period of time, and whether intended for aggregate use by one or more individuals or for separate use by the individual members of a group.

2. Replacement of Damaged Copy

The University libraries may reproduce a published work solely for the purpose of replacement of a copy or sound recording that is damaged, deteriorating, lost or stolen, if it has determined that an unused replacement cannot be obtained at a fair price.

3. Archival Reproduction

The libraries may reproduce and/or distribute a copy or sound recording of an unpublished work for the purposes of preservation and security, or for deposit for research use in another library or archives, if the copy is currently in the University libraries collections. This right extends to any type of work, including photographs, motion pictures and sound recordings.

B. RESERVE ROOM USE OF COPYRIGHTED MATERIALS

Many college, university, and school libraries have established reserve operations for readings and other materials that support the instructional requirements of specific courses. According to the American Library Association **Model Policy Concerning College and University Photocopying for Classroom, Research and Library Reserve**, the reserve unit functions as an extension of the classroom when it makes course readings available to students, and reflects an individual student's right to copy for personal scholastic use under the doctrine of fair use. When materials are included as a matter of fair use, reserve systems should constitute an ad hoc or supplemental source of information for students, beyond a textbook or other materials. If included with permission from the copyright owner, however, the scope and range of materials is potentially unlimited, depending upon the permission granted. The following provisions governing such use are drawn from the ALA **Model Policy**:

1. General Provisions

At the request of a faculty member, the University libraries may copy and place on reserve excerpts from copyrighted works in its collection in accordance with the guidelines governing classroom distribution (discussed in Section II of this document). In general, library employees may copy and/or accept copies of materials for reserve room use for the convenience of students both in preparing class assignments and in pursuing educational activities which higher education requires, such as advanced independent study and research. Audio cassettes, video cassettes, and other media titles may be placed on reserve if they are legal copies with appropriate copyright notice, e.g. date and creator.

2. Restrictions

a. Single Copies Placed on Reserve

If the request calls for a single copy to be placed on reserve, the library may copy an entire article, an entire chapter from a book, or an entire poem.

The amount of material should be reasonable in relation to the total amount of material assigned for one term of a course, taking into account the nature of the course, and its subject matter and level.

b. Multiple Copies Placed on Reserve

Requests for multiple copies to be placed on reserve should meet the following guidelines:

the number of copies should be reasonable in light of the number of students enrolled, and the difficulty and timing of assignments;

the material should contain a notice of copyright as described in Section III. A. 1. above;

the effect of copying the material should not be detrimental to the market for the work (in general, the libraries should own at least one copy of the work).

c. Course Packs

The University libraries will not accept course packs of readings for reserve unless the libraries receive proof from the faculty member that permission has been obtained from the copyright holder(s). See Section II.C.

d. Repeated Use

Copies of copyrighted materials may not be retained on reserve for more than one term for any faculty member unless the library has proof that permission to reproduce and distribute copies in this fashion has been granted by the copyright holder and that said reproduction is in accordance with all copyright laws.

See Section IX.C for guidance in seeking permission for reserve use.

e. Electronic Reserve

When requested by faculty members, the libraries will make copyrighted works available electronically for student use. Permission to mount the work electronically is necessary before it is made available (if not covered by Fair Use). If requested, the libraries will seek this permission for the faculty member and pay reasonable royalty fees required for such mounting.

All copyrighted materials mounted by the libraries for reserve use will be restricted to campus Internet Protocol addresses. Publishers may also require that access to the materials be protected by password as well.

C. INTERLIBRARY LOAN

The National Commission on New Technological Uses of Copyrighted Works (CONTU) prepared a set of guidelines governing copying and interlibrary arrangements in conjunction with Section 108 of the copyright law. Its provisions are as follows:

1. Restrictions on Number of Copies

a. Periodicals

The Interlibrary Loan units should not submit, during any calendar year, more than five requests for copies of articles from a particular periodical title if those requests are from issues published within the last five years. No restrictions are placed on the number of copies of articles requested for materials exceeding five years of age. Requests in excess of the above limits are subject to the copyright permissions process and payment of royalties, where applicable.

2. Record-Keeping Requirements

The requesting library must maintain records of all such requests and fulfillment of requests for the current calendar year plus three previous calendar years.

3. Notice

All copies made by the Interlibrary Loan units and interlibrary loan order forms must bear a notice of copyright as described in Section III. A. 1. above.

D. UNSUPERVISED REPRODUCTION EQUIPMENT

Equipment capable of reproducing copyrighted works are publicly available in unsupervised settings. In accordance with Section 108, a library is free from copyright infringement for unsupervised photocopying if the library posts a notice of copyright near all unsupervised photocopiers. The sign should say: "Notice: Making a copy may be subject to the Copyright Law." A similar notice should be placed on:

photocopiers
printers
microform printers
computers
VCRs
tape recorders
scanners
all other equipment technically capable of reproducing copyrighted materials

A similar notice should also be placed on the campus network so that a user is warned about the possibility of using copyrighted material.

The office where equipment is located is responsible for posting the appropriate notice, obtainable from the Printing Center.

Washington & Lee University | *Leyburn Library* | *Table of Contents* | *Top*

IV. Guidelines for the Use of Films and Video

A. CLASSROOM USE

Possession of a film or video does not confer the right to show the work. The copyright owner specifies, at the time of purchase or rental, the circumstances in which a film or video may be "performed". Section 110 (1) of the Copyright Act of 1976 creates an exception to the copyright holder's exclusive right of performance.

The "face-to-face" exception allows an educator to perform a work (including home use video) in class, as long as the following criteria are met:

> they must be shown as part of the instructional program;

> they must be shown by students, instructors, or guest lecturers;

> they must be shown either in a classroom or other school location devoted to instruction such as a studio, workshop, library, gymnasium, or auditorium if it is used for instruction;

> they must be shown either in a face-to-face setting or where students and teacher(s) are in the same building or general area;

> they must be shown only to students and educators;

> they must be shown using a legitimate copy with the copyright notice included.

Further, the relationship between the film or video and the course must be explicit. Films or videos, even in a face-to-face classroom setting, may not be used for entertainment or recreation, without the copyright holder's permission, whatever the work's intellectual content.

B. USE OUTSIDE THE CLASSROOM

Besides use in classrooms, video cassettes and videodiscs that are owned by the University may ordinarily be viewed by students, faculty or staff at workstations or in small-group rooms in the libraries. These videos may also be viewed at home (e.g. in a dorm room) so long as no more than a few friends are involved. Larger audiences, such as groups that might assemble in a residence hall or fraternity/sorority living room, require explicit permission from the copyright owner for "public performance" rights. No fees for viewing a video are permitted even when public performance rights are obtained.

The University maintains a public performance site license with Films, Inc. Lists of films covered by this license and forms to record use are available from the libraries and the Dean of Students Office.

C. COPYING VIDEOTAPES/OFF-AIR RECORDING OF BROADCASTS, INCLUDING SATELLITE TV

Copying videotapes without the copyright owner's permission is illegal. An exception is made for libraries to replace a work that is lost or damaged if another copy cannot be obtained at a fair price.

Licenses may be obtained for copying and off-air recording. Absent a formal agreement, **Guidelines for Off-the Air Recording of Broadcast Programming for Educational Purposes**, an official part of the Copyright Act's legislative history, applies to most off-air recording:

1. Videotaped recordings may be shown to students only within the **first 10 school days** of the 45-day retention period, set forth below.

2. Videotaped recordings may be kept for no more than **45 calendar days** after the recording date, at which times the tapes must be erased. The taped recordings may be viewed after the 10-day period only by instructors for evaluation purposes, that is, to determine whether to include the broadcast program in the curriculum in the future.

3. Off-air recordings must be made only **at the request** of an individual instructor for **instructional** purposes, not by staff in anticipation of later requests.

4. The recordings are to be shown to students no more than two times during the 10-day period, and the second time only for necessary instructional reinforcement.

5. If several instructors request videotaping of the same program, duplicate copies are permitted to meet the need; all copies are subject to the same restrictions as the original recording.

6. The off-air recordings may not be physically or electronically altered or combined with others to form anthologies, but they need not necessarily be used or shown in their entirety.

7. All copies of off-air recordings must include the copyright notice on the broadcast program as recorded.

8. C-SPAN

See C-SPAN policy in Section II.A.5.

‖*Washington & Lee University* ‖*Leyburn Library* ‖*Table of Contents* ‖*Top* ‖

V. Guidelines for the Use of Images

The current state of understanding among visual resources people about the Conference on Fair Use guidelines is one of intense dissatisfaction, not with the idea of fair use per se, but with the fair use guidelines, specifically. The guidelines are regarded as having been drafted primarily for the protection of the vendors, and primarily in the context of printed materials rather than visual images. The controversy concerns the extent to which a photograph or slide of a public domain art work or scientific drawing is protected by copyright.

The proposed CONFU guidelines, the committee believes, place unnecessary restrictions on what is currently permitted as fair use. For example, none of the fair use factors puts time limits on use, but the guidelines do.

Given the lack of consensus on this matter among visual resources professionals, many issues remain unsolved. Since there is no consensus for using copyrighted images, the University recommends that copying be done pursuant to the fair use factors.

A. DEFINITIONS

1. **Visual image** is a unique photographic representation of an object (e.g., an "original" 35 mm slide) or a photographic reproduction of an object ("duplicate" slide), usually issued in multiple copies. The term "visual image" is used here to refer to representations or reproductions of works of art (painting, sculpture, decorative or craft objects, graphics media, drawings, collages, mixed media, and electronic media) and architecture, and also includes maps, diagrams, charts, and scientific drawings. Images are typically surrogates for the represented works; their intrinsic value is primarily as documentation of the original object (e.g., a slide representation of the Mona Lisa, a photograph of the Eiffel Tower, a color reproduction of an anatomical chart).

2. **Image archive** is a collection of images, acquired and maintained by an organization such as a non-profit library, museum, or school. An image archive can be a collection of collections in different formats, of which slides and CD-ROMs are but two examples. Images in archives derive from numerous sources: from commercial vendors of images, from work-for-hire, from donation by amateur and professional photographers, and from copy photography.

3. **Copy photography** is making slides from reproductions in books or journals. This widespread and long-standing practice in the community has been a necessity for teaching, and frequently is a reason for the purchase of a book rather than an interference with the market for a book.

4. An **Electronic image** is a digital representation or reproduction of a photographic representation or reproduction of an object described above (under visual image). Electronic (digital) images are essentially the same as

analog images. The content is the same; only the format for delivery and the ease with which they can be copied are different.

5. **Electronic image archives** is a collection of electronic (digital) images of art and architecture or other subjects that may be part of a larger image archives.

B. FAIR USE AND IMAGE ARCHIVES

Visual images are typically sold by image brokers (commercial vendors) who have made photographic reproductions pursuant to a non-exclusive right with the creator of the object, or who have acquired a reproduction license to market images made from public domain objects owned or controlled by museums or corporations.

Visual images made from reproductions in books and journals for purposes such as teaching or research are understood to be fair use when photographic representations of the objects are no longer available or reasonably accessible from commercial vendors, the object's creator, or the owner of the work. The practice of reproducing images included with copyrighted text for the uses specified above is a longstanding practice in education and the subject of vigorous debate within the community, although there have been no cases addressing this practice.

Current practice recognizes the need to use large quantities of projected images in a classroom (a typical art history lecture requires an average of 25- 50 different images per class period). It is not uncommon for various images to be used the next time the course is offered. Multiple versions of the same object are commonly also presented. In practice, images are typically arranged in sequences or sets for comparison or contrast.

Assuming a fair use of copyrighted materials in providing images for the purposes listed above, permissions are not necessary. Permission is required only if the use of the copyrighted image is for other purposes, such as publication, or in circumstances where profit and/or commercial advantage is the motive for the use.

1. Image photocopying

The photocopying of images for classroom use or in the preparation of class assignments or papers is acceptable under the fair use guidelines.

2. Slides

a. Purchase, whenever possible. Subsequent duplication of purchased slides is not acceptable. b. Guidelines for copy photography, when a purchase is not possible: Follow fair use factors (see statement at the beginning re Fair Use Guidelines).

Make only one copy of a reproduction; making multiple copies is not acceptable.

Shooting every plate in a book is not acceptable.

Slides made in this way are to be used for educational purposes.

Once a slide has been added to the slide collection of an academic department, by either purchase or copy photography, it becomes the property of Washington and Lee University. If a slide is loaned, it may not be duplicated in any form. It is implicit in the lending that the borrower agrees not to authorize duplication or reproduction of these slides and assumes all responsibility for that restriction.

3. Clip art

Clip art is sold to be copied; use it, taking care to note any limitations that accompany it (e.g., some clip art may be used in printed works, but the license expressly forbids digital distribution; therefore, it may not be used to liven up web pages).

4. Fair Use and Electronic Images

a. Fair use is inadequately defined for images in general, and thus poorly understood for most transmissions of images.

b. During transmission, a copy of the image is made. This adds another layer to the already multi-layered ownership issues surrounding an image. Is the image of an artwork the property of the creator (if still under copyright) or the photographer or the repository maintaining it? This is never as self-evident as it is with a text object such as a book or a journal article.

c. It is in the immediate and long range interests of Washington and Lee that digitized images be readily and inexpensively available for teaching and research.

5. Copying which is permitted:

a. One or a small number of images is retrieved from a large collection and used so that the intrinsic value of the original collection is in no way diminished.

b. Use of "thumbnail-size" images, for no purpose other than as a reference or as a mnemonic device.

6. Copying which requires permission:

a. Using without compensation any sizable archive that someone else has collected with considerable expenditure of time, energy, and money.

b. Acquiring images that are free or quite inexpensive, and then charging an unreasonable amount for their use.

7. Notice

a. Check for the copyright symbol ("copyright" or "<©>") and the name of the copyright owner (which should be attached directly on, under, or around a digital work); it should be visible to anyone who will be using the excerpted material. Works 1989 - present, may be under copyright whether or not a copyright symbol is present; no copyright symbol has been required since 1989.

b. Put the copyright symbol, name, and date on each copy, even if the material is only being used once for a class presentation or project; this is important in case you change your mind and decide to use material for commercial or extended purposes; you would then have a record of the copyright information and of when and where you found the material.

| *Washington & Lee University* | *Leyburn Library* | *Table of Contents* | *Top* |

VI. Guidelines for Use of Copyrighted Music

In 1975, **Guidelines for Educational Use of Music** was developed by a group of music educators and publishers to clarify the intent of the copyright law with respect to music and to amplify the concept of fair use. These guidelines were submitted to Congress and became part of the legislative history of the 1976 Copyright Act.

A. REPRODUCTION OF COPYRIGHTED MUSIC

1. Copying Which Is Permitted:

a. Emergency copying to replace purchased copies which for any reason are not available for an imminent performance, provided purchased replacement copies shall be substituted in due course.

b. Multiple copies of excerpts of works may be made for academic purposes other than performance provided that such excerpts do not comprise a performable unit, provided that such copying does not exceed 10% of the work and no more than one copy per student is made.

c. Printed copies which have been purchased may be edited or simplified provided that the fundamental character of the work is not distorted or the lyrics altered or lyrics added.

d. A single copy of recordings of performances by students may be made for evaluation or rehearsal purposes and may be retained by the educational institution or instructor.

e. A single copy of a sound recording (such as a tape, disc, or cassette) of copyrighted music may be made from sound recordings owned by an educational institution or instructor for the purpose of constructing aural exercises or examinations and may be retained by the educational institution or instructor. This pertains only to the copyrights of the music itself and not to any copyright which may exist in the sound recording.

2. Copying For Which Permission is Required:

a. Copying to create or replace or substitute for anthologies, compilations, or collective works.

b. Copying of or from works intended to be "consumable" in the course of study or teaching such as workbooks, exercises, standardized tests, answer sheets, and like material.

c. Copying for the purpose of performance, except as noted in "permissible uses" above.

d. Copying for the purpose of substituting for the purchase of music except as noted in "permissible uses" above.

e. Copying without inclusion of the copyright notice which appears on the printed copy.

B. RECORDING

The copyright owner has the exclusive right to reproduce copyrighted works in phono records. Limited exceptions to this right are set forth in the guidelines as outlined above. Once phono records of a non-dramatic musical work have been distributed to the public in the U.S. under authority of the copyright owner, any other person may obtain a compulsory license to record the work by complying with certain procedures and by payment of the royalty as provided in 17 U.S.C. §115. This compulsory license requirement applies when a music educator wishes to record a student performance as part of the learning process and distribute copies of the recording within the community. Bear in mind that the first recording of a work and its distribution in recorded form requires the consent of the copyright owner.

C. PREPARATION OF DERIVATIVE WORKS
The copyright owner has the exclusive right to make arrangements of a piece of music. However, the guidelines describing what is considered to be fair use of music material set forth the following exceptions:

1. Printed copies which have been purchased may be edited or simplified, provided that the fundamental character of the work is not distorted or the lyrics altered or lyrics added;

2. The compulsory license for recording includes the privilege of making a musical arrangement of a work to the extent necessary to conform it to the style or manner of interpretation of the performance involved, but the arrangement

shall not change the basic melody or fundamental character of the work. This privilege is not meant to extend to "serious" compositions.

D. DISTRIBUTION The one exception to the exclusive right of the copyright owner to distribute copies is set forth in the compulsory license requirement relative to phono records at Section B. above.

E. PERFORMANCE The copyright owner has the exclusive right to control the performance of a musical work. However, music educators and others have special needs which are addressed in 17 U.S.C. §110 as limitation on the exclusive right of performance. The following uses are NOT infringements:

1. Performance of any copyrighted work by instructors or students in the course of face-to-face teaching activities, in a non-profit educational institution, in a classroom or similar place devoted to instruction.

2. Performance of non-dramatic literary or musical work on closed circuit television to other classrooms or to disabled students for teaching purposes only if the transmission is part of the systematic instructional activities of a non-profit educational institution, and only if the performance is directly related and of material assistance to the teaching content of the program.

3. Performance of a non-dramatic literary or musical work at a school concert if there is no purpose of direct or indirect commercial advantage, no fee or compensation paid to the performers, promoter or organizers, and no admission charge; if there is an admission charge, all of the proceeds must be used only for educational or charitable purposes; and the performance may not take place if the copyright owner objects in writing seven days before the performance.

4. Performance of non-dramatic literary or musical works or of dramatic-musical works of a religious nature, in the course of services at places of worship or at a religious assembly.

F. LICENSES The University maintains licenses with the performing rights organizations for the use of much copyrighted music on campus. These licenses are on file in the Treasurer's Office.

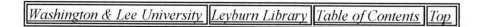

Washington & Lee University | *Leyburn Library* | *Table of Contents* | *Top*

VII. Guidelines for the Use of Computer Software

A. USE OF COPYRIGHTED COMPUTER PROGRAMS (SOFTWARE) Copying not only entails duplicating software but includes transferring a program from one medium (CD, floppy, hard disk for example) or transmitting over a local area network, or a long distance line.

Unauthorized reproduction, distribution, or adaptation of computer programs is governed by the same rules as other end-uses and will be considered infringement unless it constitutes fair use under §107 of the Copyright Act or is exempted under §117 which is explained below.

Please note that the guidelines for classroom copying in not-for-profit educational institutions are explicitly limited to books and periodicals, and do not encompass other types of copyrighted works, including computer programs.

1. Copying

A University department purchasing a program may adapt the program so it can be used on the office machines. This use qualifies for the §117 exemption; the owner of a lawfully acquired copy of a computer program is permitted to make an adaptation of a computer program "as an essential step in the utilization of the computer program in conjunction with the machine and it is used in no other manner."

A department may not obtain a single machine license for a program and then make it available via a department network or through the campus-wide computer system that any number of students, faculty, and staff may access simultaneously either on or off campus. Despite the non-commercial purpose of such distribution, because the entire program is reproduced, there is a serious commercial effect caused by lost license fees and pirated copies.

2. Lending

Under §109(b)(2)(A) of the Copyright Act, a computer program may be loaned for non-profit purposes by nonprofit libraries. All copies that are loaned by a library must contain a warning of copyright in accordance with the requirements prescribed by the Register of Copyrights.

A library may lend a book with the supplemental software on a disk in the book pocket, so long as this is lent for a non-profit purpose and the library affixes to the book or the disk the required copyright warning.

3. Archiving copies

Under §117 of the act, libraries and schools may lawfully make one copy under the following conditions: one copy is made, the original copy is stored. If the possession of the original ceases to be lawful, all copies must be destroyed. Only the number of copies purchased or licensed may be in use at any given time.

4. Licensing

Many computer programs are acquired under licenses rather than purchases.

License agreements govern many of the activities that a user of a computer-related work may conduct. These agreements are contracts between the owner or vendor of the copyrighted work and the user of the work. Contracts are governed by state law. The terms of the license agreement may broaden or narrow the rights that a user has under the Copyright Act. Such agreements usually specify restriction on the user's rights to copy the software, to access electronic information, to download information. It may specify what constitutes legitimate uses of information. If the University licenses rather than purchases a computer program, then the user should refer to the license agreement or contact the copyright owner before making an adaptation.

5. Areas of caution

> a. Use of software may be restricted to a particular computer at a particular site. You should not assume that simultaneous use of a server copy of software is permitted under single copy license restrictions.

> b. Employees may not make copies of software licensed or owned by the University for their personal use except where explicitly allowed by the software vendor. (Check with University Computing.)

> c. If the University supplies licensed software to students in the course of instruction in a classroom, then sufficient licenses must be held by the University.

> d. Shareware is easily identifiable through explicit statements and software documentation. Unless the explicit statements identify the software as shareware, the user should assume that it may NOT be duplicated. Like other information, software not containing a copyright notice is not necessarily in the public domain.

B. COPYRIGHT AND THE WEB

Copyright law applies equally to works electronically available on the web. The fact that you can view, download or print text and graphics does not mean that the material is unprotected. Nor does it mean that you are free to disseminate that work to others either electronically or in hard copy.

1. Reading, watching or listening

There is controversy at the moment about the extent to which you can read, watch or listen to a copyrighted work without permission and/or royalties and whether fair use applies.

If a work is copyrighted and you have authorized access, you are free to read, watch or listen. There are some convincing arguments that fair use applies even if your use is not authorized.

2. Downloading

When you download material to your computer you make an electronic copy.

Unless your copy falls within fair use, you may not make this copy without authorization of the copyright owner. The owner may have given permission to download.

You may be searching a commercial database that charges a fee for searching and may also authorize you to download or print the material. Such authorization is usually limited to a single copy for your personal use.

3. Home Pages

a. You may put your own created text, graphics, audio or video on your web page.

b. If you use an item created by someone else whose copyright has not expired, then you should seek permission.

c. By creating a web page you probably have given implied permission to others to link to your web page. You may link to another URL because links are like street addresses and may not be copyrightable. However, a list of links may be copyrightable under a compilation copyright and if you copy the entire list to your web page, it probably is a copyright violation.

| *Washington & Lee University* | *Leyburn Library* | *Table of Contents* | *Top* |

VIII. Departmental and Printing Services Responsibilities

Departmental offices and University Printing Services are required to abide by this policy with respect to duplication of copyrighted materials. Printing or photocopying in excess of fair use, without permission, is prohibited. Departmental and Printing Services staff should be familiar with the University copyright policy and the fair use guidelines, and are authorized to make a good faith application of the guidelines to individual instances of photocopying. These requirements pertain to all manner of duplication, including course packets, departmental copying, and individual copying, and apply to both single and multiple copies.

IX. How to Obtain permission

If it is determined that a particular instance of copying will require the permission of the copyright owner, staff or faculty members should request permission or have it requested on their behalf. Bear in mind that permission must be obtained each time an item is used unless a blanket permission has been secured. Complete documentation of all permissions, denials, and other correspondence is to be kept for a period of three years.

A. OBTAINING PERMISSION DIRECTLY

Persons wishing to procure their own permissions should apply directly to the copyright owner. Faculty members are responsible for seeking permission to use copyrighted material

http://library.wlu.edu/copyrightpolicy.html   2/22/2008

for their own publications or presentations. Communication of complete and accurate information will facilitate the request; the Association of American Publishers has offered the following suggestions. A sample permissions request letter appears in the Appendix to expedite the permissions process.

To determine who owns the copyright on the material, consult the copyright page and/or the acknowledgement page for information on copyright ownership. If the address of the publisher does not appear with the material, it may be obtained in such publications as **Books in Print**, the American Bookseller's Association's Publisher's **Directory**, **The Literary Marketplace**, **The International Literary Marketplace**, or **Ulrich's International Periodicals**, available in the University libraries.

When requesting permission to duplicate, include a complete bibliographic citation of the material to be used, including title, author and/or editor, copyright or publication date, volume and/or issue and/or edition of the publication, chapter or article title, exact page numbers of the material to be used, and number of copies to be made. Also indicate the type of use to be made of the copies (e.g., course material). Remember to allow sufficient lead time for the publisher to respond to the request.

Permission must be obtained each time an item is used, unless a blanket or extended permission has been secured. (Because rights to copyrighted material are frequently transferred, it is often difficult to secure permission for more than a one-time use.) When requesting permission for subsequent uses of copyrighted material, remember that the rights holder will not necessarily be able to process your request any more quickly than the first time, and allow sufficient lead time accordingly.

B. OBTAINING PERMISSION FOR COURSE PACKS AND OTHER COURSE MATERIALS

A copyright permissions service exists on campus to assist University faculty in obtaining permission to copy copyrighted material for course pack and other course related purposes. Faculty members must provide sufficient information in a timely manner. Persons interested in utilizing this service should call Karen Lyle, 8798.

C. OBTAINING PERMISSION FOR RESERVE

If the faculty member can easily secure permission, for example from a colleague, he/she should do so and keep a written record. If the faculty member has not sought permission, the libraries will seek permission if the work is registered with the Copyright Clearance Center (CCC). The libraries will assume the expense of reasonable royalty fees paid to the CCC. For works not registered with the CCC, the libraries will attempt to obtain permission for materials to be placed on reserve if the faculty member provides sufficient information in a timely manner and if the copyright holder's address is available through directories in the libraries.

Wheaton College

library > copyright >

Copyright

. . . .

Copyright Defined

Copyleft Defined

TEACH Act

FERPA
    Sample Form

DMCA

. . . .

Fair use
    Multimedia
    Internet/Computer
    Interlibrary Loan
    Services

. . . .

Online Course
Readings
    Blackboard or
    Websites
    Seeking Permission

Reserve Copyright
Policy

. . . .

FAQs

. . . .

HELIN Catalog

Library Search

Library Home

Academics

COPYRIGHT

The intent of copyright law is to advance learning and encourage the dissemination of knowledge.

The Digital Millennium Copyright Act (PL105-304) became law on October 28, 1998. This law updates and replaces the **Copyright Revision Act** of 1976. This Library web site provides information about provisions for personal, classroom, and reserve copy usage, as well as conditions for the *fair use* of educational multimedia. The Library staff has prepared this information to help keep users informed about current accepted policies and practices, which serve to respect the rights of creators and copyright holders and the rights of the public.

Copyright Defined

Copyright provides protection provided by United States law (title 17, U.S. Code) to the authors or creators of literary, dramatic, musical, artistic and other intellectual works. Copyright applies to electronic resources, including the Internet, to the same extent it applies to materials in traditional formats. Please note that copyright law is interpretative; the following guidelines have no force of law. The intent of copyright law is to advance learning and encourage the dissemination of knowledge. When an original work is created in any medium, its creator owns a "copyright" on it. That authors and inventors benefit from copyright is a side effect of the law.

There are some things that copyright law will not protect. Copyright will not protect the title of a book or movie, nor will it protect short phrases such as "Make my day". Copyright protection also doesn't cover facts, ideas or theories. These things are free for all to use without permission.

The creation of new works is encouraged by granting the creator the exclusive right to:

- reproduce (i.e. duplicate, photocopy, etc.) the work
- prepare a derivative work
- distribute copies of the work
- perform the work publicly
- display the work publicly

The copyright holder can also sell or assign any of these rights to someone else, such as a publisher or distributor.

Copyleft Defined

Copyleft is a method for making an intellectual work (i.e.: weblogs/blogs or other online writings) available to others so that they have the freedom to make modifications as long as the same liberty is passed along. Note that copyleft licenses are copyright licenses and there are many ways to fill in the particulars; the copyright holder chooses the terms. Such licenses help reserve copyright while allowing certain uses of a work given the stated limitations. See the GNU Project Website or the Creative Commons Website for further licensing information.

Technology, Education and Copyright Harmonization Act - **TEACH Act of 2002** (P.L. 107-273, 11/02/02)

The TEACH Act updates copyright law for digital online education addressing the use of digital technologies in distance education (for example: e-reserve use.) Digital materials can be used for teaching if the use is a *fair use*. Certain requirements must be met before exemptions may be used:

- Works must be lawfully made and acquired;
- Teaching must occur at an accredited, non-profit educational institution;
- The electronic information should only be available to students enrolled in the class by taking reasonable steps to prevent retransmission;
- Use of the work is limited to a small portion of the work;
- Works must be labeled with the notice of copyright.

Family Educational Rights and Privacy Act - FERPA

If copies of a student's papers or projects are made available to the community, both the student and the professor must sign a statement giving permission. See the college's official Family Educational Rights and Privacy Act Policy for more specific information of this law and the college's procedure to implement it.

Further Web Resources for Copyright Information

- American Library Association Washington Office Copyright Education Program
- Campus Guide to Copyright Compliance
- CONFU: The Conference on Fair Use
- Copyright Clearance Center
- Copyright Decision Map
- Copyright on the Internet, Franklin Pierce Law Center
- Cyberlaw Encyclopedia
- Electronic Frontier Foundation
- United States Copyright Office
- University of Minnesota Copyright Information & Education

Print Sources for Copyright Information

Bielefield, Arlene and Lawrence Cheeseman. *Technology and Copyright Law*. New York: Neal-Schuman, 1999.

Bruwelheide, Janis H. *Copyright Primer for Librarians and Educators*. Chicago, IL: American Library Association, 1995.

Hoffman, Gretchen McCord. *Copyright in Cyberspace*. New York: Neal-Schuman, 2001.

Russell, Carrie. *Complete Copyright*. American Library Association, 2004.

Talab, R.S. *Commonsense Copyright*. Jefferson, CA: McFarland, 1999.

Questions about copyright law?
Contact:
Deryl Freeman
Catalog & Metadata Librarian
Wallace Library
x3716 or dfreeman@wheatonma.edu

The creator of this page provides the Wheaton College campus with copyright information and guidelines but it is not offered as professional legal advice.

This page is maintained by Deryl Kenney. Last updated on 7/2/07.
Questions about this page? Use our query form.

Wheaton College
Copyright Guide

DRAFT ONLY
Lisa Richmond
latest revision: February 21, 2005

Table of Contents

A. Introduction

B. Meaning of copyright

C. Purpose of copyright

D. Copyright exemptions
1. The Fair Use exemption
2. Reproduction by libraries and archives
3. Certain performances and displays
a) Works used "in the course of face-to-face teaching activities"
b) Performances and displays in distance education or on WebCT
c) Performances of non-dramatic literary or musical works not as part of classroom teaching or distance education
d) Performances of dramatic literary or musical works not as part of classroom teaching or distance education

E. Computer software

F. Course packs sold in bookstore

G. Library reserves

H. Works "made for hire"

I. How to seek permissions

J. If you violate copyright

K. Handling your own copyright
1. Contracts with publishers
2. Registering your copyright
3. Granting permissions
4. Joint copyright

L. When works pass into the public domain

M. Checklist for Fair Use

N. Suggested notices and warnings
1. Notice for interlibrary loan orders and copies made for library patrons
2. Notice for copies made for library patrons, or for digital copies made for purposes described in section D.3
3. Notice for copying equipment

P. Sample permission request letter

Q. Sample scenarios with suggested answers

A. Introduction

The purpose of this guide is to provide basic information about U.S. copyright law to professors, staff, and students at Wheaton College. Unless a footnote states otherwise, all quotations are taken from the *U.S. Copyright Act*, Title 17, U.S. Code, as amended. The full text of the Act is available at http://lcweb.loc.gov/copyright/title17/.

It is important to know the law and apply it in good faith, not only in order to keep ourselves from wrongdoing, but also so that we may confidently exercise the rights we have as users of copyrighted works. The exercise of these rights is important for the flourishing of our academic and campus life. And for those of us who are also authors and creators, knowledge of the law will help us to manage our copyrights well, and encourage others to seek permission to use our works when it is necessary for them to do so.

This guide provides a lay understanding and a summary of complex legal matters. For help in specific circumstances, please consult one of the people named below, who will seek legal advice as necessary:

> ***General questions, Fair Use, library reserves, classroom and distance learning, non-curricular events:***
> Gregory Morrison, Buswell Library (x5847 or Reference@wheaton.edu)

> ***Course packs:***
> Wyatt Waterman, Bookstore (x5325 or Wyatt.W.Waterman@wheaton.edu)

> ***Campus computer network:***
> George Poynor, Computing Services, (x5222 or George.V.Poynor@wheaton.edu)

> ***Public performances of videos or films:***
> Andy Saur, Buswell Library (x5620 or Andy.J.Saur@wheaton.edu)

> ***Digital Millennium Copyright agent for Wheaton College:***
> Terry Huttenlock, Buswell Library (x5352 or Terry.Huttenlock@wheaton.edu)

B. Meaning of copyright

Copyright is a limited, statutory monopoly granted to creators of "original works of authorship fixed in any tangible medium of expression."

> A work is considered original if it "embodies some minimum amount of creativity."[1] For example, a translation of *The Lonely Planet Guide to Tasmania* and a particular arrangement of data may both be considered original works.

> "Fixed" means that the work exists in a form that has "more than transitory duration." A cake decorated with a happy birthday message is unlikely to be fixed, but a Web site almost certainly is.

> And finally, a "tangible medium of expression" refers to what can be seen, heard, or felt, either directly or with the assistance of a machine.

Copyright law is about more than just copying. It establishes the rights that creators have in relation to their works, as well as the rights others may have to reproduce, distribute, modify, display, or perform them.

The works in question include:

- literary works (this covers works composed of words and/or numbers, such as books, articles, Web sites, and software programs)
- musical works, including any accompanying words
- dramatic works, including any accompanying music
- pantomimes and choreographic works
- pictorial, graphic and sculptural works
- motion pictures and other audio-visual works
- sound recordings
- architectural works

Whether published or unpublished, such works are protected by copyright automatically at the time of their creation. It is not necessary for the creator to affix a copyright notice to the work or to register it with the U.S. Copyright Office in order to have copyright of it.

Copyright does not cover any "idea, procedure, process, system, method of operation, concept, principle, or discovery."

---

[1] Kenneth D. Crews. *Copyright Essentials for Librarians and Educators.* Chicago: American Library Association, 2000, p. 9.

Global reach of the law
Because of international treaties the U.S. has signed, works created or published in countries other than the United States are subject to the U.S. Copyright Law when used in the United States.

Length of copyright
Generally speaking, copyright lasts for the life of the author or creator, plus seventy years. Once this time is passed, works are said to enter the "public domain." For more information, see section L.

Copyright not physical ownership
The copyright adhering to a work is not the same as ownership of a particular copy of that work. For example, if you own a music CD, the "right of first sale" allows you to sell it, lend or give it away, and even destroy it, but you do not have the right to copy it unless your copy can be justified by an exemption granted in the copyright law.

Copyright not plagiarism
Respecting copyright is not the same as giving proper attribution to the author or creator of a work you use. For example, it may be a violation of copyright to post on your Web site an image that you copied from elsewhere on the Web, even if your posting states clearly where the image was taken from.

Copyright not contract
Licensed works (generally, software programs and databases) are governed by contract law. Contract laws supersede the provisions of the U.S. copyright law and may give users more or fewer rights than the copyright law does.

C. Purpose of copyright

Copyright exists to "promote the Progress of Science and useful Arts, by securing for limited Times to Authors and Inventors exclusive Right to their respective Writings and Discoveries."

U.S. Constitution, art. 1, sec. 8

"The primary objective of copyright is not to reward the labor of authors, but to promote the Progress of Science and useful Arts. To this end, copyright assures authors the right to their original expression, but encourages others to build freely upon the ideas and information conveyed by a work. This result is neither unfair not unfortunate. It is the means by which copyright advances the progress of science and art."

Supreme Court Justice Sandra Day O'Connor[2]

"The constitutional purpose of copyright is to facilitate the flow of ideas in the interest of learning. The primary objective of our copyright law is not to reward the author, but rather secure for the public the benefits from creations of authors."

U.S. House Report, Berne Convention Implementation Act of 1988.[3]

---

[2] Quoted in Carrie Russell, "Current Copyright Issues Facing Academic Librarians," a seminar offered by the American Library Association, 2004.

[3] Ibid.

D. Copyright exemptions

Exemptions are rights granted to users of copyrighted material. This guide outlines the exemptions most commonly used in college settings.

1. The Fair Use exemption
(§107, *Copyright Act*)

Many activities of college life may fall under the Fair Use exemption of the Act. This exemption states in part:

"…the fair use of a copyrighted work, including such use by reproduction in copies…for purposes such as criticism, comment, news reporting, teaching (including multiple copies for classroom use), scholarship, or research, is not an infringement of copyright. In determining whether the use made of a work in any particular case is a fair use the factors to be considered shall include—

> (a) the purpose and character of the use, including whether such use is of a commercial nature or is for nonprofit educational purposes;
>
> (b) the nature of the copyrighted work;
>
> (c) the amount and substantiality of the portion used in relation to the copyrighted work as a whole; and
>
> (d) the effect of the use upon the potential market for or value of the copyrighted work."

How do you apply Fair Use?

Each situation must be decided by analysis of the four factors. To date, the courts have provided very little guidance in the interpretation of Fair Use in college contexts. It is generally understood, however, that no one factor is automatically given more weight than another, and a use that is opposed by some of the factors may still be justified if the other factors favor it.

Congress has stated that "the doctrine [of fair use] is an equitable rule of reason, no generally applicable definition is possible, and each case raising the question must be decided on its own facts."[4] The more clearly each factor favors your intended use, the more confident you may be that the use is fair.

---

[4] House Committee on the Judiciary, Report on Copyright Law Revision, 94th Congress, 2d session, 1976, House Report 94-1476, 65. Quoted in United States Copyright Office, *Circular 21*, "Reproduction of Copyrighted Works by Educators and Librarians." Cp. Kenneth D. Crews: "Rules about word counts and

A helpful amplification of the four factors is provided in the Checklist for Fair Use in section M. This checklist has no legal standing, however, and does not replace the need for you to apply "an equitable rule of reason" in any given situation.

What if Fair Use is not applicable?

Consider whether one of the other exemptions applies (see parts 2 and 3 below). If no exemption covers your intended use, you must request permission from the copyright holder (see section I).

2. **Reproduction by libraries and archives**
   (Summary of §108, *Copyright Act*).

Remember that libraries and archives may also avail themselves of the Fair Use exemption (see section D.1).

In each of the following cases, the library or archives:

✓ may not charge more than what is necessary to cover the cost of making the copy.

✓ must include a notice of copyright on the copy made, or in the absence of a notice, a warning that the material may be protected by copyright. For suggested notices and warnings, see section N.

✓ will not be held liable, nor will an employee of the library or archives be held liable, for copyright infringement resulting from unsupervised copying by patrons, provided that copying equipment displays a notice that the making of a copy may be subject to copyright law. For suggested notices, see section N.

✓ may not engage in systematic or concerted copying or distribution of copies.

The libraries and archives at Wheaton College may:

✓ make up to three copies of an unpublished work in their collections solely for purposes of preservation and security or for deposit for research use in another library or archives. If the copy is made in digital format, it may not be made

---

percentages have no place in the law of fair use. At best, they are interpretations intended to streamline fair use." *Copyright Essentials for Librarians and Educators*, p. 55.

available to the public in that format outside the premises of the library or archives.

✓ make up to three copies of a published work solely for the purpose of replacement of a copy that is damaged, deteriorating, lost, or stolen, or if the existing format in which the work is stored has become obsolete, *if*:
  ✓ the library or archives has determined, after a reasonable effort, that an unused replacement cannot be obtained at a fair price, *and,*
  ✓ a copy made in digital format is not made available to the public in that format outside the premises of the library or archives.

✓ make one copy for a patron or to fulfill an interlibrary loan request of no more than one article or other contribution to a copyrighted collection or periodical issue, or a small part of any other copyrighted work, *if*:
  ✓ the copy becomes the property of the user and the library or archives has had no notice that the copy would be used for any purpose other than private study, scholarship, or research; *and*
  ✓ the library or archives displays prominently, at the place where orders are accepted, and includes on its order form, a warning of copyright. For suggested notices, see section N.

✓ make one copy for a patron or to fulfill an interlibrary loan request of an entire work or a substantial part of it, *if*:
  ✓ the library or archives has determined, after a reasonable effort, that the work cannot be obtained at a fair price; *and*
  ✓ the copy becomes the property of the user and the library or archives has had no notice that the copy would be used for any purpose other than private study, scholarship, or research; *and*
  ✓ the library or archives displays prominently, at the place where orders are accepted, and includes on its order form, a warning of copyright. For suggested notices, see section N.

3. **Certain performances and displays**
(Summary of §110, *Copyright Act* as amended by the Technology Education and Copyright Harmonization TEACH Act of 2002)

Remember that some performances and displays may also be justified under the Fair Use exemption (see section D.1).

a) **Works used "in the course of face-to-face teaching activities":**

✓ Performance or display of non-dramatic literary or musical work (such as poetry and symphonies) or reasonable and limited portions of other (i.e.

dramatic) works (such as stage plays and operas), is permitted in a classroom or similar place devoted to instruction, unless the copy used was not lawfully made and the person using it knew or had reason to believe it was not lawfully made.

b) Performances and displays in distance education or on WebCT

This area of the law is complex. Please note that this section does not address electronic reserves (see section G). To be permitted under this exemption, the performance or display:

✓ must be "made by, at the direction of, or under the actual supervision of" the professor, and be part of "mediated instructional activities" that are necessary to the course, and analogous to the kinds of performances or displays that would occur in the classroom setting. (This means that you cannot post an article on WebCT, for example, unless it is something you would otherwise have provided as a handout in the physical classroom.)

✓ must not substitute for the purchase of books or other materials readily available on the market for a fair price.

✓ must not be of works that are marketed "primarily for the purpose of display as part of mediated instructional activities transmitted via digital networks." In other words, where such works already exist, they should be purchased.

✓ must include a notice of copyright, or in the absence of a notice, a warning that the material may be protected by copyright. For suggested notices and warnings, see section N.

✓ must not be made from a copy that was not lawfully made and that the college knew or had reason to believe it was not lawfully made.

In addition:

✓ analog work may be digitized for performance or display if the work is not already available on the market in digital form.

✓ the performance of non-dramatic literary and musical works (such as poetry and symphonies) may be used in their entirety, but the performance of other works (such as stage plays, operas, or audio-visual recordings) must be used only in "reasonable and limited portions." The display of any work "in an amount comparable to that which is typically displayed in the course of a live classroom session" is permitted.

✓ to the extent reasonable and technologically feasible:
    ✓ the transmission must be limited to enrolled students only.
    ✓ the copy must be made inaccessible after the class is finished.
    ✓ the copy must not be further disseminated.

✓ the college must not engage in any activities that would decrypt or otherwise interfere with technological measures already employed by the copyright holder to prevent retention or unauthorized distribution of the work.

c) **Performances of non-dramatic literary or musical works** (such as symphonies) **not as part of classroom teaching or distance education**:

Such performances are permitted without obtaining copyright permission, as long as:

✓ there is no admission fee, or, if admission is charged, the proceeds are used exclusively for educational, religious, or charitable purposes.

✓ the performers or organizers are not paid.

d) **Performances of dramatic literary or musical works** (such as films) **not as part of classroom teaching or distance education**:

This is a grey area of the law. Wheaton College interprets the law as follows.

If the purpose of the performance is *primarily educational*, we consider it an instance of fair use, as long as:

✓ there is no admission fee.

✓ the copy (e.g. of the film being shown) was lawfully made.

If the purpose is *primarily entertainment*, we consider that there is no applicable copyright exemption. You must get permission from the copyright holder for such performances, unless the college already has public performance rights for the particular work, or you are inviting only a small number of family or friends. For more information, see section I.

E. Computer Software
(§117, *Copyright Act*)

Most computer software is subject to licenses rather than the copyright law. If the *Copyright Act* is applicable, however, remember that many uses of computer software may be justified under the Fair Use exemption (see section D.1).

In addition, the law states specifically that you may:
- ✓ Make a "back-up" copy to protect software against damage or deletion.
- ✓ Modify software to enable it to be used on a particular computer.

But you may not:
> engage in any activity that would decrypt or otherwise interfere with technological measures already employed by the copyright holder to prevent retention or unauthorized distribution of the work.

F. Course packs sold in the bookstore

This policy is based on the college's interpretation of a grey area of the copyright law. It applies to copyrighted works, or parts or works, which are photocopied and sold to students in the college bookstore.

Works produced in course packs should be intended as *primary reading material* (serving as a "textbook") for the course. If intended as *supplemental* readings, library reserve should be used instead (see section G).

✓ Course packs are compiled and sold at the professor's request. (The bookstore will provide faculty with instructions for compiling course packs at the time that it distributes textbook requisition information.)

✓ Course packs are not intended to substitute for the purchase of books or other materials readily available on the market for a fair price. In particular, no copies of works considered "consumable," such as workbooks and test booklets, will be included in course packs.

✓ Short portions of works, up to and including single chapters from books or single articles from journals, may be duplicated for course packs without copyright permission, as long is it is the first time that the particular professor has used the chapters or articles in teaching the particular course. Second and subsequent uses will require copyright permission, as will portions of works greater than single chapters or single journal articles.

✓ The bookstore staff will seek copyright permission where necessary. Any permission fees will be passed on to the buyer of the course pack. (Please note that publishers generally deny requests for 20% or more of the content of a book. In such cases, students will be required to purchase the whole book.)

✓ Remember that many journal articles are available in full text online through Buswell Library. In such cases, it will likely save your students money, and be simpler, to have them locate and print the article themselves. (To determine which journals, volumes, and years are available online, go to http://library.wheaton.edu and click on "Journal List.")

✓ Each work or part of a work that is included in the course pack will include a notice of copyright, or in the absence of a notice, a warning that the material may be protected by copyright. For suggested notices and warnings, see section N.

✓ Each pack will be sold "at cost," i.e. for the cost of production and any permission fees.

For more information, please consult Wyatt Waterman in the bookstore (x5325 or Wyatt.W.Waterman@wheaton.edu).

G. Library reserves

This policy is based on the college's interpretation of a grey area of the copyright law. It applies to copyrighted works, or parts of works, that are copied in order to be put on reserve at the library. This policy applies equally to paper and electronic reserves, including music reserves.

Works placed on reserve should be intended to serve as *incidental or supplemental reading material* for the course. If intended as primary readings (serving as a "textbook") for the course, a course pack should be prepared instead (see section F).

The Library also requests that works intended as *optional* or *recommended* readings not be placed on reserve at all, since student demand for these can usually be met by leaving the material in the library stacks.

✓ Copies will be placed on reserve only at the professor's request.

✓ No copy will be placed on reserve if it is intended to substitute for the purchase of books or other materials readily available on the market for a fair price. In particular, no copies of works considered "consumable," such as workbooks and test booklets, will be placed on reserve.

✓ Copies will be reproduced from materials lawfully obtained by the library or the professor. If the library does not own a copy of the work, the subject liaison will attempt to purchase a copy for the library collection.

✓ The number of copies of the item placed on reserve will be the lowest number the library believes is necessary to adequately serve the class.

✓ Short portions of works, up to and including single chapters from books, single articles from journals, or single pieces of recorded music, may be placed on reserve without seeking copyright permission. Copies beyond these amounts will not be placed on reserve without copyright permission unless the library believes there to be Fair Use justification.

✓ The library staff will seek copyright permission where necessary. Any permission fees will be passed on to the academic department the course belongs to.

✓ In cases where a greater amount of the book, journal, or disc is needed, the volume itself can be placed on reserve at the Reserve Desk.

✓ If a journal article is available in full text online through one of the library's research databases, it will not also be placed on reserve, since students already have a means of locating and printing the article. (To determine which journals, volumes, and years are available online, go to http://library.wheaton.edu and click on "Journal List.")

✓ Each copy will include a notice of copyright, or in the absence of a notice, a warning that the material may be protected by copyright. For suggested notices and warnings, see section N.

✓ In the case of electronic reserves, to the extent reasonable and technologically feasible:
  ✓ Access to the copy will be limited to enrolled students only.
  ✓ The copy will be made inaccessible after the course is finished.
  ✓ The copy will not be further disseminated.

For more information, please consult Gregory Morrison in Buswell Library (x5847 or Reference@wheaton.edu).

H. Works "made for hire"

Works "made for hire" are created by employees as part of their regular duties. Administrative reports, committee minutes, the college catalog and magazine, this copyright guide, and software programs written for college activities are examples of works made for hire. The college is deemed to hold the copyright to such works.

As an important exception to this rule, colleges normally recognize that the copyright to scholarly works created by faculty (such as books, articles, musical compositions, and art, as well as course notes, lectures, and exams) generally belongs to the faculty member. Of course, the college and the faculty member may enter into an agreement at any time to re-assign some or all of these rights in particular cases.

College administrators are advised to consider the question of copyright when using the services of independent contractors. Independent contractors are generally not considered employees for copyright purposes, and thus their work is not made for hire. For example, a film production company that is hired to make a promotional film about the college will retain copyright of that film unless it assigns the copyright to the college. Make sure the rights that will be assigned to the college are clearly stated, in writing, before such projects begin.

I. How to seek permissions

Remember that you should seek permission to use a work *only when*:

✓ the work is protected by copyright (see section L), *and*

✓ you've checked the work itself to see if permission for use has already been given (for example, the copyright page of some scholarly journals provides blanket permission for certain educational uses), *and*

✓ your intended use does not fall under one of the copyright exemptions given in this guide, or is not permitted by the license governing use of the work.

How do you get permission for your intended use?

If your intended use is the public performance of an audio-visual work as described in section D.3.c and d, please speak to the Video Coordinator in Buswell Library (x5620 or Andy.J.Saur@wheaton.edu).

Otherwise:

1. Identify the copyright holder or an agency that is authorized to give permissions on behalf of the copyright holder. Many works provide this information in a copyright notice. You may also find the following sources helpful:

   U.S. Copyright Office records (http://www.copyright.gov/).

   Copyright Clearance Center (http://www.copyright.com).

   For music:
   ASCAP (http://www.ascap.com/licensing/)
   BMI (http://www.bmi.com/licensing/), or
   SESAC (http://www.sesac.com/licensing/licensing1.asp).

   For movies:
   Motion Picture Licensing Corporation (http://www.mplc.com/index2.htm).

   For plays:
   Dramatists Play Service, Inc. (http://www.dramatists.com/text/licensing.html), or
   Baker's Plays (http://www.bakersplays.com).

2. Check the Creative Commons (http://www.creativecommons.org/) Web site to see if the copyright holder has already granted permission for certain uses. Currently the number of authors and creators using the Creative Commons is small, but it is

a good endeavor to support. Most of the works included are ones that have been published on the Web.

3. If the Creative Commons doesn't provide for your need, request permission directly from the copyright holder or licensing agency. If the copyright holder or agency doesn't have a Web site with an online request form, send a written letter as shown in section P. The copyright holder may decide to charge you for permission. You are free to negotiate the price. Permissions received through agencies will almost certainly come with a non-negotiable fee.

4. Keep records of all correspondence. If you receive oral permission from the copyright holder, follow it up with a letter, confirming the conversation.

5. It is good form to thank copyright holders for permissions received, in the acknowledgement section of the new work you create or publish.

6. Remember that failure to receive permission (for example, when the copyright holder does not respond to your request) does not necessarily justify the use of a work.

J. If you violate copyright

Who's responsible?

Responsibility to avoid violating the copyright law rests primarily upon you, not the college. It is important therefore that you make a good-faith effort to understand the law and comply with it.

What if your good-faith efforts prove wrong?

The only way to know for sure that you've applied the law incorrectly would be a court ruling against you. It is reassuring to know, however, that in the unlikely event you are taken to court, the law states that college employees acting within the scope of their employment will not be held liable for the statutory damages of copyright infringement if they "reasonably believed and had reasonable grounds for believing that [their] use was fair use" (§504 c. 2, *Copyright Act*).

For guidance in any particular circumstance, please consult one of the people listed in section A.

What if you are notified that you have violated copyright?

The responsibility to monitor copyright compliance rests with the copyright holder. If a copyright holder believes that you have infringed copyright, that person or his/her lawyer will most likely send you a "cease and desist" letter. If you receive such a letter but do not wish to comply because you believe your use is justified under the law, please notify one of the people listed in section A. In some cases, it will be important for the college to get legal advice.

K. Handling your own copyright

1. Contracts with publishers

When your book, article, image, or other work is accepted for publication, the publisher will give you a contract to sign. This contract usually transfers to the publisher all copyright of your work. In such cases, the publisher is granted not only the exclusive right to publish your work, but also the exclusive right to enter into contracts or give permission for future uses of your work (such as its inclusion in *ATLA Religion Index* or *JSTOR*, its re-publication, or its use by individual people) and to charge permission fees for such uses. Once you transfer your copyright to a publisher, even you, the author, must seek the publisher's permission for uses beyond what is permitted by Fair Use and the other exemptions specified in the law.

Although it usually proves difficult, you are entitled to negotiate the contract. For example, you may want to assign to a publisher the right to publish your article in a scholarly journal, but reserve the right to make it available on the Web in an open access archive after a certain length of time has passed.

Some publishers permit professors and students to freely copy works or parts of work for many academic uses. Other publishers have restrictive policies and require high permission fees. Which publication model do you want to support? Copyright is one consideration among many to bear in mind when deciding where to send your manuscript.

This is not to say that publishers who charge permission fees are acting unfairly. Each publisher has a legitimate interest in how the works it publishes are made available and used, and at what price. The copyright law is concerned with balancing the interests of copyright holders and users of copyrighted works, in order to "promote the progress of science and the useful arts" (see section C). The better you understand copyright law, the better equipped you are to encourage publishers to maintain this balance.

2. Registering your copyright

To register your copyright, follow the instructions provided by the U.S. Copyright Office at http://www.copyright.gov.

It is not necessary to register your copyright in order to assert it. It is recommended that you do so, however, for the following reasons:

✓ If you want to encourage people to seek your permission for uses beyond what the law grants them, you should make it possible for them to find out who you are and how you may be reached.

✓ If you do not register your copyright with the U.S. Copyright Office, you may not be able to collect damages in the event of a lawsuit.

3. Granting permissions

When you hold copyright of a work, you may assign or license all or only some of your rights to others. For example, you may decide to allow unlimited copying and distribution of your work with the proviso that the uses made of it be strictly non-commercial. Or, you may allow one theatre club to perform your play but not give permission to other clubs.

Exclusive rights must be granted in writing, but nonexclusive rights (that is, rights you give to more than one party) can be granted orally as well as in writing.

If you are publishing your work on the Web, or making a copy of it available there, consider registering your work under a Creative Commons license to spell out specifically how you will permit others to use it. For more information, please consult http://www.creativecommons.org/license/.

4. Joint copyright

You may hold copyright jointly with other creators or authors of a work. In such cases, the parties are free to exercise their rights independently, including the right to grant *non-exclusive* rights to new parties, as long as profits are shared equally. One party cannot re-assign copyright or grant an *exclusive* right to new parties, however, without the consent of the others.

If you embark upon a work of joint authorship, you are advised to consider the copyright question carefully. You and your colleague(s) should put your copyright agreement in writing, before the project begins.

L. When works pass into the public domain

(From Carrie Russell, *Complete Copyright: An Everyday Guide for Librarians*. American Library Association. 2004. Used by permission.)

Time of Publication	Conditions	Public Domain Status
Before 1923	None	In public domain
Between 1923 and 1978	Published without a copyright notice	In public domain
Between 1978 and 1 March 1989	Published without a notice, and without subsequent registration	In public domain
Between 1978 and 1 March 1989	Published without a notice, but with subsequent registration	70 years after death of author *
Between 1923 and 1963	Published with notice, but copyright was not renewed	In public domain
Between 1923 and 1963	Published with notice and copyright was renewed	95 years after publication date
Between 1964 and 1978	Published with notice	70 years after death of author *
Between 1978 and 1 March 1989	Published with notice	70 years after death of author *
After 1 March 1989	None	70 years after death of author *

* If the work is of corporate authorship, copyright endures for the shorter of 95 years from publication, or 120 years from creation.

M. Checklist for Fair Use

(Modified from Carrie Russell, *Complete Copyright: An Everyday Guide for Librarians*. American Library Association, 2004. Used by permission.)

See section D for assistance in interpreting this checklist.

Fair Use more likely	*Fair Use less likely*

Purpose:

Teaching (including multiple copies for classroom use)	Commercial activity
Research or scholarship	Profiting from the use
Nonprofit educational institution	Entertainment
Criticism or comment	Bad-faith behavior
News reporting	Denying credit to original author
Transformative or productive uses (changes the work for new utility)	
Restricted access (to students or other appropriate group)	
Parody	

Nature:

Published work	Unpublished work
Factual or nonfiction based	Highly creative work (art, music, novels, films, plays)
Important to favored educational objectives	Fiction

Amount:

Small quantity	Large portion or whole work used
Portion used is not central or significant to entire work	Portion used is central to work or the "heart of the work"
Amount is appropriate to favored educational purpose	

Effect:

User owns lawfully acquired or purchased copy of original work	Could replace sale of work
One or few copies made	Significantly impairs market or potential market for work or derivative
No significant effect on the market or potential market for copyrighted work	Reasonably available licensing mechanism
No similar product marketed by the copyright holder	Affordable permission available for using work
Lack of licensing mechanism	Numerous copies made
	You made it accessible on the Web or in other public forum
	Repeated or long term use

N. Suggested notices and warnings

1. **Notice for interlibrary loan orders and copies made for library patrons**

   This notice must be printed prominently on interlibrary loan order forms and posted at locations where copies are made for patrons.

   "Notice: Warning concerning copyright restrictions. The copyright law of the United States (Title 17, United States Code) governs the making of photocopies or other reproductions of copyrighted material. Under certain conditions specified in the law, libraries and archives are authorized to furnish a photocopy or other reproduction. One of these specific conditions is that the photocopy or reproduction is not to be "used for any purpose other than private study, scholarship or research." If a user makes a request for, or later uses, a photocopy or reproduction for purposes in excess of "fair use" that user may be liable for copyright infringement. This institution reserves the right to refuse a copying order if, in its judgment, fulfillment of the order would involve violation of copyright law."[5]

2. **Notice for copies made for library patrons, or for digital copies made for purposes described in section D, part 3**

   This notice must be affixed to copies made, unless the copy already contains a notice of copyright.

   "This material may be protected by copyright."

   A better notice, recommended especially for works delivered by electronic reserve in the library or on WebCT, is:

   "This material is made available at this site for the educational purposes of students enrolled in [course] at Wheaton College. The material is subject to U.S. copyright law and is not for further reproduction or transmission."[6]

3. **Notice for copying equipment**

   This notice must be posted on or near all photocopiers and other similar equipment on campus.

   "Notice: The copyright law of the United States (Title 17, U.S. Code) governs the making of photocopies or other reproductions of copyrighted material. The person using this equipment is liable for any infringement. For more information

---

[5] Code of Regulations, Title 7, §201.14.
[6] Suggested in Kenneth D. Crews, *Copyright Essentials for Librarians and Educators*, p. 71.

about the copyright law, please consult the Wheaton College Copyright Guide at [insert intranet URL]."

P. Sample permission request letter

[date]

[copyright owner's or agent's name and address]

Dear [copyright owner or agent]:

I am writing to ask your permission to use [give full citation of the work] for the purpose of [describe the intended use in sufficient detail].

Please complete and return this form to me at your earliest convenience. Thank you very much for your consideration.

Sincerely yours,

[your name, position, and contact information]

I do _____ do not _____ grant permission for my work to be used for the purpose stated above.

Name _____

Signature _____

Date _____

Q. Sample scenarios with suggested answers

For professors:

Q: Can I photocopy an article from a newspaper or journal and hand it out to my students in class?

A: Yes. §107 of the *Act* explicitly permits multiple copies for classroom use.

Reference: Section D.1

Q: Can I include a cartoon, graph, or other image on my WebCT page or PowerPoint slides?

A. Yes. For your PowerPoint slides, §110 of the *Act* explicitly permits the display of most works by a teacher in the classroom. For WebCT, §110 of the *Act* permits display of most works that are "necessary to the course" and "analogous to the kinds of displays that would occur in the classroom setting."

Reference: Section D.3.a/b

Q: I want to show Hitchcock's *North by Northwest* in class. Is that OK?

A: Yes. Showing films in class (as part of your teaching activity) is explicitly permitted in §110 of the *Act*.

Reference: Section D.3.a

Q: I published an article in a scholarly journal a few years ago. Can I post a copy of it on WebCT or on my personal web site and direct my students to it?

A: Yes, if you own the copyright to it. Otherwise the answer is Maybe. The first thing to do is check if the library already makes available a copy of the article in full text online. If so, there is no problem with linking that library URL to your WebCT or other web page. If the article is one that you would have otherwise given to your students as a handout in class, you can post it without getting copyright permission as long as you comply with the requirements listed in section D.3.b. If the article is one that you would otherwise have included in a course pack or given to the library to be placed on reserve, you should not post it without getting permission. Or, you could try to make a case for this as an instance of fair use.

Reference: Section D.1 and 3.b

Fair Use analysis:

Purpose: favorable. The purpose is scholarship.

Nature: favorable. The work in question was published and is factual, non-fiction and is important to the educational objective.

Amount: moderately unfavorable. The whole work is being copied, but the amount is "appropriate to favored educational purpose."

Effect: unfavorable. If you are posting this article as a means of circumventing the course pack or library reserve procedures, you may be replacing sales of the work or impairing the market for the work. There is likely a "reasonably available licensing mechanism" and "affordable permission" available that you should use instead.

Q: The orchestra I conduct is planning to perform Mozart's *Requiem*. Can I photocopy the sheet music and distribute it to the performers?

A: This is tricky. The *Requiem* itself is not copyright-protected, since it was composed so long ago, but the sheet music itself may be. Consult section L for guidance. If the music you want to use is protected, you will need to get permission from the copyright holder if you do not wish to buy copies of it for everyone. Alternatively, you could look for another edition of the music that is not protected.

Reference: Section D.1 and 3.c

Fair Use analysis:

Purpose: moderately favorable. The use is being made at a non-profit educational institution but the purpose is primarily entertainment.

Nature: moderately unfavorable. The *Requiem* is a highly creative work.

Amount: unfavorable. The whole work is being copied.

Effect: unfavorable. The photocopying is replacing sales of the work and numerous copies are being made.

Q: The orchestra I conduct is planning to perform Mozart's *Requiem*. Do I have to get copyright permission for the performance?

A: No permission is necessary. The use is permitted by §110 of the *Act*.

Reference: Section D.3.c

For staff:

Q: I'm creating a PowerPoint presentation for an upcoming meeting. Can I include an image I found on the Web?

A: Probably, but it would be better to try to find an image that is being offered on the Web explicitly for copying.

Reference: Section D.1

Fair Use analysis:

Purpose: moderately favorable. Your use is for an activity of a non-profit educational institution, but it isn't for the purpose of teaching or scholarship.

Nature: moderately unfavorable. The image was published on the Web and is creative rather than factual.

Amount: unfavorable. You want to use the whole work.

Effect: favorable. You are making only one copy, and there is no significant effect of the market or potential market for the image. You are making the image available only for a limited time.

For students:

Q: I want to host a showing on campus of *The Lord of the Rings: The Return of the King*. Do I need to get copyright permission?

A: If the primary purpose of the showing is entertainment or club/team bonding, you must get permission. (*Note:* if you are inviting only a small circle of friends to watch the film with you in your residence hall room, house, or apartment, you do not need permission.) If the primary purpose of the showing is educational, you do not need permission. As a first step, ask yourself the clarifying question, "What is my intent for showing this film?" and then contact Buswell Library's video coordinator (x5620) for further guidance in reaching a conclusion.

Please note: inviting a professor to lead a discussion before or after the film does not automatically turn entertainment into education. Call the video coordinator for guidance.

Reference: Section D.3.d

Fair Use analysis:

Purpose: unfavorable or unfavorable, depending upon whether the showing is primarily entertainment or education.

Nature: unfavorable. The film is a highly creative work of fiction.

Amount: unfavorable. The whole work is being shown.

Effect: unfavorable. Showing the film could replace sale of the work (e.g., movie tickets or rentals from video stores). Also, you are showing the film in a public setting.

Q: I'm creating a poster to advertise my club's event. I found a graphic on the Web that I'd like to download and use on my poster. Is that OK?

A: Probably not, unless the image is being offered on the Web explicitly for copying.

Reference: Section D.1

Fair Use analysis:

Purpose: moderately unfavorable. The purpose of your event is cultural or social, not educational.

Nature: moderately unfavorable. The image was published on the Web and is creative rather than factual.

Amount: unfavorable. You want to use the whole work.

Effect: moderately favorable. You are making only a few copies of your poster, and there is no significant effect of the market or potential market for the image. You are making the image available in a public forum, but it is only for a limited time.

Q: My drama club wants to perform Dorothy Sayers' play, *The Zeal of Thy House* (published in 1937). Do we have to get copyright permission?

A: Consult section L for guidance. From the information provided there, you will learn that a work published in 1937 is in the public domain (is not protected by copyright) if it was published without a copyright notice. Check the physical item: does it contain a copyright notice? If not, you're in the clear. If there is a copyright notice, section L instructs that it may still be in the public domain if the copyright was not renewed. Since there is no easy way of determining this, the best course of action is to get permission from the copyright holder, or look for another printed edition of the play that is not protected.

Reference: Section D.1 and 3.d

Fair Use analysis:

Purpose: unfavorable. The purpose of your event is primarily entertainment, not education.

Nature: unfavorable. The work is highly creative.

Amount: unfavorable. You want to use the whole work.

Effect: moderately unfavorable. This is a public performance (i.e., anyone is welcome is attend) and a licensing mechanism or affordable permission is likely available. The fact that you are neither charging admission nor paying the actors has no effect on the situation.

Q: For my history of art course I am writing an essay on Francisco Goya. I want to include some images of his paintings in my essay. Is there any problem with that?

A: No problem.

Reference: Section D.1

Fair Use analysis:

Purpose: favorable. The purpose of your use is "criticism," "comment," or "scholarship."

Nature: moderately favorable. The work is highly creative, but images of the paintings have been published and your use is important to educational objectives.

Amount: moderately favorable. You want to provide images of the whole painting(s) but that amount is appropriate to the educational objective.

Effect: favorable. Only one copy of each image will be made, and there in no significant effect of the market for the work (e.g. your use will not decrease sales for the book you got the images from). You are not making your copy publicly accessible, since only you and your professor will view it.

Winthrop University

115 Tillman Hall, Rock Hill, SC 29733 • 803/323-2228 • 803/323-4036 (Fax)

Winthrop University Intellectual Property Rights Policy

Approved by Winthrop University Board of Trustees June 6, 2003

I. Introduction

The fundamental mission of Winthrop University embraces teaching, research, and service, both to enhance and advance knowledge and to serve the public good. To do so, Winthrop University recruits and maintains a diverse faculty of national caliber. It "supports its faculty as they enhance their abilities as effective teachers and as they develop and enrich their knowledge and skills as scholars, researchers, practitioners and creative artists in their disciplines. Moreover, Winthrop ... support[s] high quality instruction and research in every field of study offered by developing and maintaining at an appropriate level its classrooms, studios and performance spaces, as well as its informational and instructional technology resources. "[1]

Thus, it is in the interest of all members of the university community to foster the creation of the highest quality intellectual properties that further the academic mission of the University; foster the dissemination of new knowledge and the maintenance of high academic standards to improve the education we provide our students and the service we provide to the citizens of the State of South Carolina; and to provide incentives for university faculty, staff, and students to participate fully in the use and creation of intellectual properties. Strong mutual interests are shared among the university, the faculty, the staff, and the students in the appropriate allocation of the ownership rights associated with such intellectual properties; and the rights that belong to the owners of intellectual properties should be allocated so as to optimally support the mutual interests of the university, faculty, staff, and students. [2]

From the pursuit of this mission should emerge creations and discoveries that are subject to, or eligible for, intellectual property protection. The stewardship of such intellectual property is an important responsibility of both those who create these byproducts of human knowledge and the University sponsoring them. Because of the advent of new technologies and the ability to mass-produce them at will, questions about the ownership of intellectual property created by members of the Winthrop community have arisen. Thus, as part of the Academic Program Initiatives in the 2002-2003 *Vision of Distinction,* the University has undertaken to "implement revisions to University policies regarding intellectual property issues and trends." This document sets forth Winthrop University 's Intellectual Property Rights Policy concerning the stewardship of these various creations. It will supersede the version ratified by the Board of Trustees in October 1992.[3]

II. Definitions

For the purpose of this document, **intellectual property** is defined as "any product, new or useful process, or idea resulting from scholarly or creative activity regardless of whether it is eligible for protection under provisions of copyright, patent or trademark law." Examples of intellectual property include (but are not limited to) writings, art works, musical compositions and performances, literary works, architecture, new or improved devices, circuits, chemical compounds, drugs, genetically engineered biological organisms, cell lines, data sets, software, musical processes, or unique and innovative uses of existing inventions. Intellectual property is created when something new and useful has been conceived or developed, or when unusual, unexpected, or non-obvious results, obtained with an existing invention, can be practiced for some useful purpose. Intellectual property can be created by one or more individuals, each of whom, to be a creator, must have conceived of an essential element or have contributed substantially to its conceptual development.[4]

Creators of intellectual property are defined as faculty, staff, or other persons employed by Winthrop University,[5] whether full- or part-time, or serving in an adjunctive capacity. Creators also include visiting faculty and researchers and any other persons, including students, who create or discover intellectual property using University development and resources as outlined below and whose role in its creation has been agreed upon through previously signed statements.

III. Policy

The Winthrop University Intellectual Property Rights Policy applies to all University employees in each constituent academic or administrative unit and department, both full and part –time, including faculty, staff, and to students of each constituent academic or administrative unit or department. Except as stated in Categories III.2, 3, and 4 below, intellectual property will be the sole property of the originator (faculty, staff, or student as inventor, author, creator, or designer).

Ownership of and rights to intellectual property invented, authored, or designed by Winthrop faculty, staff, or student employees and subject to protection by patent, copyright, or trademark law shall be categorized as follows:

1. individual scholarly/aesthetic product,
2. University –assisted product,
3. University –commissioned product ("Work-for-Hire"),
4. third-party sponsored/contracted product.

1. Individual Scholarly/Aesthetic Products

Intellectual property that is produced outside of the terms of primary employment and not part of a directed assignment at Winthrop and that makes no more than incidental use of Winthrop resources considered part of the employee's usual academic environment (such as the usual office, studio, laboratory, computer, and library privileges) shall be owned by the faculty, staff, or student employee who produces the individual product. (The general obligation of faculty to produce scholarly works *does not* constitute such a directed assignment.)

The items most commonly considered as individual scholarly/aesthetic products are those created by faculty members, non-faculty researchers, or students as part of their ongoing intellectual inquiry, creative impulses, and pedagogical activities and are disseminated among the scholarly and creative communities primarily for the advancement of knowledge. Typically these works reflect research and/or creativity that, within the University, are considered as evidence of professional advancement or accomplishment and are submitted in partial fulfillment for the granting of tenure and awarding of promotion. Such works include scholarly publications, journal articles, reports (contracted or otherwise), research bulletins, monographs, books, plays, poems, and works of art. In some scholarly disciplines, they may include products such as (but not limited to) software,[6] biological and chemical compounds, data sets, and instructional materials.[7]

Such items are usually protected by copyright rather than patent; copyright protects such products from the moment of their fixation in a tangible medium of expression, that is, instantly and automatically. They may be created spontaneously or take years to develop. If the creation of an individual scholarly/aesthetic project will involve the use of significant institutional resources (as defined in the next section), the creator and the University should agree before the project begins on the use of facilities, allocation of rights to use the work, and the recovery of expenses and/or sharing of benefits from commercialization of the work.

Our faculty enjoy royalties on various creative expressions (whether in print, tangible form, or electronically reproduced). Nothing in this policy should be interpreted to impinge upon or constrict those royalties. One hundred percent of any royalty, sale, or licensing gross income accruing from individual scholarly/aesthetic products shall belong to the employee. If the creator of such individual scholarly/aesthetic products should leave the University, he or she retains the rights to any such products created at Winthrop unless he or she has assigned the rights elsewhere. Winthrop will assert no ownership to individual scholarly/aesthetic products created before the creator was employed by or enrolled at Winthrop University.

Faculty will report any new creations (or uses) to their chairs or deans. The disclosure should be less formal than that involved for discoveries, inventions, and patents but should come early in the creation process and will normally be reflected in the faculty member's Annual Report. Only with such disclosure can the University have a good sense of how new information technologies are being used and how the administration can fulfill its obligation to support such work.

2. University-Assisted Products

Some intellectual property will be produced outside of the terms of primary employment at Winthrop that will make significant use (other than incidental use as defined above) of university resources not usually assigned to an employee as part of his/her ordinary appointment and that consequently requires specific, case by case permission of one's Dean and/or department head prior to use of those resources. Such products will be deemed university-assisted products. Examples of such products include, but are not limited to, those for which the creator is granted additional research funding or support; those for which time is reassigned from the creator's usual employment responsibilities; or those for which the creator is provided additional equipment, space, supplies, travel, staff, marketing support, use of University-owned technologies, or similar resources. Such university assisted-products shall be owned jointly by the faculty, staff, or student employee who produced the intellectual property and by the University.

Because new technologies and works created with them (as, for example, distance education or web-based courses) are always in a state of ongoing creation, they commonly involve collaborative ownership and significant use of University resources. For instance, a faculty member may use her or his knowledge and expertise to develop the content of a web-based course in her or his field, then collaborate with other University employees such as programmers, graphic artists, video technicians, marketing specialists, and financial professionals in order actually to deliver the course. Such creations would be an example of significant use of University resources to create or develop a university-assisted product. In such cases, the parties should execute an agreement regarding the sharing arrangement before starting the project that will result in creation of the intellectual property.

Royalties, sales or license fee gross income from the university-assisted product shall be shared between the employee and Winthrop as agreed at the time written permission for significant use of the Winthrop resources is given. In no case shall the employee's share of the gross income be less than 50 percent. Responsibility to file copyright, patent, or trademark claims shall be negotiated and included in the authorization from one's Dean and/or department head. In the event Winthrop funds the copyright, patent, or trademark application process, Winthrop shall have a paid-up, non-exclusive license to use, without other cost, the work for educational purposes.

When income generated from various discoveries and creations in teaching and research is small (under $25,000), asserting University ownership will doubtless discourage innovation. Faculty, therefore, will retain any generated revenue up to and including $25,000. Sharing beyond that limit for creations in which University resources are instrumental in the production is set in the table below.

The first $25,000 in income for any individual item of intellectual property shall be paid to the creator/inventor in full, after which distribution is as follows:

	$25,001 – $50,000	$50,001 – $75,000	$75,001 – $100,000	$100,001 – $125,000	Over $125,000
Creator	70%	65%	60%	55%	50%
Winthrop	20%	25%	25%	28%	30%
Reinvestment [8]	10%	10%	15%	17%	20%

In the case of the death of the creator, any unpaid royalties shall be paid to the creator's estate unless otherwise specified.

In all cases of university-assisted products, the University must specify before the task is undertaken for how long and over how many iterations of said creation its ownership exists *before* that creation is forthcoming. Any university-assisted product that the University has expressed no interest in owning *ab initio*, cannot, at a later date, be declared owned by the University. The University's interest should not be asserted when there is noncommercial use of new information technologies by faculty or for the commercial use of such technologies until the revenues generated are substantial.

The University will normally exert copyright and/or ownership for three years on any university-assisted project. At the end of the three years, the University has the right to renew its claim for two more years, provided it pays an appropriate royalty to the creator. The University may continue to renew its claim every two years. If the University does not renew its claim, the creation becomes the full possession (including copyright) of the creator.

Many university-assisted products will fall under the category of patentable, rather than copyrightable, works. Since publication of an idea embodied in a patentable product bars the filing of a patent application in every country in the world except the United States and starts a very specific clock running on the right to file that patent application, it is crucial that the University be aware of the potential development of such products long before they are completed in order to comply with the requirements for applying for patent, trade secret, or other legal protections for the product. Therefore creators of such potentially-patentable products must inform their Deans or department heads in writing before the work to produce such products is undertaken, and comply with all the appropriate policies and responsibilities set out in sections iv and v of this document to protect the rights of both the creator and the University.

More and more, Winthrop faculty are working outside the University in consulting capacities. In such settings they have access to resources they might not otherwise have access to on campus. Nevertheless, when creations (especially those curricular-related ones) are produced that the University has either substantially supported or provided release or reassigned time for and wishes to use in other educational outreaches, the University shares ownership. This should be made clear early on in this process and *before* the faculty member has signed any consulting agreements.

3. University-Commissioned Products

Intellectual property produced as the primary employment task or as temporarily-reassigned full–time Winthrop activity, when that task or activity explicitly is to produce a specific work subject to protection as intellectual property, shall be owned by Winthrop. In some cases this will be clear from the job description or the contract of employment. One hundred percent of any royalties, sales, or licenses accruing from such commissioned products shall belong to Winthrop. Such directed work assignments must be defined by written contractual agreement before the work is undertaken by the employee.

4. Third-Party, Sponsored/Contracted Products

Intellectual property produced as part of a grant or contract for a third party under an agreement with Winthrop and the employee shall adhere to the terms of the specific contract. All such contracts should be developed before the work is undertaken, must contain an intellectual property ownership clause, and must be approved and signed by the employee's dean and/or department head and by the vice president of the employee's area or by the appropriate administrative officer of Winthrop.

IV. Responsibilities

1. Exercising Rights

The University shall not exercise intellectual property rights in any work created or discovered by a creator other than works meeting the definition of university-assisted products, university commissioned products, or third-party contracted products, unless such rights are voluntarily transferred by the creator or secured through licenses set forth in this policy.

Winthrop University shall have the right to determine the disposition of applicable intellectual property which it holds or in which shares ownership under this policy. That determination shall include the interests of the University, the public, and the creator, including the creator's professional or ethical convictions concerning the use of intellectual property. Responsibility for disposition of intellectual property resides with the Academic Affairs Office, subject to the policies developed by the University Research Committee.

2. Creators' Responsibilities

Creators must promptly disclose to the University (or dean or chair) any applicable jointly-held intellectual property creation as detailed in section III.2 above. Disclosure shall be made on *Intellectual Property Rights Form 1A*. Copies must be sent to the Academic Vice-President, Department Chairperson and College Dean. The Academic Affairs Office shall routinely report all disclosures to the President.

Creators may not assign or license rights of intellectual property that is jointly held with the University to third parties without the written consent of the University. All assignments must be in writing and shall conform with the requirements of this Policy. Creators of jointly-held intellectual property shall assist the University to obtain statutory protection for the intellectual property and to perform all obligations to which it may be subject, including executing appropriate assignments and other documents required to set forth effectively the ownership of, and rights to, said intellectual property.

The creator retains responsibility for intellectual stewardship of his or her intellectual property. The creator shall have agreed, or not, to be identified as the creator by the University and by subsequent licensees and assignees, as required by law. Because premature or unauthorized disclosure may defeat legal protection of intellectual property, the University must inform creators of the consequences of premature or unauthorized disclosures. The University and creators must work together to facilitate both scholarly disclosures and the acquisition of appropriate intellectual property protection.

3. University Administration of Intellectual Property

Primary responsibility for identifying, protecting, and managing applicable intellectual property resides with the Academic Affairs Office, under policies developed and supervised by the University Research Council and the Vice President for Academic Affairs. All disclosures shall be submitted to the Academic Affairs Office. The Academic Affairs Office will determine whether Winthrop University desires to obtain protection for jointly-held intellectual property or otherwise make use of the intellectual property. The Academic Affairs Office shall consult, as it deems necessary, with the University Research Council concerning such decisions and other matters relating to technology transfer and the implementation of the policy. The Academic Affairs Office or the University Research Council may request a recommendation from the University Research Policy Committee regarding the disposition of jointly-held intellectual property.

The Academic Affairs Office shall notify the creator promptly after it has determined whether it is in the best interest of Winthrop University to seek protection for jointly-held intellectual property. If Winthrop University decides to seek protection for such property, it shall proceed either through its own efforts or those of an appropriate private firm or attorney to obtain protection and/or manage the intellectual property. In those instances where delay would jeopardize obtaining the appropriate protection for the intellectual property, the creator may request that the Academic Affairs Office expedite its decision whether or not it shall seek statutory intellectual property protection.

4. Specific Responsibilities

The University acknowledges the importance of transferring intellectual property appropriately, effectively, and frugally. To that end, the University shall establish efficient mechanisms for technology transfer in order to maximize any value of intellectual property to the faculty and the University.

1. The University administration shall:

   A. Provide oversight of intellectual property and technology transfer according to this policy and any other pertinent University policies;

   B. Assist Colleges in aiding and abetting effective transfers and College policies and procedures consistent with University policies;

   C. Provide legal services and cooperate with the Colleges in promoting and licensing intellectual property; and

   D. Take appropriate actions to protect the University's intellectual property.

2. The Deans of the Colleges shall:

   A. Promote intellectual property transfers consistent with the College's objectives and academic environment;

   B. Establish policies and procedures for intellectual property transfers, avoiding conflicts of interests consistent with University policies; and

   C. Review and approve all agreements that convey or affect the University's rights to intellectual property originating in that College as specified in this policy.

3. Creators of intellectual property shall:

   A. Disclose to appropriate University or College officials the creation of intellectual property;
   B. Conduct intellectual property transfer activities consistent with University and College policies and procedures, including those governing conflicts of commitment and conflicts of interest; and,
   C. Cooperate with the University in defending and prosecuting patents and in legal actions taken in response to copyright infringement.

5. Faculty Responsibility to Enrolled Students

Faculty must make every effort to accommodate not only different styles of learning but also the needs of differently abled students in their courses through the use of technology. Limited, fair use of web-based materials (following the three major tests of spontaneity, brevity and cumulative use) is protected under both the *Copyright Act of 1976* and the *Digital Millennium Copyright Act of 1998.* However, as specified in both acts, the materials should be used only for a specified course and *repeated use requires written permission.* Materials for students at remote locations are also covered under this act and should abide by the copyright acts cited above. Faculty must make every effort to ensure their use of such materials is in compliance with federal and state statutes governing copyright.

Students retain their own intellectual property rights unless signed away, and this includes any print or non-print posting of papers (even for use as examples) by current or former students. Written permission of students who are the creators of papers, projects, research, and similar materials used in this way is required. Student engaged in research guided or directed by faculty that will later be used either commercially, or beyond the current semester, are subject to all contractual agreements between the parties.

6. Material Made Available for University Use

In the course of their contractual duties, many faculty, staff, and students create materials that are subject to intellectual property protection, and that are voluntarily made available for the use of the University without expectation of further compensation.[9] The University shall retain a non-exclusive, royalty-free license to use such material made available for the use of the University, provided that significant contributions of the creator(s) are acknowledged and there is mutual, *written* consent. Such licenses shall not include the right to exploit the work for profit outside of the University but may include its use in distance education delivery.

7. Licenses for Non-Commercial Research and Teaching

With passage of the Digital Millennium Act, and preexisting copyright laws, many faculty, staff, and students encounter not only high costs but also considerable inconvenience in obtaining permission to use material that is subject to intellectual property protection for research and teaching. Creators of intellectual property are, therefore, encouraged to seek from publishers and other persons who assign rights to intellectual property a non-exclusive, royalty-free license for their own non-commercial research and teaching and, where possible, for anyone within the University to use that intellectual property for non-commercial research and teaching. [10] Appropriate units shall work to assist creators in securing such licenses.

8. Assignment or Licensing of Intellectual Property by the Creator(s)

A. Owners

Winthrop University may, at its discretion, permit the creator(s) to assign or license jointly-held applicable intellectual property. The University may not withhold consent for assignment or licensing unless the University intends to pursue protection for such jointly-held intellectual property. Such assignments or licenses shall be subject to the following provisions, unless *waived in writing* by the University.

- Winthrop University shall retain for itself a royalty-free license to use jointly-held intellectual property for non-commercial research and teaching within the University.

- Winthrop University shall receive a share of all proceeds generated from commercialization of university-assisted products after the creator has recovered documented out-of-pocket costs for obtaining legal protection for the intellectual property. The shares of such proceeds will be governed by the formula in Section III.2 (above).

B. Creators

In the event the creator(s) receives a specific request for assignment or licensing of applicable jointly-held intellectual property, he or she must promptly provide the University with sufficient information to determine the marketability of the applicable intellectual property. The University shall notify the creator in writing of any objection to the proposed assignment or licensing no later than 45 business days after receiving the creator's request to assign or license and the supporting information

9. Intellectual Property Transfer/Commercialization Agreements

Winthrop University welcomes agreements with third parties for the development, use, dissemination, and commercialization of intellectual property, consistent with the University's mission and its policies on intellectual property. Any agreement to license or transfer ownership of Winthrop University's intellectual property by means of sale, assignment, or exchange shall be subject to this Policy and shall include the terms necessary to fulfill the requirements of this Policy. Agreements relating to the development and/or commercialization of intellectual property may provide that the contracting entity bear the costs of obtaining protection for intellectual property. Any intellectual property held by Winthrop may not be transferred without written consent of the University.

V. Procedures

Ownership and gross income rights can be defined by any of the above categories and are dependent on the specific written contractual terms agreed upon by all parties.

Each Winthrop employee has the responsibility to protect intellectual property during development. The employee must establish intellectual property rights within 60 days of initiating development work by providing written notice to the Dean or department head of his or her area, who will report it promptly to the Academic Vice President. The Vice President must then provide within 30 days a written determination of Winthrop's intent to pursue or to relinquish any rights to the subject intellectual property. In the event Winthrop elects to relinquish its intellectual property rights, the rights will be assigned to the creator.

The University has an interest in how its name is used. Faculty members may not decide whether the University should sponsor a program. Use of the University name for non-sponsored research or creation must be approved in writing by the Office of the President and in advance of use.

VI. Dispute Resolution

The creator of intellectual property may appeal any adverse determination concerning the identification, protection, and/or management of intellectual property to the University Sponsored Programs and Research Office, whose determinations may be appealed to the Vice President for Academic Affairs and Dean of the appropriate college. Further appeals are subject to existing University policy concerning review of administrative decisions.

In the event of a dispute over the judgment that assigns a particular product to one of the four categories of intellectual property as outlined in Section III above, the dispute is to be adjudicated by the Committee on Faculty Personnel, augmented by additional members:

- If the dispute involves a faculty member, the Committee will be augmented by an administrator or professional staff member outside the faculty member's academic department and two additional faculty members, all three agreed upon by the committee chair and the Vice President for Academic Affairs;

- If the dispute involves a non-faculty employee, the Committee will be augmented by three professional staff members outside the staff member's administrative division.

The augmented committee on Faculty Personnel will make its recommendation to the Vice President for Academic Affairs or, in the case of a dispute involving a non-faculty employee, to the vice president of the employee's area.

---

[1] *A Vision of Distinction, 2002-2003.*

[2] The principles set out in this paragraph are based on those recommended by CETUS' (Consortium for Educational Technology in University Systems') "University Guidelines for Intellectual Property" (**http://www.cetus.org/fair3.html**).

[3] This draft borrows generously from the draft of 4/29/02 developed by Dean Mark Herring of Dacus Library, which in turn was based on parts of the following successful university polices already in place: The University of Indiana; The University of Georgia, Johns Hopkins University, Harvard University and The University of Arizona.

[4] Elements of this definition are borrowed, verbatim, from *Intellectual Property Guidelines, The Johns Hopkins University Intellectual Property Policy*, I. Intellectual Property: Definition; and from *The Regents' Rules and Regulations Part II, Chapter XII, "Intellectual Property,"* of the University of Texas.

[5] Winthrop University or the University shall refer to Winthrop University and to any foundation associated with Winthrop University.

[6] Software is defined as that which accomplishes a task or produces, manages, analyzes, or otherwise manipulates a product, such as data text, a physical object, or other software. Such software acts as a partner in the accomplishment of such a tasks or in the creations or management of such a product or result. It also includes any web-based courses and/or curriculum materials developed specifically for distance education or that might be used in the execution of web-base courses instruction delivery. Information software is defined as software likely to provide information to the user. Such software mimics the reproduction or display of material, as might be found in a library reference tool, for example.

[7] Instructional materials are defined as works whose primary use is for the instruction of students. Such works include textbooks, syllabi, and study guides, web-base courses, or helps to same. If these works have depended on the *significant* use of Winthrop resources for production, they fall under the category of University -assisted products.

[8] "Reinvestment" refers to a research and development fund that will either be created or named. This fund will be for the exclusive use of faculty involved in research.

[9] The following are examples of such materials but are not inclusive of all such productions or creations: intellectual property contributions of creators to University committee reports, musical or dramatic performances or productions, and departmental lecture note files.

[10] In a recent case, for example, it was determined that the author of a scholarly article did not have the right to repeated use of said article for routine class distribution without written permission from the publisher. Examples of language that may be included in contracts to ensure such rights may be found in the University of Texas "Policy and Guidelines for Management and Marketing of Copyrighted Works," available at **http://www.utsystem.edu/ogc/intellectualproperty/copymgt.htm.**

INTELLECTUAL PROPERTY RIGHTS POLICY FORM (.doc)